Complete
VEGETARIAN
Cookbook

Complete

VEGETARIAN

Cookbook

Janet Hunt

HAMLYN

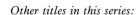

Other titles in this series:

Complete Indian Cookbook
Cooking with a Wok · Jewish Cookbook
Mexican Cookbook · Regional Chinese Cookbook

Front cover photograph by Graham Miller
Back cover photograph by Paul Kemp
Photography by Paul Kemp

Published in 1983 by
Hamlyn Publishing
a division of The Hamlyn Publishing Group Limited
Bridge House, London Road, Twickenham, Middlesex, England
© Copyright The Hamlyn Publishing Group Limited 1983
Fourth impression 1985

ISBN 0 600 322742

Phototypeset in 9/9½ pt and 10/11 pt Plantin Light by
Servis Filmsetting Limited, Manchester
Printed in Spain

Contents

Useful Facts and Figures

Notes on metrication

In this book quantities are given in metric and Imperial measures. Exact conversion from Imperial to metric measures does not usually give very convenient working quantities and so the metric measures have been rounded off into units of 25 grams. The table below shows the recommended equivalents.

Ounces	Approx g to nearest whole figure	Recommended conversion to nearest unit of 25	Ounces	Approx g to nearest whole figure	Recommended conversion to nearest unit of 25
1	28	25	11	312	300
2	57	50	12	340	350
3	85	75	13	368	375
4	113	100	14	396	400
5	142	150	15	425	425
6	170	175	16 (1 lb)	454	450
7	198	200	17	482	475
8	227	225	18	510	500
9	255	250	19	539	550
10	283	275	20 ($1\frac{1}{4}$ lb)	567	575

Note When converting quantities over 20 oz first add the appropriate figures in the centre column, then adjust to the nearest unit of 25. As a general guide, 1 kg (1000 g) equals 2.2 lb or about 2 lb 3 oz. This method of conversion gives good results in nearly all cases, although in certain pastry and cake recipes a more accurate conversion is necessary to produce a balanced recipe.

Liquid measures The millilitre has been used in this book and the following table gives a few examples.

Imperial	Approx ml to nearest whole figure	Recommended ml	Imperial	Approx ml to nearest whole figure	Recommended ml
$\frac{1}{4}$ pint	142	150 ml	1 pint	567	600 ml
$\frac{1}{2}$ pint	283	300 ml	$1\frac{1}{2}$ pints	851	900 ml
$\frac{3}{4}$ pint	425	450 ml	$1\frac{3}{4}$ pints	992	1000 ml (1 litre)

Spoon measures All spoon measures given in this book are level unless otherwise stated.

Can sizes At present, cans are marked with the exact (usually to the nearest whole number) metric equivalent of the Imperial weight of the contents, so we have followed this practice when giving can sizes.

Oven temperatures

The table below gives recommended equivalents.

	°C	°F	Gas Mark		°C	°F	Gas Mark
Very cool	110	225	$\frac{1}{4}$	Moderately hot	190	375	5
	120	250	$\frac{1}{2}$		200	400	6
Cool	140	275	1	Hot	220	425	7
	150	300	2		230	450	8
Moderate	160	325	3	Very hot	240	475	9
	180	350	4				

Notes for American and Australian users

In America the 8-oz measuring cup is used. In Australia metric measures are now used in conjunction with the standard 250-ml measuring cup. The Imperial pint, used in Britain and Australia, is 20 fl oz, while the American pint is 16 fl oz. It is important to remember that the Australian tablespoon differs from both the British and American tablespoons; the table below gives a comparison. The British standard tablespoon, which has been used throughout this book, holds 17.7 ml, the American 14.2 ml, and the Australian 20 ml. A teaspoon holds approximately 5 ml in all three countries.

British	American	Australian	British	American	Australian
1 teaspoon	1 teaspoon	1 teaspoon	$3\frac{1}{2}$ tablespoons	4 tablespoons	3 tablespoons
1 tablespoon	1 tablespoon	1 tablespoon	4 tablespoons	5 tablespoons	$3\frac{1}{2}$ tablespoons
2 tablespoons	3 tablespoons	2 tablespoons			

NOTE: When making any of the recipes in this book, only follow one set of measures as they are not interchangeable.

Introduction

I should have been a life-long vegetarian, but in fact it was only ten years or so ago that I actually got around to giving up meat. For years I had picked at it, liking only those processed varieties that came in squares or slices and tasted very little like the real thing, if at all.

One day it suddenly occurred to me that if I didn't want to eat meat, I didn't have to. That there were (surprise, surprise) other cranks who had given up meat and yet still managed to live healthy, happy lives. That I wouldn't have to give up the real gustatory pleasures of life – avocados, wine and chocolate cake . . . nor would I have to grow my hair and wear thong sandals.

It was a fantastic revelation.

After the euphoria, however, came the realisation that if I didn't eat meat, I'd have to eat something else. I started reading cookery books and health magazines avidly, experimented with such traditional foods as nut cutlets and raw beetroot – and filled up on bread and jam. I gained weight and lost heart, but not enough to give up. Eventually I learned how to turn simple ingredients into delicious dishes by using different combinations, fresh herbs and exotic spices; by being adventurous with the many vegetables and fruits that now flood into our shops from around the world; and by introducing into my cookery such exciting (but at first baffling!) ingredients as miso, tofu and tahini. Apart from anything else, I began to see meat as extremely boring.

My husband, too, is now a vegetarian. This means I've had to learn to cook for his tastes as well as my own, so widening my scope. To write this book I've widened it still further, including rather more special dishes for entertaining; conventional foods for vegetarian youngsters who may be shy about standing out from the crowd and prefer to eat much as their friends do; a special chapter on vegan cooking; plus scrumptious baked goodies and desserts.

Although written principally for people who want to eat well without eating meat, I hope that the following pages will have something to offer everyone. The majority of people in this world are vegetarian most of the time because of circumstances – it is only in the affluent West that meat is served daily. From the poorer countries come imaginative ways of using basic non-meat ingredients, recipes that have been passed on not just for years, but through the centuries. Many of these dishes, the Indian and Chinese ones, for instance, are already familiar to people in the West. You may well enjoy trying some of these recipes, and find it easy to banish meat from the table for at least a couple of days each week – a practice that you will find not only enjoyable but also economical.

The fact that vegetarian cookery is often linked with poverty shouldn't make you think of such dishes as being inferior – in fact they offer all the nutrients you will need, providing you vary them in your diet, and are probably much better for you and your family than many of the colourful (but nutritionally empty) convenience foods that fill the supermarket shelves.

Vegetarians can, of course, live on these junk foods just as easily as anyone else; they may even feel fit and look good. Personally, I like my foods as natural as possible. As my interest in vegetarian cookery has grown, so has my preference for wholefoods – and that, too, is reflected in this book. Wholefoods are quite simply foods that have had nothing added nor taken away. They contain no chemical additives such as preservatives or colouring. They haven't been so highly processed that they need to be artificially flavoured for you to recognise what it is you're supposed to be eating. You know whether they're fresh or not because their true taste isn't swamped or disguised.

I recommend anyone switching to a vegetarian diet to incorporate at least some wholefoods into their new eating habits, though be careful about being fanatical.

I'm not obsessed about eating right – I enjoy it. Nothing makes me more mad than when some meat-eating gourmet says 'I'd love to be vegetarian too, but I enjoy my food too much', as though the fact that I've given up meat also means I've lost any interest in eating. For some vegetarians this may be true, but how sad that they should be missing out on one of life's pleasures.

Whether you agree with me or disagree, are vegetarian or not, enjoy your food or hate it, I hope you'll try some if not all of the following recipes. And enjoy them. And just in case you want to go a step further and have a go at following a complete vegetarian wholefood diet for a while, here are some tips to get you started.

The Foods You'll Eat

Base your meals on simple foods such as pulses, grains, fruit, vegetables and nuts. There's a growing body of nutritionists who are convinced that these are the foods for health, to keep your eyes shining and your skin clear . . . and your waistline free from those uncomfortable rolls. They aren't expensive and they're very versatile. To make them more interesting use smaller amounts of cheese, free-range eggs, tofu, yogurt – and, for special occasions, cream.

If you have a sweet tooth, indulge it with honey, molasses, a little raw brown sugar and dried fruits. All these have some nutrients to offer.

Personally I enjoy wine with my meals and use it in cooking when a dish cries out for it. Some purists may disagree about the place of alcohol in a wholefood diet, so you must make up your own mind.

Setting Up Your Kitchen

Most of the equipment you will find in any kitchen will be useful, so if you're switching from one way to another you may not need to add a thing. If you are just setting up home, the basic equipment is: a set of heavy pans with good fitting lids (enamelled iron is best, otherwise buy stainless steel or cast iron pans); a good set of knives; a wooden chopping block; a grater for cheese and breadcrumbs; a steamer (one that fits into larger pans is ideal); a strong whisk; and several wooden spoons.

I find my small coffee grinder is perfect for grinding small amounts of foods such as nuts, cheese and sunflower seeds, while a liquidiser or blender is ideal for making soups out of left-overs, blending all kinds of purées, and for grinding raw brown sugar to a fine powder. And I intend, one day soon, to treat myself to a pressure cooker (it cuts the time needed to cook pulses by at least half). I also find my yogurt maker and bean sprouter invaluable – but that's because I'm especially fond of yogurt and bean sprouts! If you can't afford to buy all these items at once, start at the beginning of the list and add to your equipment as you go along and your cookery becomes more adventurous.

Buying In Bulk

Many wholefoods can be bought in bulk, which saves you time and money. Cereals and beans, sugar, honey, tahini, nut butters – all keep exceptionally well. Wholemeal flour is the main exception to this as it still contains the wheatgerm which can easily go rancid. Buy it in smaller amounts and store it carefully, or split larger quantities with like-minded friends. Nowadays there are quite a lot of bulk buying co-operatives around which mean you get very cheap goods and make new friends. Ask at your local wholefood shop, library, or various societies – or set one up yourself?

Freezing Wholefoods

As I like my food fresh, I don't have a freezer. But the main advantage of the freezer to a vegetarian is that you can freeze surplus vegetables from your garden or buy them when they are at rock-bottom prices and freeze them to use when they are in short supply. You can do this with some fruits, too.

The exceptionally busy cook can make larger quantities of dishes when there is time to spare and heat them up in minutes when needed. Flans and quiches, more complicated pasta dishes and pizzas, rice and bean dishes all freeze well.

Vegetable stock, always useful, can be frozen into ice cubes and stored in polythene bags. Ready-made sauces, fresh herbs, breads and cakes will also usually freeze well. Cooked pancakes are especially useful as they de-frost quite quickly and can be made into a meal in minutes.

There are, however, some foods to avoid putting into the freezer. Very watery vegetables like tomatoes and marrow (summer squash), for example, completely lose their shape when thawed. Curry gets stronger in flavour but not everyone sees that as a disadvantage! Cubed or sliced potatoes, if added to stews which are then frozen, may well distintegrate into a mush when re-heated.

Many foods that people store in freezers can, in any case, be kept quite well in the refrigerator for a reasonable time. Fresh breadcrumbs will refrigerate well for up to 2 weeks, while dried breadcrumbs can be kept in a screw-topped jar for a good deal longer. Many cooked dishes can also be covered with cooking foil and chilled for some days. This is one of the advantages of vegetarian food, in fact. Meat becomes suspect in a very short time, whereas dishes made out of beans, vegetables and the like rarely cause problems, providing of course they are well covered and kept in the cool.

I hope I have given you some idea of the pleasures of vegetarian cooking as well as the techniques. Now you can start to put them into practice!

Janet Hunt

If you would like any more information on any aspect of vegetarianism, write to:
The Vegetarian Society,
53 Marloes Road,
London,
W8 6LA.

Sunshine Breakfasts

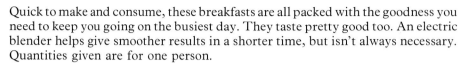

Breakfasts-in-a-Glass

Quick to make and consume, these breakfasts are all packed with the goodness you need to keep you going on the busiest day. They taste pretty good too. An electric blender helps give smoother results in a shorter time, but isn't always necessary. Quantities given are for one person.

Yogurt and Bran Breakfast

METRIC/IMPERIAL	AMERICAN
1 (150-g/5.3-oz) carton natural yogurt	$\frac{2}{3}$ cup plain yogurt
1 heaped teaspoon bran	1 heaped teaspoon bran
1 heaped teaspoon wheatgerm	1 heaped teaspoon wheatgerm
1–2 tablespoons fruit purée or	1–2 tablespoons fruit purée or
concentrated fruit juice (blackcurrant,	concentrated fruit juice (blackcurrant,
apple, pineapple)	apple, pineapple)
honey to taste (optional)	honey to taste (optional)

Combine all the ingredients, adding enough fruit purée or juice to give the yogurt a good flavour. If the fruit you are using is not very sweet, you may need to add a little honey.

Mix well by hand or in a liquidiser or blender and drink straight away.

Soya Banana Shake

METRIC/IMPERIAL	AMERICAN
1 ripe banana	1 ripe banana
200 ml/7 fl oz soya milk	$\frac{3}{4}$ cup soy milk
maple syrup or honey to taste	maple syrup or honey to taste
generous pinch of cinnamon	generous pinch of cinnamon
25 g/1 oz walnuts, coarsely chopped	$2\frac{1}{2}$ tablespoons coarsely chopped walnuts

Peel and slice the banana. Put all the ingredients except the nuts together into a liquidiser or blender and blend until thick and smooth. Transfer the mixture to a glass and chill briefly. Just before drinking, sprinkle with the nuts and a little extra cinnamon, if liked.

Orange and Egg Whip

METRIC/IMPERIAL	AMERICAN
1 egg	1 egg
200 ml/7 fl oz fresh orange juice	$\frac{3}{4}$ cup fresh orange juice
1–2 teaspoons honey	1–2 teaspoons honey
1 teaspoon brewers yeast	1 teaspoon brewer's yeast

Whisk all the ingredients well together or blend them in a liquidiser or blender. Transfer the mixture to a glass and drink immediately.

Frullata (Italian Fruit Purée)

Illustrated on page 18

Although there is no protein in this mixture, it makes an excellent cleansing breakfast, rich in vitamins and natural sugars. You can use most fruits in whatever combination you fancy, just make sure they are fresh (preferably in season). Leave the peel on whenever possible too, as this contains a good deal of vitamins.

METRIC/IMPERIAL	AMERICAN
6 strawberries	6 strawberries
$\frac{1}{4}-\frac{1}{2}$ small melon	$\frac{1}{4}-\frac{1}{2}$ small melon
1 small peach	1 small peach
1 small apple	1 small apple
generous squeeze of lemon	generous squeeze of lemon

Hull the strawberries. Remove the seeds from the melon and cut the flesh into chunks. Chop the peach, discarding the stone. Core and slice the apple. Put all the fruit into a liquidiser or blender, add the lemon juice and blend just long enough to make a thick fruit purée rather than a liquid.

Tip at once into a glass or a bowl and eat with a spoon.

Grapefruit Cocktail

METRIC/IMPERIAL	AMERICAN
150 ml/$\frac{1}{4}$ pint fresh grapefruit juice	$\frac{2}{3}$ cup fresh grapefruit juice
1 teaspoon ground almonds	1 teaspoon ground almonds
1 teaspoon soya flour	1 teaspoon soy flour
honey or maple syrup to taste	honey or maple syrup to taste

Whisk the grapefruit juice with the almonds and soya flour, or blend the ingredients together in a liquidiser or blender. Adjust the sweetening to taste and drink at once.

Hot Carob Drink

METRIC/IMPERIAL	AMERICAN
200 ml/7 fl oz milk	$\frac{3}{4}$ cup milk
1 tablespoon carob powder	1 tablespoon carob flour
1 teaspoon honey or to taste	1 teaspoon honey or to taste
pinch each of ground cloves, cinnamon and grated nutmeg	pinch each of ground cloves, cinnamon and grated nutmeg
1 teaspoon whipped double cream (optional)	1 teaspoon whipped heavy cream (optional)

Whisk all the ingredients together except for the cream. Pour the mixture into a pan and heat gently until hot enough to drink. Do not allow it to boil. Pour the drink into a cup and top with an extra sprinkling of spices and the cream, if used.

Sunflower Muesli

A slightly different version of everybody's favourite breakfast cereal.

METRIC/IMPERIAL	AMERICAN
225 g/8 oz medium oat flakes	2¼ cups rolled oats
50 g/2 oz wheatgerm	½ cup wheatgerm
100 g/4 oz sunflower seeds, ground to a meal	1 cup sunflower seeds, ground to a meal
100 g/4 oz dried apricot pieces	⅔ cup dried apricot pieces
2 bananas	2 bananas
milk to serve	milk to serve
raw brown sugar or honey to taste	raw brown sugar or honey to taste

In a large bowl, mix together the oat flakes, wheatgerm, ground sunflower seeds and apricot pieces. Peel and slice the bananas. Divide the muesli between four individual bowls, pour in the milk and top each with a few slices of banana. Serve at once and add sweetening and extra milk as liked. **Serves 4**

VARIATION

Banana goes well with the sunflower seeds and apricots but you can also use apple or whatever fruits you prefer.

NOTE You can make up a large amount of this muesli and store it in an airtight jar, ready for use. But if it is likely to be around for several weeks, leave the sunflower seeds whole and omit the wheatgerm altogether; sunflower seeds retain their flavour better if left whole, while wheatgerm does not keep well over a long period of time. Add it instead with the fruit and milk.

Malt Granola

Another favourite breakfast dish, a handful of granola also makes a crunchy, energy-packed nibble, especially popular with children. The only problem is stopping at one handful . . . . .

METRIC/IMPERIAL	AMERICAN
4 tablespoons oil	⅓ cup oil
175 g/6 oz malt extract	½ cup malt extract
225 g/8 oz jumbo oat flakes	3 cups rolled oats
100 g/4 oz barley flakes	1½ cups barley flakes
100 g/4 oz rye flakes	1⅓ cups rye flakes
100 g/4 oz chopped mixed nuts	⅔ cup chopped mixed nuts
100 g/4 oz wheatgerm	2 cups wheatgerm
50 g/2 oz sunflower seeds	½ cup sunflower seeds
100 g/4 oz sultanas	⅔ cup seedless white raisins

In a large, heavy pan, heat together the oil and malt extract and add the oat, barley and rye flakes. Stir the cereals together until well mixed and thoroughly coated in the oil and malt mixture. Turn the heat down as low as possible and continue cooking, stirring occasionally, for 20–30 minutes.

Add the nuts and cook for a further 10 minutes. Stir the wheatgerm and sunflower seeds into the mixture and continue cooking gently for 2–3 minutes until golden. For a delicately flavoured granola, remove it from the heat as soon as it has reached this point. If you like a richer flavour, continue cooking until the mixture is a deeper brown.

Once you have finished cooking, stir in the sultanas (seedless white raisins) and leave the mixture to cool. Store the granola in an airtight container and serve it at breakfast time with milk, yogurt or fruit juice as liked. **Makes 1 kg/2 lb**

Sesame Crunch Cereal

METRIC/IMPERIAL	AMERICAN
6 tablespoons honey	½ cup honey
4 tablespoons oil	⅓ cup oil
1 tablespoon vanilla essence	1 tablespoon vanilla extract
450 g/1 lb medium oat flakes	4½ cups rolled oats
175 g/6 oz sesame seeds	1 cup sesame seeds
50 g/2 oz soya grits (optional)	⅔ cup soy grits (optional)
100 g/4 oz desiccated coconut	1⅓ cups shredded coconut
pinch of salt	pinch of salt

Set the oven at moderate (180 C, 350 F, gas 4). Stir the honey, oil and vanilla essence together in a pan and heat gently. Add all the remaining ingredients, including the soya grits, if used, and mix as thoroughly as possible so that everything is coated in the honey mixture.

Transfer the cereal to a large, shallow baking tin or pan and bake it in the oven for about 15–20 minutes or until lightly browned. Check the cereal frequently to make sure it does not stick or burn and stir it every 5 minutes.

Remove the cereal from the oven, allow to cool and transfer it to a storage jar. Serve it with milk. Fresh fruit also goes well with this high-protein, crunchy cereal. **Makes 1 kg/2 lb**

Hot Fruit Crunch
Illustrated on page 18

METRIC/IMPERIAL	AMERICAN
100 g/4 oz dried apricots	⅔ cup dried apricots
100 g/4 oz prunes	⅔ cup prunes
4 small dessert pears	4 small dessert pears
1 teaspoon mixed spice	1 teaspoon mixed spice
juice and finely grated rind of ½ lemon	juice and finely grated rind of ½ lemon
1–2 tablespoons honey	2–3 tablespoons honey
25 g/1 oz sunflower seeds	¼ cup sunflower seeds
25 g/1 oz pumpkin seeds	¼ cup pumpkin seeds
25 g/1 oz hazelnuts	¼ cup hazelnuts

Cover the apricots and prunes with water and leave them to soak overnight. If they are still rather firm, bring them to the boil in a pan and simmer them for a few minutes until soft. Peel, core and slice the pears.

Set the oven at moderate (180 C, 350 F, gas 4). Combine the three fruits and arrange them in an ovenproof dish. Sprinkle the mixed spice, lemon juice and lemon rind over the top and trickle with honey. (If the pears are sweet and ripe, you won't need to add much, unless you have an especially sweet tooth.)

Coarsely chop the seeds and nuts, mix them well together and spread the topping evenly over the fruit. Bake for 20–30 minutes or until well browned. Serve the fruit crunch hot or warm, with natural (plain) yogurt if liked. **Serves 4**

VARIATION
Substitute a generous sprinkling of Sunflower Muesli, Malt Granola or Sesame Crunch Cereal for the seeds and nuts.

Kasha Porridge

Roasted buckwheat is often called kasha after a Russian dish of that name.

METRIC/IMPERIAL	AMERICAN
175 g/6 oz kasha (roasted buckwheat)	1 cup kasha (roasted buckwheat)
450 ml/¾ pint water or milk	2 cups water or milk
pinch of salt	pinch of salt
a little creamy milk (optional)	a little creamy milk (optional)
honey to serve (optional)	honey to serve (optional)

Place the kasha in a pan and add the water or milk and salt. Bring to the boil, cover the pan and simmer for 10 minutes or until soft.

Adjust the liquid to make a thicker or thinner porridge according to taste and serve it with creamy milk and honey, if liked. **Serves 4**

NOTE If you cannot obtain kasha, buy ordinary buckwheat and dry roast it in a pan over a medium heat for 3–5 minutes until it begins to brown. You will need to stir it frequently so that it colours evenly.

Scrambled Eggs with Cream

Illustrated on page 18

A very luxurious version of an everyday dish.

METRIC/IMPERIAL	AMERICAN
6 eggs	6 eggs
salt and pepper	salt and pepper
4–6 tablespoons single cream	⅓ cup light cream
fresh chives	fresh chives
25 g/1 oz butter or margarine	2 tablespoons butter or margarine

Beat the eggs together lightly and season with salt and pepper to taste. Whisk the cream well into the mixture (a rotary whisk does the job best). Finely chop the chives. Keep a little on one side and sprinkle the rest into the egg mixture.

Melt the butter or margarine in a pan and pour in the egg mixture. Cook gently, stirring up the mixture from the bottom of the pan all the time until the eggs begin to set. Remove the pan from the heat and leave the eggs for a minute or two, during which time they will set more firmly. (If you continue cooking until the eggs are completely set, a delay of one or two minutes before serving can allow the eggs to become overcooked in the hot pan.) Turn the eggs out on to four individual plates and garnish each serving with a sprinkling of chives. Eat with toast, oatcakes or Sesame Wheatgerm Crackers (see page 137). **Serves 4**

Kedgeree

Most people tend to think of Kedgeree as a fish dish. In fact it is based on the Indian Khichri *which was originally a dish made from rice and lentils or split peas. I prefer the original version.*

METRIC/IMPERIAL	AMERICAN
225 g/8 oz brown rice	1 cup brown rice
50 g/2 oz butter or margarine	4 tablespoons butter or margarine
1 onion, chopped	1 onion, chopped
225 g/8 oz split peas, soaked in water overnight	1 cup split peas, soaked in water overnight
salt and pepper	salt and pepper
3 hard-boiled eggs	3 hard-cooked eggs
chopped fresh parsley to garnish	chopped fresh parsley to garnish

Wash the rice in cold water and leave to drain. Melt the butter or margarine in a pan, add the onion and fry gently until transparent. Drain the split peas and add them to the pan together with the rice, stirring so that the ingredients are well mixed. Fry the mixture over a low heat for 3–5 minutes. Pour in just enough water to cover, bring to the boil and cover the pan. Reduce the heat and simmer for 40 minutes or until all the water has been absorbed and the rice and split peas are cooked. Season generously with salt and pepper.

Slice the eggs. Turn the kedgeree out into a serving dish and top with the eggs and chopped parsley. **Serves 4**

VARIATIONS

For a more exotic kedgeree, fry 1 teaspoon cumin and a pinch of chilli powder with the onion. Alternatively, stir in ½ teaspoon garam masala just before serving.

Not everyone, however, can face such fancy foods at breakfast time. If you like the idea but not the timing, try one of the spiced versions for dinner with a big crisp salad and a yogurt side dish.

Rieska (Finnish Quick Bread)

You can prepare the dough for this the night before and just pop it into the oven in the morning.

METRIC/IMPERIAL	AMERICAN
225 g/8 oz rye or barley flour	2 cups rye or barley flour
2 teaspoons baking powder	2 teaspoons baking powder
pinch of salt	pinch of salt
25 g/1 oz butter or margarine	2 tablespoons butter or margarine
2 teaspoons demerara raw brown sugar	2 teaspoons light raw brown sugar
200 ml/7 fl oz creamy milk	1 cup creamy milk

Set the oven at hot (220 C, 425 F, gas 7). Sift the flour, baking powder and salt together into a bowl. Melt the butter or margarine. Stir the sugar into the flour mixture followed by the milk and the butter or margarine. Mix thoroughly, then knead briefly with floured hands to make a smooth dough. Roll this into a ball.

Grease a baking sheet and press the dough ball down on to it to make a large circle about 1 cm/½ in thick. Prick this lightly and bake for 10–15 minutes until golden brown. Cut it into wedges and serve the Rieska while still warm. **Serves 4**

Bran Muffins

Illustrated on page 18

A much nicer way of taking your daily bran than most.

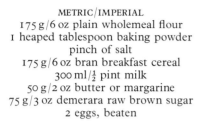

METRIC/IMPERIAL	AMERICAN
175 g/6 oz plain wholemeal flour	1½ cups wholewheat flour
1 heaped tablespoon baking powder	1 heaped tablespoon baking powder
pinch of salt	pinch of salt
175 g/6 oz bran breakfast cereal	2½ cups bran breakfast cereal
300 ml/½ pint milk	1¼ cups milk
50 g/2 oz butter or margarine	¼ cup butter or margarine
75 g/3 oz demerara raw brown sugar	½ cup light raw brown sugar
2 eggs, beaten	2 eggs, beaten

Set the oven at hot (220 C, 425 F, gas 7). Mix together the flour, baking powder and salt. In a separate bowl, soak the bran cereal in the milk for 5 minutes. Melt the butter or margarine, combine it with the sugar and stir in the eggs followed by the bran and milk mixture. Gradually stir in the dry ingredients. Beat the batter well to lighten it.

Grease 15 deep patty tins or muffin pans and fill each one two thirds full with batter. Bake the muffins for about 20 minutes or until well risen. Eat while still warm, with honey or jam; nut butters and Apple Spread (see page 75) also go well. **Makes 15**

Corn Bread Rolls

METRIC/IMPERIAL	AMERICAN
175 g/6 oz cornmeal	1¼ cups cornmeal
50 g/2 oz plain wholemeal flour	½ cup wholewheat flour
1 teaspoon baking powder	1 teaspoon baking powder
1 teaspoon bicarbonate of soda	1 teaspoon bicarbonate of soda
½ teaspoon salt	½ teaspoon salt
2 eggs	2 eggs
50 g/2 oz butter or margarine	¼ cup butter or margarine
about 200 ml/7 fl oz milk	1 cup milk

Set the oven at moderately hot (200 C, 400 F, gas 6). Mix the cornmeal, wholemeal flour, baking powder, bicarbonate of soda and salt together in a bowl. Lightly beat the eggs. Melt the butter or margarine and add this to the dry ingredients followed by the eggs and enough milk to make a thick batter.

Divide the mixture between 12 greased patty tins or muffin pans and bake for about 20 minutes or until a skewer inserted in the rolls comes out clean. Turn out and serve at once with savoury dishes or with honey, molasses or jam. **Makes 12**

VARIATION

Savoury Corn Bread Rolls Stir 2 teaspoons chopped fresh mixed herbs or 1 teaspoon dried mixed herbs into the dry ingredients and mix in half a small onion, very finely chopped, with the eggs.

Some basic ingredients. Clockwise from the top: split peas, chickpeas (garbanzos beans), red lentils, tofu, black-eye beans, aduki beans, wholewheat lasagne, wholewheat spaghetti, tahini, mung beans, kidney beans, olive oil, soya beans. On the plate: lasagne verdi, buckwheat macaroni, wholewheat macaroni, spaghetti verdi.

Danish Pastries

The typical New Yorker's breakfast when served with fresh fruit juice and strong, creamy coffee, Danish pastries come in a wide variety of shapes and flavours. Here is the basic recipe with two of my favourite fillings. This quantity should make 12–15 assorted pastries.

METRIC/IMPERIAL	AMERICAN
25 g/1 oz demerara raw brown sugar	3 tablespoons light raw brown sugar
150 ml/¼ pint lukewarm milk	⅔ cup lukewarm milk
15 g/½ oz fresh yeast or 2 teaspoons dried yeast	½ cake compressed yeast or 2 teaspoons active dry yeast
100 g/4 oz butter or margarine	½ cup butter or margarine
225 g/8 oz plain wholemeal flour	2 cups wholemeal flour
pinch of salt	pinch of salt

Dissolve 1 teaspoon of the sugar in the milk, stir in the dried (active dry) yeast, if used, and set the mixture aside until it becomes frothy. Cream fresh (compressed) yeast with the milk.

Cut the butter or margarine into small pieces. Sift the flour into a mixing bowl with the salt, reserving the bran for another recipe. Stir in the remaining sugar followed by the yeast mixture and mix well together.

Knead the dough on a lightly floured surface until smooth and roll it out to an oblong measuring about 35.5 × 18 cm/14 × 7 in. Lightly mark the oblong into thirds and dot the top two thirds with the fat. Fold the bottom third over the middle and the top third over the bottom, press the edges together to seal and turn the pastry so that the sealed edges are facing you. Roll it out again to an oblong of roughly the same size and fold once more into three. Place the pastry on a well-floured plate and chill in the refrigerator for 30 minutes. Repeat this rolling, folding and chilling process three more times to give your pastry a light texture, then chill for a further 30 minutes before rolling it out and cutting it into shapes.

Apple Danish

Set the oven at hot (220 C, 425 F, gas 7). Roll the dough out thinly on a lightly floured surface and cut it into 13-cm (5-in) squares. Place a little coarsely chopped dessert apple mixed with ground mixed spice and honey or raw sugar jam in the centre of each, fold the pastry, corner to corner, to make a triangle and press the edges together to seal. Arrange the pastries on a lightly greased baking sheet and leave them to rise for 1 hour. Bake them for 10–15 minutes. Spread the tops with more honey or jam while the pastries are warm and sprinkle with chopped nuts.

Almond Whirl Danish

Set the oven at hot (220 C, 425 F, gas 7). Roll the dough out thinly to an oblong and spread it sparingly with a good quality marzipan (almond paste). Roll it up lengthways like a Swiss roll (jelly roll) and cut it into 1-cm/½-in thick slices to make whirls. Arrange these on a greased baking sheet, allow to rise for 1 hour and bake them for 10–15 minutes. Top with glacé cherries, if liked.

Orange and Molasses Marmalade (page 21); Frullata (page 11); Bran Muffins (page 16) with Dried Apricot Spread (page 21); Hot Fruit Crunch (page 13); Yogi Tea (page 20); Scrambled Eggs with Cream (page 14).

Oatcakes

METRIC/IMPERIAL	AMERICAN
100 g/4 oz plain wholemeal flour	1 cup wholemeal flour
1 teaspoon baking powder	1 teaspoon baking powder
generous pinch of salt	generous pinch of salt
225 g/8 oz medium oatmeal	1⅓ cups medium oatmeal
50 g/2 oz butter or margarine	¼ cup butter or margarine
about 150 ml/¼ pint water or milk	about ⅔ cup water or milk
25 g/1 oz coarse oatmeal	1 tablespoon coarse oatmeal

Set the oven at moderate (160 C, 325 F, gas 3). Mix the flour, baking powder and salt together in a large bowl. Mix in the medium oatmeal. Rub the butter or margarine into the dry ingredients with your finger tips until you have a crumb-like mixture. Gradually pour in enough water or milk to make a firm but pliable dough.

Knead the dough for a few minutes on a lightly floured board. Roll it out to about 5 mm/¼ in thick and use a glass or a plain biscuit (cookie) cutter to cut out rounds. Place these at intervals on a greased baking sheet and lightly press a little coarse oatmeal on top of each.

Bake the oatcakes for about 25 minutes or until just beginning to colour. Serve them while still warm, if possible, with butter, jam, honey, cheese or eggs as liked. **Makes 18**

VARIATION

For sweeter oatcakes mix 25–50 g/1–2 oz (2–4 tablespoons) raw brown sugar in with the medium oatmeal.

Yogi Tea

Illustrated on page 18

In India, this is a perfect way to finish a meal. It is warming, soothing and aids digestion. Try it and you'll find it a nice way to start the day, too.

METRIC/IMPERIAL	AMERICAN
1 litre/1¾ pints water	4 cups water
1 tablespoon sliced root ginger	1 tablespoon sliced ginger root
2 sticks cinnamon	2 sticks cinnamon
8 cloves	8 cloves
8 peppercorns	8 peppercorns
4 cardamom seeds	4 cardamom seeds
3–6 teaspoons tea or tea bags to taste	3–6 teaspoons tea or tea bags to taste
honey and milk	honey and milk

Pour the water into a large pan and add the ginger, cinnamon, cloves, peppercorns and cardamoms. Bring to the boil, reduce the heat and simmer for about 30 minutes. Add the tea and continue simmering for a further 15 minutes. Strain into cups and serve with milk and honey to taste.

This tea will keep for several days in the refrigerator. If you store it without straining it first, the spices will continue strengthening it, so you may need to dilute it with more water before serving.

Use as many tea bags as you like for this tea, but do remember that you will swamp the delicate flavour of the spices if the tea is too strong. **Makes about 900 ml/1½ pints (4 cups)**

Dried Apricot Spread

Illustrated on page 18

This tastes like real fresh fruit, a lovely way to start the day.

METRIC/IMPERIAL	AMERICAN
225 g/8 oz dried apricots	1½ cups dried apricots
1 tablespoon lemon juice	1 tablespoon lemon juice
1 tablespoon thick honey (optional)	1 tablespoon thick honey (optional)

Soak the apricots in enough water to cover for a few hours. Drain, chop them into small pieces and put them into a saucepan with the lemon juice. Cook over a low heat for 5–10 minutes until soft, stirring from time to time with a wooden spoon, pressing the spoon against the side of the pan to break the fruit. You may need to add more juice or water, but be careful not to add too much, as you want to end up with a thick, smooth purée. Now stir in the honey if liked, not so much as a sweetener but to give the spread a softer texture.

Rinse out a jam jar with hot water, dry well and pack the apricot spread into it. Seal firmly and store in the refrigerator. Eat within a week. **Makes 225 g/8 oz**

NOTE If you have a liquidiser or blender, you can make this spread without cooking the apricots. Simply soak them as directed, drain and blend them to a purée with the lemon juice.

Orange and Molasses Marmalade

Illustrated on page 18

METRIC/IMPERIAL	AMERICAN
450 g/1 lb Seville oranges	1 lb Seville oranges
1 lemon	1 lemon
2 litres/3½ pints water	7 cups water
1.5 kg/3 lb demerara raw brown sugar	8 cups light raw brown sugar
2 tablespoons molasses	3 tablespoons molasses

Wash the oranges and lemon and put them into a large pan with the water. Bring to the boil, lower the heat and simmer gently for 1–2 hours or until the fruit is soft enough to pierce easily with a skewer or knitting needle.

Lift the fruit out of the pan with a straining spoon and allow it to cool slightly, then cut it in half and remove the pips. Tie these in a piece of muslin (cheese cloth) and return them to the pan. Slice the fruit coarsely, put it back in the pan and cook gently for 10 more minutes. Remove the pan from the heat. Lift out the bag containing the pips, squeezing it to release any liquid into the pan, then discard it. Stir the sugar and molasses into the mixture with a wooden spoon and continue stirring until completely dissolved. Return the pan to the heat, bring the mixture to the boil and boil it rapidly for 10–15 minutes or until setting point is reached.

To check this, remove the pan from the heat. Spoon a little of the marmalade on to a saucer and leave it to cool slightly, then push it gently to one side to see if it wrinkles. When it does so, it is ready. Test frequently as marmalade can be ruined both in flavour and texture if cooked too long, and once it has been cooked beyond its setting point it will turn to a liquid that will never set.

Allow the marmalade to cool in the pan for 5–10 minutes until it begins to stiffen, then stir it to distribute the peel as evenly as possible. Pour it into 4 or 5 dry, warmed jars and top at once with waxed paper rounds. When cold, seal the jars with pieces of cellophane held in place with elastic bands.

Store the marmalade in a cool, dry, dark spot. **Makes 1.75–2.25 kg/4–5 lbs**

Super Soups and Starters

Vegetable Stock

Generally, water which vegetables have been cooked in will make good vegetable stock, especially spinach, broccoli, courgette (zucchini), marrow (summer squash) and potato water. Or you can make a basic stock from vegetable trimmings which can be varied according to what you have handy.
Alternatively, just use a vegetable stock cube!

METRIC/IMPERIAL	AMERICAN
Vegetable trimmings (broccoli leaves and stalks, celery tops, spinach and parsley stalks, Brussels sprout and cauliflower leaves, mushroom stalks)	Vegetable trimmings (broccoli leaves and stalks, celery tops, spinach and parsley stalks, Brussels sprout and cauliflower leaves, mushroom stalks)
1 onion	1 onion
1 carrot	1 carrot
1 tablespoon oil	1 tablespoon oil
1 clove garlic, crushed (optional)	1 clove garlic, crushed (optional)
1 bay leaf	1 bay leaf

Thoroughly wash all the vegetable trimmings and leave to drain. Slice the onion and carrot. Heat the oil in a large pan and sauté the onion and garlic, if used, until softened but not browned. Add the carrot, vegetable trimmings and bay leaf, cover with water and bring to the boil. Cover the pan and simmer over a low heat for 30–45 minutes, then strain and use as required.

Watercress Soup with Yogurt

METRIC/IMPERIAL	AMERICAN
2 tablespoons vegetable oil	3 tablespoons vegetable oil
1 large onion, chopped	1 large onion, chopped
1 clove garlic, crushed	1 clove garlic, crushed
1 large bunch watercress	1 large bunch watercress
225 g/8 oz potatoes	$\frac{1}{2}$ lb potatoes
900 ml/1½ pints Vegetable Stock (above)	3¾ cups Vegetable Stock (above)
1 (150-g/5.3-oz) carton natural yogurt	$\frac{2}{3}$ cup plain yogurt
salt and pepper	salt and pepper
a little paprika	a little paprika

Heat the oil in a large pan, add the onion and garlic and sauté them gently for 5 minutes or until the onion is soft but not discoloured. Remove any coarse or discoloured stems from the watercress, keep a little on one side for garnishing, and chop the rest. Put it into the pan and continue cooking for a few minutes. Peel and finely slice the potatoes and add them to the pan.

Cook for a few more minutes before pouring in the stock. Bring to the boil, cover and simmer for 8–10 minutes, until the potatoes are soft.

Take the pan off the heat and stir in the yogurt. To make the soup creamy and smooth, either blend it in a liquidiser or blender or rub it through a sieve. Return it to the pan and heat gently; do not allow it to boil. Season the soup to taste and serve at once garnished with the reserved sprigs of watercress and a little paprika.
Serves 4

Celery and Peanut Soup

METRIC/IMPERIAL	AMERICAN
1 small head celery with leaves	1 small bunch celery with leaves
450 ml/¾ pint water	2 cups water
1 small onion	1 small onion
50 g/2 oz butter or margarine	¼ cup butter or margarine
25 g/1 oz plain wholemeal flour	¼ cup wholewheat flour
50 g/2 oz smooth peanut butter or to taste	¼ cup smooth peanut butter or to taste
600 ml/1 pint milk	2½ cups milk
salt and pepper	salt and pepper
a little paprika	a little paprika

Wash the celery and cut off the leaves. Keep a few leaves on one side for a garnish and put the rest in a pan with the water. Bring to the boil and simmer gently for 10 minutes, then strain the liquid, discarding the leaves, and set it on one side.

Finely chop the onion and the celery stalks. Melt the butter or margarine in a separate pan and sauté the onion and celery for a few minutes. Add the flour and continue cooking briefly. Stir in the peanut butter, milk and the reserved celery water and bring the soup to the boil, stirring continuously. Lower the heat and simmer for 15–20 minutes until the vegetables are tender. Season to taste and serve sprinkled with a little paprika and garnished with the reserved celery leaves. **Serves 4**

Tomato Soup with Tofu

This is an unusual soup, rich in protein. You can serve it either hot or chilled.

METRIC/IMPERIAL	AMERICAN
450 g/1 lb tomatoes	1 lb tomatoes
2 tablespoons oil	3 tablespoons oil
1 onion, chopped	1 onion, chopped
½ clove garlic, crushed	½ clove garlic, crushed
2 teaspoons chopped fresh or 1 teaspoon dried basil	2 teaspoons chopped fresh or 1 teaspoon dried basil
750 ml/1¼ pints Vegetable Stock (page 22)	generous 3 cups Vegetable Stock (page 22)
150 ml/¼ pint milk	⅔ cup milk
3 tablespoons tomato purée	4 tablespoons tomato purée
275 g/10 oz tofu, diced	1¼ cups diced tofu
salt and pepper	salt and pepper
chopped fresh parsley to garnish	chopped fresh parsley to garnish

Cut a cross in the bases of the tomatoes. Plunge them briefly into boiling water, then into cold water and peel away the skins.

Heat the oil in a pan. Add the onion and garlic and sauté for a few minutes. Chop the tomatoes and add these to the pan with the basil. Continue cooking for a few minutes, then stir in the vegetable stock, the milk and the tomato purée and bring to the boil. Lower the heat and simmer for 15–20 minutes.

Take the pan off the heat, add the diced tofu and transfer the ingredients to a liquidiser or blender. Purée the mixture to a smooth, thick liquid. Season with salt and pepper to taste and add a little more stock or milk if the consistency is too thick. Return the soup to the pan and heat through gently if it is to be served hot; chill it for a few hours if you want to serve it cold. Garnish with plenty of chopped fresh parsley. **Serves 6**

Cream of Chestnut Soup

METRIC/IMPERIAL	AMERICAN
450 g/1 lb chestnuts	1 lb chestnuts
900 ml/1½ pints Vegetable Stock (page 22)	3¾ cups Vegetable Stock (page 22)
1 teaspoon cornflour	1 teaspoon cornstarch
salt and pepper	salt and pepper
1 (142-ml/5-fl oz) carton single cream	⅔ cup light cream
1 Brussels sprout or a pinch of freshly grated nutmeg to garnish	1 Brussels sprout or a pinch of freshly grated nutmeg to garnish

Cut a cross in the side of each chestnut and place the nuts in a saucepan with water to cover. Bring to the boil, reduce the heat and simmer for 10 minutes. Drain the chestnuts and allow to cool until they can be handled. Remove the outer shells and inner skins.

In a clean pan heat all but 2 tablespoons of the stock, add the chestnuts and simmer them until soft (which can take anything from 20 minutes – 1 hour, depending on how fresh they are). Blend these ingredients to a thick sauce in a liquidiser or blender and return the soup to the pan. Whisk the cornflour (cornstarch) into the reserved stock, add to the pan and bring the soup to the boil. Simmer gently for 5–10 minutes, stirring occasionally, and season with salt and pepper to taste. Remove the pan from the heat and, very carefully, stir in the cream.

Slice the Brussels sprout, if used, into rings. Turn the soup into four individual bowls and serve sprinkled with nutmeg or the rings of Brussels sprout. **Serves 4**

Mushroom Egg Drop Soup

A light, delicately flavoured soup to serve before a more substantial main course or a Chinese meal.

METRIC/IMPERIAL	AMERICAN
15 g/½ oz butter or margarine	1 tablespoon butter or margarine
225 g/8 oz mushrooms	2 cups mushrooms
1 onion, chopped	1 onion, chopped
1 litre/1¾ pints Vegetable Stock (page 22)	4½ cups Vegetable Stock (page 22)
bouquet garni (parsley, thyme, bay leaf)	bouquet garni (parsley, thyme, bay leaf)
1 tablespoon soy sauce or to taste	1 tablespoon soy sauce or to taste
50 g/2 oz canned sweet corn	⅓ cup canned corn
salt and pepper	salt and pepper
2 eggs	2 eggs

Melt the butter or margarine in a pan. Slice the mushrooms thinly and sauté them with the onion for 5 minutes. Add the stock, bouquet garni, soy sauce and sweet corn. Bring the soup to the boil, lower the heat and simmer gently for 10–15 minutes or until the mushrooms are cooked but still firm. Remove the bouquet garni and season the soup to taste with salt and pepper.

Beat the eggs together in a small bowl until frothy. Bring the soup once more to the boil and, very slowly, pour in the egg, a drop at a time, stirring continuously, so that it breaks up into cooked strands. Serve the soup at once. **Serves 4**

Cabbage Soup
with Miso and Noodles

METRIC/IMPERIAL	AMERICAN
1 tablespoon oil	1 tablespoon oil
2 small onions	2 small onions
2 carrots	2 carrots
$\frac{1}{2}$ medium cabbage	$\frac{1}{2}$ medium cabbage
1 tablespoon miso or to taste	1 tablespoon miso or to taste
1.15 litres/2 pints water	5 cups water
50 g/2 oz buckwheat noodles	$\frac{1}{4}$ cup buckwheat noodles
salt and black pepper	salt and black pepper

Heat the oil in a large pan. Peel and chop the onions and carrots and slice the cabbage. Sauté the vegetables in the oil for 5–10 minutes, stirring frequently. Dissolve the miso in a little of the water, add the rest of the water and pour the mixture into the pan.

Bring the soup to the boil, break the noodles into pieces and sprinkle them into the pan. Stir once and simmer over a low heat for 15 minutes or until the noodles are cooked. Season to taste; as the miso is salty and strongly flavoured, you may need to add only a little freshly ground black pepper. Serve at once. **Serves 6**

Pumpkin Soup

Illustrated on page 35

METRIC/IMPERIAL	AMERICAN
1 (1-kg/2-lb) pumpkin	1 (2-lb) pumpkin
25 g/1 oz butter or margarine	2 tablespoons butter or margarine
1 large onion, chopped	1 large onion, chopped
600 ml/1 pint Vegetable Stock (page 22)	$2\frac{1}{4}$ cups Vegetable Stock (page 22)
600 ml/1 pint milk	$2\frac{1}{4}$ cups milk
25 g/1 oz plain wholemeal flour	$\frac{1}{4}$ cup wholewheat flour
salt and pepper	salt and pepper
soy sauce	soy sauce
4 tablespoons single cream	$\frac{1}{3}$ cup light cream

Peel the pumpkin, remove the seeds and chop the flesh into cubes. Melt the butter or margarine in a large pan and sauté the onion with the pumpkin for about 10 minutes, stirring occasionally. Pour in the stock, bring to the boil, reduce the heat and simmer the vegetables, covered, for about 30 minutes or until very tender.

Press the ingredients through a sieve to make a thick purée or blend them in a liquidiser or blender. Return the purée to the pan with three-quarters of the milk and heat through. Whisk the flour into the rest of the milk and gradually add this to the soup, stirring well until smooth. Bring the soup to the boil and simmer for a few minutes more until thick and creamy, season to taste with salt and pepper and soy sauce, stir in the cream and serve at once with wholemeal croûtons (see below). Pumpkin Soup can also be served chilled. **Serves 6–8**

Wholemeal Croûtons

Cut the crusts from slices of wholemeal bread and slice the bread into cubes. Sauté in a little butter or margarine until crisp and golden.

Black Bean Soup

Not a soup for the conventional. Personally, I like the exotic look of black beans . . . and it's certainly a good conversation starter.

METRIC/IMPERIAL	AMERICAN
100 g/4 oz black beans	½ cup black beans
4 sticks celery	4 stalks celery
2 onions	2 onions
2 tablespoons oil	3 tablespoons oil
1 clove garlic, crushed	1 clove garlic, crushed
1.15 litres/2 pints Vegetable Stock (page 22) or water	5 cups Vegetable Stock (page 22) or water
1 teaspoon chilli powder or to taste	1 teaspoon chilli powder or to taste
salt and pepper	salt and pepper
4 tomatoes	4 tomatoes

Soak the beans overnight in plenty of water. Drain and place them in a pan with fresh water, bring them to the boil and simmer them until almost tender. This can take anything from 1–2 hours, depending on the size and freshness of the beans.

Coarsely chop the celery and onions. Heat the oil in a separate pan and gently fry the garlic, celery and onions for 10 minutes. Pour in the stock or water and sprinkle in the chilli powder and salt and pepper to taste. Drain the beans and add them to the pan. Bring the soup to the boil, cover the pan and simmer for 30 minutes – 1 hour, until all the ingredients are cooked but still firm. At the very last minute, quarter the tomatoes and stir them into the soup so that they are warmed through but not cooked. Serve at once. **Serves 6**

Chickpea, Rice and Parsley soup

METRIC/IMPERIAL	AMERICAN
100 g/4 oz chickpeas, soaked in water overnight	½ cup garbanzos beans, soaked in water overnight
100 g/4 oz brown rice	½ cup brown rice
1 litre/1¾ pints Vegetable Stock (page 22)	4½ cups Vegetable Stock (page 22)
2 teaspoons fresh or 1 teaspoon dried crushed rosemary	2 teaspoons fresh or 1 teaspoon dried crushed rosemary
1–2 teaspoons yeast extract or to taste	1–2 teaspoons yeast extract or to taste
salt and pepper	salt and pepper
2 tablespoons chopped fresh parsley	3 tablespoons chopped fresh parsley

Drain and rinse the chickpeas (garbanzos). Thoroughly wash the rice and allow to drain. Combine all the ingredients except the parsley in a saucepan and bring to the boil. Cover the pan and simmer for 1–2 hours until the chickpeas are just cooked.

Add the parsley, reserving a little on one side for garnishing, and blend the soup very briefly in a liquidiser or blender to give a thick liquid that still retains some of the crunchiness of the chickpeas. Return this to the saucepan and heat it through gently. Taste and adjust the seasoning, turn the soup into four individual bowls and serve it topped with the reserved parsley. **Serves 4**

NOTE Perhaps the best time to make this soup is when you have some cooked chickpeas and rice left over from another dish. Simply blend all the ingredients together as above and heat through gently.

Winter Hotchpotch

Illustrated on page 35

METRIC/IMPERIAL	AMERICAN
1 large onion	1 large onion
2 carrots	2 carrots
1 large potato	1 large potato
1 small turnip or swede	1 small turnip or rutabaga
2 sticks celery	2 stalks celery
2 leeks	2 leeks
½ small cauliflower	½ small cauliflower
4 tomatoes	4 tomatoes
2 tablespoons oil	3 tablespoons oil
1 clove garlic, crushed	1 clove garlic, crushed
1.15 litres/2 pints Vegetable Stock (page 22)	5 cups Vegetable Stock (page 22)
2 teaspoons chopped fresh mixed herbs or 1 teaspoon dried mixed herbs	2 teaspoons chopped fresh mixed herbs or 1 teaspoon dried mixed herbs
50 g/2 oz wholewheat macaroni	¼ cup wholewheat macaroni
50 g/2 oz frozen peas (optional)	⅓ cup frozen peas
salt and pepper	salt and pepper
75 g/3 oz Cheddar cheese, grated (optional)	¾ cup grated Cheddar cheese (optional)

Prepare all the vegetables first. Peel the onion, carrots, potato and turnip or swede (rutabaga) and cut them into even-sized cubes. Wash and slice the celery and leeks. Divide the cauliflower into florets. Peel the tomatoes (see Tomato Soup with Tofu, page 23) and coarsely chop the flesh.

Heat the oil in a large pan and sauté the onion and garlic for just a minute or two. Put the celery, carrot and turnip in the pan and cook for a few minutes longer, stirring frequently. Now add the stock, herbs and tomatoes, bring the soup to the boil, lower the heat and simmer for 20 minutes. Stir in the potato, leeks, cauliflower and macaroni and cook for another 15–20 minutes or until all the ingredients are tender. Five minutes before the end of cooking time, add the peas, if used. Season with salt and pepper and pour in more stock if necessary.

Serve this thick, chunky soup topped with grated Cheddar and accompanied with Wholemeal Baps (see page 120) and you are serving a complete meal in one bowl. **Serves 6**

Parsnip Vichyssoise

METRIC/IMPERIAL	AMERICAN
2 tablespoons vegetable oil	3 tablespoons vegetable oil
2 medium leeks, finely sliced	2 medium leeks, finely sliced
2 medium sticks celery, finely sliced	2 medium stalks celery, finely sliced
4 medium parsnips	4 medium parsnips
100 g/4 oz shelled fresh or frozen peas	⅔ cup shelled fresh or frozen peas
900 ml/1½ pints Vegetable Stock (page 22)	3¾ cups Vegetable Stock (page 22)
salt and pepper	salt and pepper
300 ml/½ pint creamy milk	1¼ cups creamy milk
chopped fresh chives to garnish	chopped fresh chives to garnish

Heat the oil in a pan and gently sauté the leeks and celery for a few minutes, taking care they do not brown. Peel and dice the parsnips and add them to the pan with the peas, stock and salt and pepper to taste. Bring to the boil, lower the heat and simmer gently for 10–15 minutes until the parsnips are soft.

Cool the vegetables slightly, then pass them through a sieve or blend them in a liquidiser or blender. Stir in the milk, adjust the seasoning and chill the soup in the refrigerator for 2–3 hours. Serve topped with chopped chives. **Serves 6**

Chilled Lettuce and Sorrel Soup

Illustrated on page 35

This is a delightful summer soup, at once delicate and refreshing. If you cannot obtain sorrel, try it with fresh young spinach leaves instead.

METRIC/IMPERIAL	AMERICAN
1 small lettuce	1 small lettuce
225 g/8 oz fresh sorrel leaves	½ lb fresh sorrel leaves
1 large onion	1 large onion
25 g/1 oz butter or margarine	2 tablespoons butter or margarine
1 litre/1¾ pints Vegetable Stock (page 22)	4½ cups Vegetable Stock (page 22)
salt and pepper	salt and pepper
2 egg yolks	2 egg yolks
about 4 tablespoons single or double cream	about ⅓ cup light or heavy cream
finely sliced cucumber to garnish	finely sliced cucumber to garnish

Wash, drain and shred the lettuce and sorrel leaves. Finely chop the onion. Melt the butter or margarine in a pan and sauté the onion until it begins to go transparent. Add the lettuce and sorrel and continue cooking gently for a few minutes. Pour in the stock, season to taste with salt and pepper and bring to the boil. Cover the pan and simmer over a low heat for 10 minutes.

Cool the ingredients slightly, then put them in a liquidiser or blender with the egg yolks and blend to a purée. Stir in enough cream to give the liquid a soft, pale green colour. Adjust the seasoning. Chill the soup in the refrigerator and serve, topped with sliced cucumber. **Serves 4**

Chilled Fruit Soup

Fruit soups, so popular on the Continent, are rarely served in this country. But on a hot summer's day they make a delightful start to a meal (or a finish!)

METRIC/IMPERIAL	AMERICAN
450 g/1 lb ripe strawberries	1 lb ripe strawberries
2 large dessert apples	2 large dessert apples
1 litre/1¾ pints fruit juice (orange juice, apple juice) or equal quantities fruit juice and water	4½ cups fruit juice (orange juice, apple juice) or equal quantities fruit juice and water
about 100 g/4 oz demerara raw brown sugar	⅔ cup light raw brown sugar
2 tablespoons cornflour	3 tablespoons cornstarch
4 tablespoons dry red wine (optional)	⅓ cup dry red wine (optional)
1 (150 g/5.3 oz) carton natural yogurt or whipping cream (optional)	⅔ cup plain yogurt or heavy cream (optional)

Clean and hull the strawberries. Keep four berries on one side for garnishing and press the rest through a sieve or blend them in a liquidiser or blender to make a purée. Peel, core and finely grate the apples. Put all the fruit into a pan with all but 4 tablespoons of the fruit juice and sugar to taste (the exact amount will depend on how sweet the apples are). Bring to the boil, reduce the heat and simmer for 10 minutes. Whisk the cornflour (cornstarch) into the rest of the fruit juice and add this to the pan; cook for a further 5–10 minutes, stirring continuously.

Now pour in the wine, if used. Skim any froth from the surface of the soup, allow the soup to cool and chill it thoroughly before serving.

Serve in four individual bowls, each garnished with a few pieces of fresh strawberry and a spoonful of yogurt or whipped cream, if liked. **Serves 4**

Globe Artichokes
with Mousseline Sauce

METRIC/IMPERIAL	AMERICAN
4 globe artichokes	4 globe artichokes
3 egg yolks	3 egg yolks
1 teaspoon lemon juice	1 teaspoon lemon juice
75 g/3 oz unsalted butter	$\frac{1}{3}$ cup unsalted butter
salt	salt
about 2 tablespoons double cream	about 3 tablespoons heavy cream
(optional)	(optional)

First prepare the artichokes. Break off any tough or blemished outer leaves, cut off the stems and trim the points of the leaves. Wash the artichokes well under running water, place them in a pan of boiling salted water and simmer for 30–40 minutes, until you can pull out a leaf with ease. Drain, turn the artichokes upside down to dry and cool. Now remove the small spiky inner leaves and the choke, leaving a 'bowl' of outer leaves. Stand the artichokes in a serving dish.

Beat the egg yolks in a bowl with the lemon juice and stand the bowl over a pan of water. Add a knob of butter and whisk, heating gently. When the sauce begins to thicken add another knob of butter and continue whisking over a medium heat (do not let the water boil or the sauce may curdle). Use up all the butter in this way by which time the sauce should be thick and creamy. Season with salt to taste, remove the pan from the heat and beat the sauce for a few minutes to cool it slightly. Whip the cream, if used, until stiff and fold it in.

Pour a little of the sauce into each artichoke. Transfer any remaining sauce to a sauce boat and serve it alongside. **Serves 4**

Potted Spinach

Illustrated on page 36

METRIC/IMPERIAL	AMERICAN
1.5 kg/3 lb fresh spinach	3 lb fresh spinach
175 g/6 oz butter	$\frac{3}{4}$ cup butter
4 tablespoons single or double cream	$\frac{1}{3}$ cup light or heavy cream
pinch of freshly grated nutmeg	pinch of freshly grated nutmeg
salt and pepper	salt and pepper

Wash and shred the spinach, place it wet in a pan, cover and steam it over a high heat for 1–2 minutes. Drain it thoroughly before chopping it very finely.

In a clean pan melt half the butter and add the spinach. Cook gently over a low heat for 5–10 minutes or until the spinach has absorbed most of the fat. Remove the pan from the heat and cool slightly, then stir in the cream, nutmeg and salt and pepper to taste. Mix to a thick, smooth, green paste and transfer to an attractive dish or to four individual serving pots. Level the surface with a teaspoon. Melt the rest of the butter and pour it over the top (if you want to turn the Potted Spinach out on to individual plates, omit this step). Chill for at least a few hours, preferably longer, and serve with dry crackers or melba toast (see below). **Serves 4**

Melba Toast

Lightly toast thin slices of brown wholemeal bread under a hot grill. Using a sharp knife, carefully slice the pieces of toast through the middle and toast the uncooked sides until crisp and curling.

Stilton Walnut Pâté

Illustrated on page 36

A strongly flavoured pâté that is impressive yet quick to make.

METRIC/IMPERIAL	AMERICAN
25 g/1 oz butter	2 tablespoons butter
25 g/1 oz plain wholemeal flour	$\frac{1}{4}$ cup wholewheat flour
200 ml/7 fl oz milk	$\frac{3}{4}$ cup milk
100 g/4 oz diced Stilton cheese	$\frac{2}{3}$ cup diced Stilton cheese
50 g/2 oz walnuts, chopped	$\frac{1}{3}$ cup chopped walnuts
salt and pepper	salt and pepper
about 2 teaspoons mayonnaise	about 2 teaspoons mayonnaise
4 walnut halves or a little watercress to garnish	4 walnut halves or a little watercress to garnish

Melt the butter in a pan and sprinkle in the flour. Stir and cook gently for a few minutes, then take the pan off the heat and gradually stir in the milk. Return to the heat and bring slowly to the boil, stirring continuously. Simmer gently for 1 minute until the sauce thickens. Allow to cool slightly.

Meanwhile crumble the Stilton and add it to the sauce with the chopped walnuts. Stir until the cheese melts, season to taste and add enough mayonnaise to soften the mixture without making it liquid. Turn the pâté into a serving dish or into four ramekins and top with the walnut halves, if used. Chill for a few hours, then serve garnished with a little watercress, if liked. Hot toast makes the ideal accompaniment.

VARIATION

Try this recipe with other types of cheese. Sage Derby is especially good.

Herbed Lentil Pâté

METRIC/IMPERIAL	AMERICAN
1 red pepper, deseeded	1 red pepper, deseeded
1 large onion	1 large onion
1 stick celery	1 stalk celery
225 g/8 oz brown or green lentils	1 cup brown or green lentils
2 tablespoons oil	3 tablespoons oil
25 g/1 oz butter or margarine	2 tablespoons butter or margarine
450 ml/$\frac{3}{4}$ pint Vegetable Stock (page 22)	2 cups Vegetable Stock (page 22)
2 tablespoons tomato purée	3 tablespoons tomato purée
1 teaspoon chopped fresh or $\frac{1}{2}$ teaspoon dried thyme	1 teaspoon chopped fresh or $\frac{1}{2}$ teaspoon dried thyme
$\frac{1}{2}$ teaspoon dried oregano	$\frac{1}{2}$ teaspoon dried oregano
salt and pepper	salt and pepper

Finely chop the red pepper, onion and celery. Wash and drain the lentils. Heat the oil and butter or margarine together in a pan, add the chopped vegetables and sauté for 5–10 minutes. Stir in the lentils, vegetable stock, tomato purée and herbs and bring to the boil. Cover the pan and simmer over a low heat for 30–45 minutes or until all the liquid has been absorbed and the lentils are soft. (You may need to add a little more water during the cooking process). Mash the ingredients together to make a smooth purée and season well with salt and pepper. Transfer the pâté to a dish or to four ramekins, smooth the top and chill for a few hours. Serve with thin fingers of wholemeal toast or crackers. **Serves 4**

Curry-stuffed Eggs

METRIC/IMPERIAL	AMERICAN
4 large eggs	4 large eggs
2 teaspoons mango chutney or to taste	2 teaspoons mango chutney or to taste
2 teaspoons curry powder or to taste	2 teaspoons curry powder or to taste
about 2 tablespoons Mayonnaise (page 109) or natural yogurt	about 3 tablespoons Mayonnaise (page 109) or plain yogurt
salt and pepper	salt and pepper
few leaves curly endive	few leaves chicory
Garnish	*Garnish*
sliced cucumber	sliced cucumber
wedges of tomato or red pepper	wedges of tomato or red pepper

Hard boil the eggs for 10 minutes and plunge them into cold water. When cool, shell the eggs, cut them in half lengthways and scoop out the warm yolks. Mash the yolks with a fork or press them through a sieve into a bowl. Chop the chutney. Mix the egg yolk, chutney and curry powder well together, adding just enough mayonnaise or yogurt to give the mixture a creamy texture. Season to taste with salt and pepper. Spoon the filling into the egg whites and swirl the tops into a pattern with a fork. Or, for a more professional look, pipe the filling into the whites through a star-shaped (fluted) vegetable nozzle.

Divide the endive (chicory) leaves between four small plates. Arrange two egg halves on top of each and garnish with the cucumber slices and the wedges of tomato or red pepper. **Serves 4**

Onion Soufflettes

METRIC/IMPERIAL	AMERICAN
50 g/2 oz butter or margarine	$\frac{1}{4}$ cup butter or margarine
2 large onions, chopped	2 large onions, chopped
25 g/1 oz plain wholemeal flour	$\frac{1}{4}$ cup wholewheat flour
150 ml/$\frac{1}{4}$ pint milk	$\frac{2}{3}$ cup milk
salt and pepper	salt and pepper
3 egg yolks	3 egg yolks
5 egg whites	5 egg whites
25 g/1 oz Cheddar cheese, finely grated	$\frac{1}{4}$ cup grated Cheddar cheese

Set the oven at moderately hot (190 C, 375 F, gas 5). Melt just under half the butter or margarine in a pan and add the chopped onion. Sauté gently for 5 minutes, then drain off any excess fat and put the onion into a liquidiser or blender. Blend to a purée and set on one side. Lightly grease four individual soufflé dishes, using a little more of the butter or margarine.

Sift the flour, reserving the bran for use in another recipe (you can use the whole flour in this recipe if you like, but the soufflés will be lighter in texture if you don't). Make a white sauce (see page 72) using the remaining butter or margarine, the flour and milk. Stir in the onion purée, season with salt and pepper to taste and remove the pan from the heat.

When the mixture has cooled slightly, beat in the egg yolks, one at a time. Whisk the egg whites until they hold stiff peaks. Stir 2 tablespoons of egg white into the onion mixture to soften it, then carefully fold in the rest. Spoon the mixture into the prepared dishes and top each one with a little finely grated cheese. Bake them at once for about 20 minutes, until they have risen and are nicely browned on top. Serve immediately. **Serves 4**

Nut and Pasta Salad

METRIC/IMPERIAL	AMERICAN
100 g/4 oz wholewheat spaghetti rings	½ cup wholewheat spaghetti rings
100 g/4 oz button mushrooms	1 cup mushrooms
12 stuffed olives	12 stuffed olives
50 g/2 oz almonds	½ cup almonds
about 150 ml/¼ pint Mayonnaise (page 109)	⅔ cup Mayonnaise (page 109)
salt and freshly ground black pepper	salt and freshly ground black pepper
few lettuce leaves	few lettuce leaves
parsley sprigs to garnish	parsley sprigs to garnish

Bring a pan of salted water to the boil, add the pasta rings and cook them for 10–12 minutes until just tender but still 'al dente'. Drain, rinse through with cold water and drain again. Put the pasta in a bowl.

Carefully slice the button mushrooms and olives. Coarsely chop the almonds. Mix these ingredients with the pasta rings and stir in just enough mayonnaise to coat lightly. Season to taste with salt and black pepper.

Divide the lettuce leaves between four individual plates and arrange the nut and pasta salad on top. Garnish with sprigs of parsley. **Serves 4**

Bazargan

This popular Middle Eastern dish makes an unusual starter served in small portions (it's quite filling). Or try it at a buffet party.

METRIC/IMPERIAL	AMERICAN
225 g/8 oz bulgur	1¾ cups bulgur
75 g/3 oz walnuts	¾ cup walnuts
1 tablespoon oil	1 tablespoon oil
1 large onion, chopped	1 large onion, chopped
1 tablespoon chopped fresh parsley	1 tablespoon chopped fresh parsley
1 teaspoon dried oregano	1 teaspoon dried oregano
½–1 teaspoon ground coriander	½–1 teaspoon ground coriander
½–1 teaspoon ground cumin	½–1 teaspoon ground cumin
¼ teaspoon allspice	¼ teaspoon allspice
3 tablespoons tomato purée	4 tablespoons tomato purée
salt and pepper	salt and pepper
Garnish	*Garnish*
tomato slices	tomato slices
parsley sprigs	parsley sprigs

Wash the bulgur in cold water and drain it. Place it in a bowl with water to cover and leave it to soak for 30 minutes. Drain the grains thoroughly through a fine sieve and transfer them to a bowl.

Chop the walnuts coarsely. Heat the oil in a pan and soften the onion in it for 5 minutes, taking care that it does not brown. Stir the onion into the bulgur, followed by the walnuts, herbs, spices, tomato purée and salt and pepper to taste, and mix all the ingredients thoroughly together.

Chill the Bazargan in the refrigerator for as long as possible – even overnight – so that all the flavours are absorbed by the grain. Arrange on a shallow serving dish and garnish with the sliced tomatoes and parsley. **Serves 8**

Creamy Vegetable Vols-au-Vent

Illustrated on page 36

METRIC/IMPERIAL	AMERICAN
Puff Pastry	*Puff Paste*
225 g/8 oz plain wholemeal flour	2 cups wholewheat flour
pinch of salt	pinch of salt
200 g/7 oz unsalted butter or margarine, cut into flakes	$\frac{3}{4}$–1 cup unsalted butter or margarine, cut into flakes
1 teaspoon lemon juice	1 teaspoon lemon juice
about 150 ml/$\frac{1}{4}$ pint ice-cold water	about $\frac{2}{3}$ cup ice-cold water
beaten egg to glaze	beaten egg to glaze
Filling	*Filling*
75 g/3 oz mushrooms	$\frac{3}{4}$ cup mushrooms
1 red pepper, deseeded	1 red pepper, deseeded
1 tablespoon oil	1 tablespoon oil
75 g/3 oz cream cheese	$\frac{1}{3}$ cup cream cheese
75 g/3 oz cooked peas	$\frac{1}{2}$ cup cooked peas
a little milk to mix (optional)	a little milk to mix (optional)
salt and pepper	salt and pepper
tomato quarters and watercress to garnish (optional)	tomato quarters and watercress to garnish (optional)

Sift the flour and salt into a mixing bowl, reserving the bran for use in another recipe. Rub half the fat in with your finger tips until the mixture resembles fine breadcrumbs. Stir the lemon juice into the water and add enough of this liquid to the mixture to make a light, moist dough. Knead lightly on a floured surface until smooth, then roll out to an oblong about 1 cm/$\frac{1}{2}$ in thick. Dot the rest of the fat over half the pastry; cover with the other half, pressing the side edges lightly to seal. Turn the pastry so that the side edges are facing you and roll it out again. Now fold the pastry into three, wrap it in kitchen foil and chill it for at least 30 minutes. Roll the pastry out again, fold it once more into three and chill it for another 30 minutes. Repeat this process at least once, preferably three or four times more, and chill the pastry before use.

Set the oven at hot (220 C, 425 F, gas 7). Roll the pastry out carefully on a floured surface to 1 cm/$\frac{1}{2}$ in thick. Cut out 6 rounds using a 6-cm/$2\frac{1}{2}$-in plain or fluted pastry cutter; arrange them on a wetted baking sheet. Now use a smaller, 3.5-cm/$1\frac{1}{2}$-in cutter to make shallow, circular cuts in the centres of the pastry rounds. Brush the tops of the rounds with beaten egg, keeping away from the edges.

Bake the rounds for 15–20 minutes, until well risen, crisp and golden. Use a small knife to lift off the centre lids and return the bases to the oven for 1–2 minutes to dry out. Transfer the pastry cases to a wire rack to cool completely.

Slice the mushrooms and pepper. Heat the oil in a pan and lightly sauté the mushrooms and pepper until soft; drain and mix them into the cream cheese with the peas while still warm so that the cheese melts to form a creamy sauce. Add a little milk if the mixture is too thick. Season with salt and pepper to taste and allow the filling to cool.

Divide the creamy vegetable mixture between the vol-au-vent cases and replace the lids at an angle so that the filling shows. Serve arranged on a large plate, garnished with the tomato quarters and watercress, if liked. **Serves 6**

VARIATION

For a different shape of vol-au-vent, roll the pastry out to 5 mm/$\frac{1}{4}$ in thick and cut out 12 rectangles or rhomboids instead of rounds. Bake them on a wetted baking tray as above and, when cool, sandwich the filling between two shapes at a time to make six vols-au-vents.

Deep-fried Mushrooms
with Mock Hollandaise Sauce

METRIC/IMPERIAL	AMERICAN
225 g/8 oz firm, medium mushrooms	½ lb firm, medium mushrooms
about 50 g/2 oz plain wholemeal flour	about ½ cup wholewheat flour
1 egg, beaten	1 egg, beaten
about 50 g/2 oz fine dried wholemeal breadcrumbs	about ½ cup fine dried wholewheat breadcrumbs
oil for deep-frying	oil for deep-frying

Clean and trim the mushrooms and cut each one in half. Dip them first into the flour, then into the beaten egg and finally into the breadcrumbs, making sure the breadcrumbs coat the mushrooms evenly.

Heat a good quantity of oil in a deep pan to 190 C (375 F). You can test to see if the correct temperature has been reached by dropping a cube of bread into the oil; if it turns golden brown in just under a minute, the oil is ready. Deep-fry the mushrooms a few at a time until golden and crisp – it should take only a few minutes. Put them aside to drain on absorbent kitchen paper, then serve four or five to each person with a good spoonful of Mock Hollandaise Sauce. **Serves 4**

Mock Hollandaise Sauce

METRIC/IMPERIAL	AMERICAN
50 g/2 oz plain wholemeal flour	½ cup wholewheat flour
50 g/2 oz margarine	¼ cup margarine
600 ml/1 pint milk	2½ cups milk
salt and pepper	salt and pepper
50 g/2 oz butter, cut into flakes	¼ cup butter, cut into flakes
1 egg yolk, lightly beaten	1 egg yolk, lightly beaten
juice of half a lemon	juice of half a lemon
1 teaspoon chopped fresh or ½ teaspoon dried tarragon	1 teaspoon chopped fresh or ½ teaspoon dried tarragon

Sift the flour, reserving the bran for use in another recipe. Make a white sauce (see page 72) with the margarine, flour and milk and season with salt and pepper to taste. Remove the pan from the heat and cool slightly. Add the butter, egg yolk, lemon juice and tarragon. Mix well and serve with the mushrooms. **Serves 4**

Grapefruit Brûlée with Nuts

METRIC/IMPERIAL	AMERICAN
2 large grapefruit	2 large grapefruit
4 teaspoons demerara raw brown sugar	4 teaspoons demerara raw brown sugar
4 teaspoons ground nuts (walnuts, almonds)	4 teaspoons ground nuts (walnuts, almonds)
2 teaspoons cinnamon or to taste	2 teaspoons cinnamon or to taste

Cut the grapefruit in half and run a knife around each half just inside the skin to loosen the flesh. Separate the segments too, if liked. Stir the sugar, nuts and cinnamon together and sprinkle some of the mixture over each grapefruit half. Place under a hot grill for 10 minutes until heated through. **Serves 4**

Chilled Lettuce and Sorrel Soup (page 28);
Pumpkin Soup (page 25); Winter Hotchpotch (page 27).

Guacamole

A classic dip that makes an ideal start to a meal – especially as it's so easy to do.
It's also a good way to use up avocados that are just a little too ripe.

METRIC/IMPERIAL	AMERICAN
2 large ripe avocados	2 large ripe avocados
1 small onion	1 small onion
juice of 1 lemon	juice of 1 lemon
1 teaspoon chilli powder or to taste	1 teaspoon chilli pepper or to taste
salt and pepper	salt and pepper
1 tomato	1 tomato

Peel, halve and stone the avocados and mash the flesh with a fork until it resembles thick cream. Chop the onion very finely. Mix the lemon juice, chopped onion and chilli powder into the avocado purée and season to taste with salt and pepper. Dip the tomato briefly into boiling water, plunge it into cold water and peel away the skin. Chop and mash the flesh and add it to the avocado mixture. (If you have a liquidiser or blender you can mix all the ingredients together in it and save yourself time and effort.)

Transfer the Guacamole to a covered container and chill before serving. It can be scooped up with crackers or crispbread, crusty French bread, or – best of all – corn chips, which are now available at some delicatessens and wholefood shops. **Serves 4**

Tomato Ice

A real hot-weather recipe, this one.

METRIC/IMPERIAL	AMERICAN
450 g/1 lb ripe tomatoes	1 lb ripe tomatoes
½ small onion	½ small onion
1 tablespoon tomato purée	1 tablespoon tomato purée
generous squeeze of lemon	generous squeeze of lemon
4 tablespoons double cream or	⅓ cup heavy cream or Mayonnaise
Mayonnaise (page 109)	(page 109)
salt and pepper	salt and pepper
sprigs of mint and watercress to garnish	sprigs of mint and watercress to garnish

Chop the tomatoes and onion, put them into a pan, cover and cook very gently for 30 minutes or until soft. Rub the mixture through a sieve into a bowl and add the tomato purée, lemon juice and cream or mayonnaise. Mix very well and season to taste with salt and pepper. (If you have a liquidiser or blender, you can simply put everything into it without cooking the tomatoes first. The texture will not be so smooth, but it's delicious made either way.)

Turn the thick, creamy mixture into an ice tray or a plastic box and freeze for about 1 hour or until just beginning to set. Beat the mixture lightly and return it to the freezer for about 4 hours until completely set.

Just before you wish to serve the Tomato Ice, remove it from the tray and crush it coarsely. Serve at once in individual chilled glasses, garnished with mint and watercress. **Serves 4**

Stilton Walnut Pâté (page 30); Potted Spinach (page 29);
Creamy Vegetable Vol-au-vent (page 33).

Crudités and Various Dips

You can use whatever vegetables you like when serving crudités – just make sure they are as young and as fresh as possible. Although at most small dinner parties they are usually served with just one favourite dip, I prefer to make small portions of two or three different dips so that all the guests find something they like. Otherwise there is always one poor soul who ends up nibbling unadorned carrot sticks!

METRIC/IMPERIAL	AMERICAN
½ small cauliflower	½ small cauliflower
4 carrots	4 carrots
4 sticks celery	4 stalks celery
½ small cucumber	½ small cucumber
small head of fennel	small head of fennel
50 g/2 oz button mushrooms	½ cup button mushrooms

Wash all the vegetables and allow them to dry. Break the cauliflower into bite-sized florets; peel the carrots and slice them into long strips; cut the celery and cucumber into small chunks; peel and slice the fennel. The mushrooms can be halved or sliced or simply left whole if they still have their stalks.

Do not prepare the vegetables too long in advance, but long enough to chill them briefly before serving, as this makes them crunchier. Arrange them around the dips. **Serves 4**

Blue Cheese and Brazil Nut Dip

METRIC/IMPERIAL	AMERICAN
75 g/3 oz soft blue cheese (Stilton, Dolcelatte, Gorgonzola)	½ cup diced soft blue cheese (Stilton, Dolcelatte, Gorgonzola)
2 tablespoons white wine	3 tablespoons white wine
25 g/1 oz finely grated brazil nuts	2½ tablespoons finely grated brazil nuts
chopped fresh chives to garnish	chopped fresh chives to garnish

Put the cheese in a bowl and mash it with a fork until completely smooth. Combine well with the wine and grated nuts and garnish with the chives. **Serves 4**

Soured Cream Dip

METRIC/IMPERIAL	AMERICAN
1 small dessert apple	1 small dessert apple
50 g/2 oz walnuts	½ cup walnuts
1 (142-ml/5 fl-oz) carton soured cream	⅔ cup dairy sour cream
salt and pepper to taste	salt and pepper to taste

Peel, core and grate the apple. Chop the nuts coarsely. Mix all the ingredients together and chill briefly. **Serves 4**

Aïoli (Garlic Dip)

METRIC/IMPERIAL
2 cloves garlic or to taste
300 ml/½ pint Mayonnaise (page 109)

AMERICAN
2 cloves garlic or to taste
1 cup Mayonnaise (page 109)

Peel and crush the garlic cloves. Mix them well into the mayonnaise and set aside for a time for the flavours to blend
This is a mild version of Aïoli – if you are especially fond of garlic, use more cloves. **Serves 4**

Tofu Tahini Dip

METRIC/IMPERIAL
100 g/4 oz tofu
2 tablespoons tahini
½ clove garlic, crushed (optional)
2 tablespoons oil
1 tablespoon lemon juice, wine or cider vinegar
salt and pepper to taste

AMERICAN
½ cup diced tofu
3 tablespoons tahini
½ clove garlic, crushed (optional)
3 tablespoons oil
1 tablespoon lemon juice, wine or cider vinegar
salt and pepper to taste

Make sure all the liquid is drained from the tofu, then mash it with the other ingredients until smooth. Chill briefly before serving. **Serves 4**

Vegetable Cocktails

You need a juice extractor to make the only kind of vegetable cocktails worth serving to guests. Use only good quality vegetables and wash and trim them well. Then chop the vegetables into pieces and put them in the juicer in any of a multitude of delicious combinations. Here are some to get you started, but do experiment with whatever vegetables and fruits you have handy. And don't forget to serve the cocktails in elegant glasses, appropriately garnished.

SUGGESTED COMBINATIONS

Equal quantities of carrots, dessert apples and celery. Serve garnished with a few chopped nuts.

Beetroot and pineapple juice, with or without a little natural (plain) yogurt.

Tomato and lemon juice to taste, with a pinch of raw brown sugar and garnished with slivers of lemon peel.

Carrot juice mixed with just a drop of orange juice; or with a little tahini to make it creamy.

One part watercress to two parts pineapple or more, depending on how sweet you like your juice.

A mixture of as many vegetables as you like, flavoured with a splash of soy sauce and topped with chopped fresh parsley.

Main Dishes

Fruit and Vegetable Kebabs

Illustrated on pages 46–47

These are fiddly to put together, but well worth it for those occasions when you want to serve up something as exotic as it is colourful. Kebabs are easiest to cook under the grill, but can also be fun to eat at a summer evening barbecue. Quantities given here are very approximate as it is difficult to judge the exact amount you'll need but you should aim to serve 3 skewers per person.

METRIC/IMPERIAL	AMERICAN
about 4 tablespoons vegetable oil	$\frac{1}{3}$ cup vegetable oil
2 thick slices wholemeal bread	2 thick slices wholemeal bread
1 large parsnip	1 large parsnip
1 (439-g/15½-oz) can pineapple pieces in natural juice	1 (15½-oz) can pineapple pieces in natural juice
3 firm bananas	3 firm bananas
3 medium courgettes	3 medium zucchini
1 large green pepper	1 large green pepper
100 g/4 oz button mushrooms	1 cup button mushrooms
350 g/12 oz cherry tomatoes	¾ lb cherry tomatoes
bay leaves	bay leaves
salt and pepper	salt and pepper

Heat 1 tablespoon oil in a frying pan. Remove the crusts from the bread, cut the bread into large cubes and sauté them until golden and crisp. Remove the bread cubes from the pan and drain them well on absorbent kitchen paper.

Trim the parsnip and cut it into thick slices – if you prefer you can steam the slices gently for a few minutes to soften them slightly, but I like them better left raw.

Drain the canned pineapple. Cut the bananas into thick chunks. Trim the courgettes and slice them also into chunks. Trim and quarter the pepper, remove the seeds and cut the quarters into large squares. Clean the mushrooms. Thread all the vegetables including the tomatoes, the fruit and the bread cubes on to 12 skewers, alternating them so that you have a good contrast of colour and texture, and adding a bay leaf every now and again.

Lay the kebabs on a baking sheet, brush them with a little oil and season well with salt and pepper. Cook them under a medium grill, turning frequently and brushing them with more oil as you do so. Be especially careful not to burn the fruit.

Serve the kebabs once the ingredients are heated through and just beginning to colour – they should still be quite firm or they will fall off the skewers. **Serves 4**

NOTE Most people serve kebabs with hot rice spiced with turmeric: sprinkle 1 tablespoon turmeric into 450 g/1 lb (2⅓ cups) rice while it is cooking and you will find that the rice absorbs both the flavour and colour.

If you want to be different, try using millet as your grain accompaniment – its sweet and delicate flavour goes especially well with kebabs that contain fruit, and a generous sprinkling of chopped roasted pistachio nuts (or almonds) adds protein as well as a crunchy texture.

Courgettes Provençale with Haricot Beans

METRIC/IMPERIAL	AMERICAN
175 g/6 oz haricot beans, soaked in water overnight	1 cup navy beans, soaked in water overnight
1 green pepper, deseeded	1 green pepper, deseeded
50 g/2 oz butter or margarine	4 tablespoons butter or margarine
1 onion, sliced	1 onion, sliced
1 clove garlic, crushed	1 clove garlic, crushed
225 g/8 oz tomatoes	½ lb tomatoes
450 g/1 lb courgettes	1 lb zucchini
salt and pepper	salt and pepper
1–2 teaspoons crushed dried rosemary	1–2 teaspoons crushed dried rosemary
1 (142-ml/5-fl oz) carton soured cream or natural yogurt	⅔ cup dairy sour cream or plain yogurt

Drain the beans and cook them in fresh boiling water for 45 minutes or until tender, drain and leave on one side.

Slice the pepper. Melt the fat in a pan and fry the sliced onion, pepper and garlic for about 5 minutes. Peel the tomatoes (see Tomato Soup with Tofu, page 23), chop the flesh and add it to the pan. Continue cooking for a few more minutes.

Trim the courgettes (zucchini), slice them into chunks and put them into the pan with the other vegetables. Sprinkle in the salt, pepper and rosemary to taste, stir well, cover the pan and simmer for 10–15 minutes until the vegetables are almost cooked. Stir in the beans and allow them to heat through. Transfer the Courgettes Provençale to a serving dish and spoon the soured cream or yogurt on top. Serve with rice or wholemeal toast and a green salad. **Serves 4**

Lentil-stuffed Courgettes

Illustrated on page 45

METRIC/IMPERIAL	AMERICAN
6 medium courgettes	6 medium zucchini
1 onion	1 onion
2 tomatoes (optional)	2 tomatoes (optional)
2 sticks celery	2 stalks celery
50 g/2 oz butter or margarine	4 tablespoons butter or margarine
100 g/4 oz red split lentils	½ cup red split lentils
salt and pepper	salt and pepper
1–2 teaspoons chopped fresh mixed herbs or ½–1 teaspoon dried mixed herbs	1–2 teaspoons chopped fresh mixed herbs or ½–1 teaspoon dried mixed herbs
50 g/2 oz grated Cheddar cheese	½ cup grated Cheddar cheese

Parboil the courgettes in boiling salted water for 2–3 minutes. Drain well, cool slightly, and cut the courgettes in half lengthways. Scoop out and chop the flesh.

Chop the onion and the tomatoes, if used. Finely slice the celery. Melt half the butter or margarine in a pan and stir in the onion, tomato, celery and chopped courgette. Sauté all the vegetables together briefly, then add the lentils and enough water to cover. Simmer for about 20 minutes until the lentils and vegetables are tender and all the water has been absorbed; season with salt and pepper to taste and sprinkle with herbs. Use the mixture to fill the courgette skins and arrange the stuffed courgettes side by side in a greased ovenproof dish. Sprinkle with cheese and dot with the remaining fat. Grill the courgettes for 5–10 minutes, until golden. Serve with young French beans or spinach. **Serves 4**

Crêpes with French Beans and Almonds

METRIC/IMPERIAL	AMERICAN
Crêpes	*Crêpes*
100 g/4 oz plain wholemeal flour	1 cup wholewheat flour
pinch of salt	pinch of salt
2 eggs	2 eggs
1 tablespoon vegetable oil	1 tablespoon vegetable oil
150 ml/¼ pint milk	⅔ cup milk
150 ml/¼ pint water	⅔ cup water
oil for frying	oil for frying
Filling	*Filling*
450 g/1 lb French beans	1 lb French beans
50 g/2 oz butter or margarine	4 tablespoons butter or margarine
50 g/2 oz almonds, coarsely chopped	⅓ cup coarsely chopped almonds
100 g/4 oz mushrooms	1 cup mushrooms
25 g/1 oz plain wholemeal flour	¼ cup wholewheat flour
300 ml/½ pint milk	1¼ cups milk
1 tablespoon chopped fresh tarragon or	1 tablespoon chopped fresh tarragon or
1 teaspoon dried tarragon	1 teaspoon dried tarragon
salt and pepper	salt and pepper
paprika for sprinkling	paprika for sprinkling

Mix the flour and salt together in a bowl. Make a well in the centre and stir in the eggs. Pour in the oil. Mix the milk and water together and gradually add it to the mixture; beat hard until all the ingredients have blended to make a smooth sauce. Stand the batter in a cool place for at least 30 minutes.

Meanwhile, prepare the filling. Trim the beans, slice them if liked and steam them over a pan of boiling water for about 15 minutes or until just tender. Melt about half the butter or margarine and sauté the chopped almonds for a few minutes until crisp and golden. Remove them from the pan and place them on one side. Clean and slice the mushrooms and sauté them briefly in the pan until cooked but still firm.

Set the oven at moderately hot (190 C, 375 F, gas 5). Make a white sauce (see page 72) with the remaining butter or margarine, the flour and milk, take the pan off the heat and stir in the cooked beans and mushrooms. Add the tarragon, season with salt and pepper to taste and keep the sauce warm.

Heat a little oil in a heavy-based frying pan until very hot. Beat the batter again and ladle a small amount into the pan, tipping it to cover the base evenly. Cook over a high heat for barely a minute or until it begins to colour, then flip it over and cook the other side. Slide the crêpe on to a plate, cover and use the rest of the batter in the same way, adding a drop more oil to the pan when necessary.

Divide the bean filling between the crêpes, roll each one up and place them side by side in a greased ovenproof dish. Brush with a little melted butter or margarine, if liked, sprinkle them with paprika and almonds and put them in the oven for 10 minutes or until heated through. Serve with a fresh green salad. **Serves 4**

Cauliflower Cheese de Luxe

METRIC/IMPERIAL	AMERICAN
1 large cauliflower	1 large cauliflower
175 g/6 oz Cheshire cheese	1 cup diced Cheshire cheese
1 (142-ml/5 fl-oz) carton soured cream	⅔ cup dairy sour cream
1 tablespoon plain wholemeal flour	1 tablespoon wholewheat flour
25 g/1 oz butter or margarine	2 tablespoons butter or margarine
25–50 g/1–2 oz dried wholemeal breadcrumbs	¼–½ cup dried wholewheat breadcrumbs
50 g/2 oz walnuts, coarsely chopped	⅓ cup coarsely chopped walnuts
1 teaspoon chopped fresh mixed herbs or	1 teaspoon chopped fresh mixed herbs or
½ teaspoon dried mixed herbs	½ teaspoon dried mixed herbs
salt and pepper	salt and pepper

Set the oven at moderate (350 F, 180 C, gas 4). Break the cauliflower into florets and cook these in boiling salted water for 5–10 minutes, until just tender. Drain and arrange in a shallow ovenproof dish.

Crumble the cheese. Stir together the soured cream, flour and cheese and spoon the mixture over the cauliflower. Melt the butter or margarine, stir in the breadcrumbs, walnuts, herbs and salt and pepper to taste, and sprinkle the cauliflower with the mixture. Bake for about 10 minutes until golden and crisp and serve with rice and a colourful salad. **Serves 4**

Leek Layer Betty

METRIC/IMPERIAL	AMERICAN
75 g/3 oz butter or margarine	⅓ cup butter or margarine
175 g/6 oz dried wholemeal breadcrumbs	1½ cups dried wholewheat breadcrumbs
4 large leeks	4 large leeks
25 g/1 oz plain wholemeal flour	¼ cup wholewheat flour
300 ml/½ pint milk	1¼ cups milk
1 egg yolk	1 egg yolk
squeeze of lemon	squeeze of lemon
salt and pepper	salt and pepper
50 g/2 oz roasted hazelnuts	⅓ cup roasted hazelnuts
a little chopped fresh sage (optional)	a little chopped fresh sage (optional)

Set the oven at moderately hot (190 C, 375 F, gas 5). Melt 50 g/2 oz (4 tablespoons) of the butter or margarine in a frying pan and fry the breadcrumbs until crisp and golden. Wash and trim the leeks and slice them into 2.5-cm/1-in wide chunks. Cook in a little boiling water for 15–20 minutes until tender.

Make a white sauce (see page 72) with the rest of the fat, the flour and milk, cool slightly and stir in the egg yolk and lemon juice. Season to taste with salt and pepper. Drain the leeks and mix them thoroughly into the sauce.

Chop the hazelnuts coarsely. Arrange half the leek mixture in the base of a small ovenproof dish, sprinkle with half the chopped nuts, then with half the breadcrumbs. Repeat these layers and finish by scattering chopped fresh sage over the top, if liked. Bake for 20 minutes. **Serves 4**

Aduki and Celery Casserole with Gravy

METRIC/IMPERIAL	AMERICAN
Casserole	*Casserole*
100 g/4 oz aduki beans, soaked in water overnight	⅔ cup adzuki beans, soaked in water overnight
2 medium potatoes	2 medium potatoes
3 sticks celery	3 stalks celery
3 hard-boiled eggs	3 hard-cooked eggs
50 g/2 oz butter or margarine	4 tablespoons butter or margarine
50 g/2 oz canned sweet corn	⅓ cup canned corn
50 g/2 oz dried wholemeal breadcrumbs	½ cup dried wholewheat breadcrumbs
1 teaspoon yeast extract or to taste	1 teaspoon yeast extract or to taste
150 ml/¼ pint Vegetable Stock (page 22)	⅔ cup Vegetable Stock (page 22)
1 teaspoon fresh marjoram or ½ teaspoon dried marjoram	1 teaspoon fresh marjoram or ½ teaspoon dried marjoram
salt and pepper	salt and pepper
Gravy	*Gravy*
25 g/1 oz butter or margarine	2 tablespoons butter or margarine
1 small onion, finely chopped	⅓ cup finely chopped onion
25 g/1 oz plain wholemeal flour	¼ cup wholewheat flour
300 ml/½ pint Vegetable Stock (page 22) or water	1¼ cups Vegetable Stock (page 22) or water
½–1 teaspoon yeast extract	½–1 teaspoon yeast extract
1 bay leaf	1 bay leaf
salt and pepper	salt and pepper

Drain the aduki beans, place them in a pan with fresh water to cover and bring to the boil. Cover the pan and simmer for about 45 minutes or until soft, drain and leave the beans on one side. Set the oven at moderate (180 C, 350 F, gas 4). Scrub the potatoes, cut them into large, even-sized chunks and steam them for about 20 minutes, until just tender (leave the skins on, unless you particularly dislike their taste – they are full of goodness and help stop the chunks disintegrating).

Wash and chop the celery. Quarter the eggs. Melt 40 g/1½ oz (3 tablespoons) butter or margarine in a pan and sauté the celery for a few minutes, stirring frequently. Add the drained potatoes and beans and mix well. Sprinkle in the sweet corn and gently stir in the quartered eggs and half the breadcrumbs. Transfer the mixture to a casserole dish. Dissolve the yeast extract in the vegetable stock, add the marjoram and salt and pepper to taste and pour the stock over the other ingredients. Spread the rest of the breadcrumbs over the casserole, dot with the remaining butter or margarine and bake for about 30 minutes or until the top is golden and crisp.

To make the gravy, melt the butter or margarine in a pan and add the chopped onion. Sauté until the onion begins to colour, then sprinkle in the flour and continue cooking for a few moments. Add the stock or water, yeast extract and bay leaf, stir well and simmer the gravy for 10 minutes or longer, until it is rich and flavourful. Season to taste and add more stock or water if necessary for a pouring consistency. Serve the gravy hot in a sauce boat along with the casserole. As this is a rather filling dish, all you need to accompany it is a salad. **Serves 4**

NOTE 175 g/6 oz (¾–1 cup) tofu or walnuts can be substituted for the eggs.

Chestnut Roll (page 54); Broccoli and Egg Salad (page 102);
Lentil-stuffed Courgettes (page 41).

Overleaf *Peanut and Spinach Loaf (page 53); Crêpes with French Beans and Almonds (page 42);*
Fruit and Vegetable Kebabs (page 40).

Basic Wholewheat Lasagne

METRIC/IMPERIAL	AMERICAN
350 g/12 oz plain wholemeal flour	3 cups wholewheat flour
1 teaspoon salt	1 teaspoon salt
3 eggs, lightly beaten	3 eggs, lightly beaten
1 egg yolk or 1–2 tablespoons water (optional)	1 egg yolk or 1–2 tablespoons water (optional)

Mix the flour and salt in a large mixing bowl and make a well in the centre. Pour in the beaten egg and mix all the ingredients thoroughly together to a smooth, firm dough. If it seems too dry, add an extra yolk or a drop of water. Wrap in greaseproof (waxed) paper and leave to stand at room temperature for 1 hour.

Divide the dough into 2–3 portions and on a floured surface roll each one out as gently and evenly as possible until paper thin. Cut the dough into 7.5 × 13-cm/3 × 5-in strips with a sharp knife and lay them on a floured surface. Use the lasagne at once, if possible, or leave it to dry and use another day. **Makes 350 g/12 oz (¾ lb)**

VARIATION
Lasagne Verdi Blend 50–75 g/2–3 oz (⅓ cup) cooked spinach to a purée in a liquidiser or blender. Mix well into the dough after adding the eggs.

Spinach Lasagne

METRIC/IMPERIAL	AMERICAN
225 g/8 oz wholewheat lasagne	½ lb wholewheat lasagne
225 g/8 oz spinach	½ lb spinach
225 g/8 oz ricotta or cottage cheese	1 cup ricotta or cottage cheese
1 egg, beaten	1 egg, beaten
generous pinch of raw brown sugar	generous pinch of raw brown sugar
1 tablespoon vegetable oil	1 tablespoon vegetable oil
1 small onion, finely chopped	1 small onion, finely chopped
50 g/2 oz Parmesan cheese, grated	½ cup grated Parmesan cheese

Set the oven at moderately hot (190 C, 375 F, gas 5). Bring a pan of salted water to the boil, add the lasagne and cook it for 5 minutes if it is home-made or 15 minutes if shop-bought, until just tender. Drain, rinse through with cold water and set aside. Wash and shred the spinach and place it wet in a pan. Cover and steam over a high heat for 5–10 minutes until tender, then drain. Beat the ricotta or cottage cheese, the egg and sugar together in a bowl. Heat the oil and sauté the chopped onion until crisp, drain and add it to the cheese mixture.

Arrange half the lasagne across the bottom of a shallow ovenproof casserole and cover with half the spinach. Spread half the cheese mixture evenly over the top. Repeat these layers and finish with a generous sprinkling of Parmesan cheese. Bake the lasagne for 30 minutes until the top is well-browned. **Serves 4**

From the top Fennel Italian-style (page 50); Gougère (page 57).

Risotto al Gorgonzola

METRIC/IMPERIAL	AMERICAN
275 g/10 oz brown rice	1½ cups brown rice
2 tablespoons vegetable oil	3 tablespoons vegetable oil
100 g/4 oz mushrooms, sliced	1 cup sliced mushrooms
1 large onion, sliced	1 large onion, sliced
100 g/4 oz Gorgonzola cheese	⅔ cup diced Gorgonzola cheese
2 tablespoons single cream	3 tablespoons light cream
2 tablespoons dry white wine	3 tablespoons dry white wine
about 4 tablespoons Vegetable Stock	about ⅓ cup Vegetable Stock (page 22)
(page 22)	salt and pepper
salt and pepper	½ cup grated Parmesan cheese
50 g/2 oz Parmesan cheese, grated	½ cup walnuts
50 g/2 oz walnuts	chopped fresh chives to garnish (optional)
chopped fresh chives to garnish (optional)	

Wash the rice well in cold water and leave to drain. Heat the oil in a heavy-based pan and lightly sauté the sliced mushrooms. Remove these and set them on one side. Put the sliced onion in the pan, adding a little more oil if necessary, and cook gently until transparent. Sprinkle in the rice and cook for a few minutes more, then pour in 750 ml/1¼ pints (3 cups) water and bring the mixture to the boil. Simmer over a low heat for 30–40 minutes until all the water has been absorbed and the rice is tender.

Meanwhile prepare the sauce. In a large bowl mash the Gorgonzola to a thick, smooth paste. Add the cream, wine and enough stock to give a fairly liquid consistency. If you like, you can adjust the quantities of cream and wine to suit your own taste. Now stir the mushrooms into the cooked rice, followed by the sauce, and season with salt and pepper to taste. Turn the mixture into a shallow ovenproof dish, sprinkle Parmesan cheese over the top and place the risotto under a hot grill for a few minutes until golden brown. Alternatively, if the rice has cooled down, bake the risotto in a moderate oven (180 C, 350 F, gas 4) for 15 minutes.

Serve sprinkled with walnuts and chopped fresh chives, if liked, and accompanied by a crisp lettuce and tomato salad. **Serves 4**

Moussaka

METRIC/IMPERIAL	AMERICAN
175 g/6 oz soya 'mince'	1 cup textured vegetable
350 ml/12 fl oz water	protein 'hamburger'
2 large aubergines	1½ cups water
3 tablespoons vegetable oil	2 large eggplants
2 large onions, sliced	4 tablespoons vegetable oil
salt and pepper	2 large onions, sliced
4 tomatoes	salt and pepper
150 ml/¼ pint Vegetable Stock (page 22)	4 tomatoes
2 tablespoons tomato purée	⅔ cup Vegetable Stock (page 22)
2 eggs	3 tablespoons tomato purée
4 tablespoons creamy milk	2 eggs
pinch of cayenne	⅓ cup creamy milk
parsley sprigs to garnish (optional)	pinch of cayenne
	parsley sprigs to garnish (optional)

Set the oven at moderate (180 C, 350 F, gas 4). Put the soya 'mince' in a pan with the water and bring to the boil. Lower the heat and simmer for 5 minutes, drain and set on one side. Thinly slice the aubergines (eggplants), heat half the oil in a pan and lightly sauté the slices for 5 minutes, turning them once. Remove them from the pan and leave them to drain on absorbent kitchen paper. Heat the rest of the oil in the pan and sauté the sliced onions until they begin to soften. Add the 'meat', stir well and cook gently for a few more minutes. Season generously with salt and pepper.

Slice the tomatoes. Arrange the onion and meat mixture in a medium-sized ovenproof dish or casserole, top with the tomato slices and finish with the aubergine. Stir together the vegetable stock and the tomato purée and pour the mixture over the ingredients. Cover the casserole, place it in the oven and bake it for 20 minutes.

Beat the eggs with the milk and the cayenne. Take the casserole out of the oven and pour in the egg mixture. Bake the moussaka uncovered for a further 15 minutes or until the eggs have set. Serve hot, garnished with parsley if liked.
Serves 4

Aubergine Italian-style

METRIC/IMPERIAL	AMERICAN
2 large aubergines	2 large eggplants
salt	salt
2 tablespoons vegetable oil	3 tablespoons vegetable oil
1 egg, beaten	1 egg, beaten
100 g/4 oz mozzarella cheese	$\frac{1}{4}$ lb mozzarella cheese
1 quantity Tomato Sauce (page 72)	1 quantity Tomato Sauce (page 72)
50 g/2 oz Parmesan cheese, grated	$\frac{1}{2}$ cup grated Parmesan cheese

Set the oven at moderately hot (200 C, 400 F, gas 6). Wash, trim and slice the aubergines (eggplants), lay the slices on a plate and sprinkle them with salt. Leave for 30 minutes, then rinse them thoroughly with fresh water and pat dry.

Heat the oil in a pan. Dip the aubergine slices into beaten egg and fry them until lightly coloured on each side. Slice the mozzarella. Arrange the aubergine, tomato sauce and mozzarella in layers in a small greased ovenproof dish until all the ingredients have been used. Sprinkle the Parmesan cheese over the top and bake the aubergine for 20 minutes or until the top begins to brown. Serve with a salad made of endive, chicory and lettuce for a fresh, crisp contrast to a rather rich dish.
Serves 4

VARIATIONS

This dish can also be prepared using other vegetables instead of the aubergines. Try substituting 2 large bulbs fennel (as illustrated on page 48) and make the dish in the same way but omitting the salting process. This is only necessary with aubergines as it removes excess water, making the aubergine easier to cook and more able to retain its shape.

Stuffed Marrow Slices

METRIC/IMPERIAL	AMERICAN
1 medium marrow	1 summer squash
225 g/8 oz tomatoes	½ lb tomatoes
1 red pepper, deseeded	1 red pepper, deseeded
½ small onion	½ small onion
½ clove garlic, crushed	½ clove garlic, crushed
50 g/2 oz raw or roasted hazelnuts	⅓ cup raw or roasted hazelnuts
50 g/2 oz fresh wholemeal breadcrumbs	1 cup fresh wholewheat breadcrumbs
1–2 tablespoons chopped mixed fresh herbs or 1 teaspoon mixed dried herbs	1–2 tablespoons chopped mixed fresh herbs or 1 teaspoon mixed dried herbs
salt and pepper	salt and pepper
1 small egg	1 small egg
50 g/2 oz butter (optional)	¼ cup butter (optional)
chopped fresh parsley to garnish	chopped fresh parsley to garnish

Set the oven at moderately hot (190 C, 375 F, gas 5). Peel the marrow (summer squash) and slice into four widthways. Scoop out the seeds, leaving a hole in the centre of each slice. Arrange the rings in a greased ovenproof dish or baking tin.

Chop the tomatoes, red pepper and onion very finely and combine them in a bowl with the garlic. Chop the nuts coarsely and add them to the bowl together with the breadcrumbs and mixed herbs. Season to taste with salt and pepper. Beat the egg and add just enough of it to the bowl to bind the other ingredients into a fairly soft mixture. Use this to fill the marrow rings. Put the lid on the dish or cover it with kitchen foil and bake the marrow for 30–40 minutes until tender.

Top each slice with a knob of butter, if used, and a sprinkling of chopped fresh parsley. Serve the marrow as it is or with a cheese or mushroom sauce (see White Sauce, page 72). Glazed carrots and jacket potatoes make good accompaniments.
Serves 4

Celery and Rice Loaf

METRIC/IMPERIAL	AMERICAN
2 sticks celery	2 stalks celery
1 small onion	1 small onion
25 g/1 oz butter or margarine	2 tablespoons butter or margarine
2 eggs	2 eggs
75 g/3 oz walnuts	¾ cup walnuts
100 g/4 oz cooked brown rice	¾ cup cooked brown rice
100 g/4 oz Cheddar cheese, grated	1 cup grated Cheddar cheese
salt and pepper	salt and pepper
1–2 teaspoons curry powder	1–2 teaspoons curry powder

Set the oven at moderate (180 C, 350 F, gas 4). Chop the celery and onion very finely. Melt the butter or margarine in a pan and sauté the onion and celery for a few minutes. Beat the eggs. Finely chop or grind the walnuts.

Mix all the ingredients including the rice and cheese well together and season to taste with salt, pepper and curry powder. Spoon the mixture into a 450-g/1-lb (7 × 3½ × 2-in) loaf tin and smooth the top. Bake for 30–40 minutes until set firm, turn the loaf out of the tin and serve with a tomato or cheese sauce (see page 72).
Serves 4

Peanut and Spinach Loaf

Illustrated on pages 46–47

METRIC/IMPERIAL	AMERICAN
4 slices wholemeal bread	4 slices wholewheat bread
150 ml/¼ pint milk	⅔ cup milk
450 g/1 lb spinach	1 lb spinach
2 eggs	2 eggs
100 g/4 oz raw peanuts	½ cup raw peanuts
175 g/6 oz Cheddar cheese, grated	1½ cups grated Cheddar cheese
salt and pepper	salt and pepper
generous pinch of grated nutmeg	generous pinch of grated nutmeg
15 g/½ oz butter	1 tablespoon butter
25 g/1 oz wheatgerm	¼ cup wheatgerm

Set the oven at moderate (180 C, 350 F, gas 4). Remove the crusts from the bread, grate the bread into crumbs and soak them in the milk for a few minutes. Wash the spinach and remove the stems. Drain well or pat dry with a paper towel and cut the leaves into fine pieces.

Separate the eggs. Grate or coarsely chop the peanuts. Drain the breadcrumbs and mix them with the spinach, cheese, nuts and egg yolks. Season with salt and pepper and nutmeg to taste. Whisk the egg whites until stiff and fold them into the other ingredients.

Spoon the mixture into a well-greased 450-g/1-lb ($7 \times 3\frac{1}{2} \times 2$-in) loaf tin and smooth the top. Melt the butter, mix it with the wheatgerm and sprinkle this over the loaf. Bake for about 1 hour, turn out of the tin and serve with a cheese or tomato sauce (see page 72). **Serves 4**

Brussels Sprout
and Wheatgerm Soufflé

METRIC/IMPERIAL	AMERICAN
450 g/1 lb Brussels sprouts	1 lb Brussels sprouts
3 eggs	3 eggs
50 g/2 oz butter or margarine	¼ cup butter or margarine
25 g/1 oz plain wholemeal flour	¼ cup wholewheat flour
25 g/1 oz wheatgerm	¼ cup wheatgerm
300 ml/½ pint milk	1¼ cups milk
generous pinch of nutmeg	generous pinch of nutmeg
salt and pepper	salt and pepper

Set the oven at moderately hot (200 C, 400 F, gas 6). Trim the sprouts and steam them for 10–15 minutes until tender, then drain.

Separate the eggs. Make a white sauce with the butter or margarine, the flour, wheatgerm and milk and beat it thoroughly with a wooden spoon. Add the nutmeg and salt and pepper to taste and allow to cool slightly. Beat in the egg yolks.

Chop the cooled Brussels sprouts or blend them to a purée in a liquidiser or blender. Stir into the sauce. Whisk the egg whites until stiff but not dry and fold them into the vegetable mixture. Pour it into a greased 15-cm/6-in soufflé dish and bake for about 30 minutes or until risen. Serve at once with potato or corn crisps and a tomato and basil salad, if liked. **Serves 4**

Green Pepper
and Cream Cheese Flan

METRIC/IMPERIAL	AMERICAN
Pastry	*Dough*
100 g/4 oz butter or margarine	$\frac{1}{2}$ cup butter or margarine
225 g/8 oz plain wholemeal flour	2 cups wholewheat flour
about 2 tablespoons cold water	about 3 tablespoons cold water
Filling	*Filling*
25 g/1 oz plain wholemeal flour	$\frac{1}{4}$ cup wholewheat flour
1 large green pepper, deseeded	1 large green pepper, deseeded
1$\frac{1}{2}$ tablespoons vegetable oil	2 tablespoons vegetable oil
275 g/10 oz cream cheese	10 oz cream cheese
2 eggs, lightly beaten	2 eggs, lightly beaten
150 ml/$\frac{1}{4}$ pint milk	$\frac{2}{3}$ cup milk
salt and pepper	salt and pepper

Cut the butter or margarine into flakes and rub them into the flour until the mixture resembles fine breadcrumbs. Add enough water to bind the ingredients into a soft dough. Knead for a minute or two, then wrap the dough in cling film (saran wrap) and chill for 30 minutes.

Set the oven at moderate (180 C, 350 F, gas 4) and place a baking sheet inside to warm up. For the filling, sift the wholemeal flour, reserving the bran for another recipe. Cut the green pepper into strips. Heat the oil in a pan and lightly sauté the pepper until soft but not browned. Drain on absorbent kitchen paper, then combine with the cheese, beaten egg, flour, milk and salt and pepper to taste.

Roll out the chilled pastry to a large round and use it to line a 23-cm/9-in flan tin or pie pan. Pour in the cheese filling. Place the flan on the hot baking sheet to ensure the pastry cooks thoroughly and bake it for about 30 minutes or until set.
Serves 4

Chestnut Roll

Illustrated on page 45

METRIC/IMPERIAL	AMERICAN
Pastry	*Dough*
100 g/4 oz butter or margarine	$\frac{1}{2}$ cup butter or margarine
225 g/8 oz plain wholemeal flour	2 cups wholewheat flour
pinch of salt	pinch of salt
2–3 tablespoons cold water	3–4 tablespoons cold water
a little milk for glazing	a little milk for glazing
Filling	*Filling*
225 g/8 oz chestnuts	$\frac{1}{2}$ lb chestnuts
25 g/1 oz butter or margarine	2 tablespoons butter or margarine
50 g/2 oz mushrooms, chopped	$\frac{1}{2}$ cup mushrooms, chopped
1 leek, finely sliced	1 leek, finely sliced
$\frac{1}{2}$ clove garlic, crushed	$\frac{1}{2}$ clove garlic, crushed
1–2 tablespoons water	2–3 tablespoons water
salt and pepper	salt and pepper
watercress to garnish	watercress to garnish

Rub the butter or margarine into the flour and salt until the mixture resembles fine breadcrumbs. Add enough water to bind the ingredients to a dough, knead lightly and wrap in kitchen foil or cling film (saran wrap). Stand the dough in the refrigerator for at least 30 minutes.

Set the oven at moderately hot (200 C, 400 F, gas 6). To make the filling, slit the shells of the chestnuts and cook them in boiling water for 15 minutes. Drain and allow to cool, then peel away both the outer shells and the inner skin. Melt the butter or margarine in a pan and sauté the mushrooms briefly, remove them and set them on one side. Put the sliced leek and garlic together into the pan and sauté gently for 5 minutes. Chop the chestnuts coarsely and add them to the pan. Pour in just enough water to moisten the ingredients, cover the pan and simmer for 10 minutes or until the nuts and leek are tender. Add more water if necessary, but not too much as the mixture must be dry. Stir in the mushrooms and remove the pan from the heat. Drain thoroughly and season to taste with salt and pepper.

On a lightly floured surface, roll the pastry out to a neat oblong measuring roughly 30 × 23 cm/12 × 9 in and spread the chestnut and vegetables over it, leaving a small space around the edges. Roll up the pastry from the longest edge, like a swiss roll (jelly roll). Dampen the edges with a little water, press them together to seal and place the roll on a lightly greased baking sheet. Brush the top with milk.

Bake the Chestnut Roll for 30–40 minutes, until the pastry is cooked. Serve it in thick slices garnished with watercress and accompanied by a creamy white sauce (see page 72) and a cucumber salad, if liked. **Serves 4**

Slimmer's Quiche

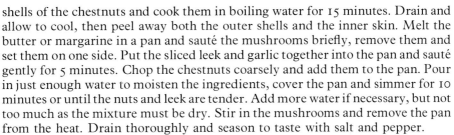

For anyone who loves quiche but wants to avoid too many fats (and calories!)

METRIC/IMPERIAL	AMERICAN
Pastry	*Dough*
225 g/8 oz plain wholemeal flour	2 cups wholewheat flour
pinch of salt	pinch of salt
100 g/4 oz soft margarine	$\frac{1}{2}$ cup soft margarine
about 2 tablespoons cold water	about 3 tablespoons cold water
Filling	*Filling*
1 tablespoon oil	1 tablespoon oil
1 small onion, chopped	1 small onion, chopped
3 eggs	3 eggs
225 g/8 oz cottage cheese	1 cup cottage cheese
salt and pepper	salt and pepper
75 g/3 oz bean sprouts	$1\frac{1}{2}$ cups bean sprouts

Set the oven at moderately hot (200 C, 400 F, gas 6) and place a large baking sheet inside to heat up. Mix together the flour and salt and rub in the margarine. Add enough water to bind the mixture to a dough, turn it on to a lightly floured surface and knead until smooth and elastic. Wrap the dough in cling film (saran wrap) and put it into the refrigerator.

Heat the oil in a saucepan and sauté the chopped onion for about 5 minutes, until just beginning to soften. Remove from the pan and drain on absorbent kitchen paper. Beat the eggs. Mash the cottage cheese until thick and creamy and combine it with the egg and salt and pepper to taste. On a lightly floured surface, roll out the pastry to a round and use it to line a 20-cm/8-in flan tin or pie pan. Mix the onion with the bean sprouts and spread these ingredients across the pastry, then pour in the egg and cheese mixture. Put the flan on the hot baking sheet to help the pastry cook and bake it in the preheated oven for 10 minutes, then turn the temperature down to moderate (180 C, 350 F, gas 4) for a further 30–40 minutes or until the filling has set. **Serves 4**

Egg and Bean Sprout Rolls

METRIC/IMPERIAL	AMERICAN
Rolls	*Rolls*
75 g/3 oz plain wholemeal flour	¾ cup wholewheat flour
pinch of salt	pinch of salt
1 egg, beaten	1 egg, beaten
about 200 ml/7 fl oz milk	¾ cup milk
2 teaspoons vegetable oil	2 teaspoons vegetable oil
150 ml/¼ pint vegetable oil for frying	⅔ cup vegetable oil for frying
Filling	*Filling*
about 1 tablespoon vegetable oil	about 1 tablespoon vegetable oil
2 eggs, beaten	2 eggs, beaten
100 g/4 oz bean sprouts	2 cups bean sprouts
salt and pepper	salt and pepper
soy sauce	soy sauce
1 egg white, beaten	1 egg white, beaten

Sift together the flour and salt, putting aside the bran for use in another recipe. Make a well in the centre, pour in the egg and mix well. Using a wooden spoon gradually beat in the milk and oil to make a smooth batter. Leave it to stand for 30 minutes. Heat a little of the oil for frying in a frying pan or skillet and, when very hot, pour in the minimum amount of batter to cover the base. Cook the pancake on one side only, remove it to a plate, and use the rest of the batter in the same way.

Now make the filling. Heat the oil in a clean frying pan and add the beaten eggs. Cook gently to make an omelette, then set it on one side. Add a drop more oil to the pan if necessary and sauté the bean sprouts for 30 seconds. Season them with salt, pepper and soy sauce to taste. Cut the omelette into little strips and mix them with the bean sprouts.

Spread the filling on the cooked side of four of the pancakes (you can freeze any extra ones) and roll the pancakes up to half way. Tuck in the sides and continue rolling to make secure packages. Seal the edges with a little egg white and secure the rolls with wooden cocktail sticks (toothpicks).

Heat the remaining oil for frying and shallow fry the rolls, turning gently, for 3–4 minutes until evenly coloured. Drain and serve piping hot with Sweet and Sour Cabbage (see below). Although rice is traditional with Chinese food, wholewheat noodles also make a tasty accompaniment. **Serves 4**

Sweet and Sour Cabbage

METRIC/IMPERIAL	AMERICAN
1 (227 g/8 oz) can pineapple segments in natural juice	1 (8 oz) can pineapple segments in natural juice
1 medium white cabbage	1 medium white cabbage
1 small onion	1 small onion
1 tablespoon cider vinegar	1 tablespoon cider vinegar
1 tablespoon clear honey	1 tablespoon clear honey
pinch of mustard powder	pinch of mustard powder
salt and pepper	salt and pepper
soy sauce	soy sauce
50 g/2 oz blanched almonds, coarsely chopped	⅓ cup coarsely chopped blanched almonds

Drain the pineapple, reserving the juice. Clean, trim, and shred the cabbage. Chop the onion very finely. Put the cabbage into a pan with the vinegar, honey, onion and about 150 ml/¼ pint (⅔ cup) of the pineapple juice. Sprinkle the mixture with the mustard and salt, pepper and soy sauce to taste, cover the pan and bring to the boil. Lower the heat and continue cooking very gently for about 10 minutes, until the cabbage is almost cooked, but still retains its crispness. Stir in the pineapple segments and chopped nuts and cook the cabbage uncovered for a few more minutes. Taste to see that the flavour is right – if it is too sweet, add more soy sauce or vinegar; if too sour, add a little honey. **Serves 4**

Gougère

Illustrated on page 48

METRIC/IMPERIAL	AMERICAN
Choux Pastry	*Choux Paste*
75 g/3 oz plain wholemeal flour	¾ cup wholewheat flour
pinch of salt	pinch of salt
50 g/2 oz butter or margarine	¼ cup butter or margarine
150 ml/¼ pint water	⅔ cup water
2 large eggs, lightly beaten	2 large eggs, lightly beaten
40 g/1½ oz Cheddar cheese, grated	⅓ cup grated Cheddar cheese
Filling	*Filling*
2 tablespoons oil	3 tablespoons oil
1 onion, finely chopped	1 onion, finely chopped
½ clove garlic, crushed	½ clove garlic, crushed
2 large courgettes	2 large zucchini
4 large tomatoes	4 large tomatoes
salt and pepper	salt and pepper
1–2 tablespoons water	2–3 tablespoons water
50 g/2 oz cooked peas	⅓ cup cooked peas
chopped fresh parsley or chives to garnish (optional)	chopped fresh parsley or chives to garnish (optional)

Set the oven at moderately hot (200 C, 400 F, gas 6). Sift the flour with the salt, reserving the bran for another recipe. Combine the fat and water in a small saucepan and heat gently until the fat melts. Then bring the mixture to the boil and immediately add the flour. Beat the ingredients quickly with a wooden spoon until the mixture forms a dough and comes away from the side of the pan. Leave to cool for a few minutes, then gradually beat in the eggs, a little at a time, and continue beating until the mixture is thick and glossy in texture.

Place the dough in a piping bag fitted with a large plain nozzle (tip) and pipe choux buns around the inside edge of a round, greased ovenproof dish. Sprinkle with grated Cheddar and bake for 30–40 minutes or until well risen.

Heat the oil in a pan and sauté the chopped onion and garlic for 5–10 minutes. Slice the courgettes (zucchini) and the tomatoes and add them to the pan with salt and pepper to taste. Sauté the vegetables briefly, then pour in enough water to moisten the pan, cover and simmer the vegetables for 15–20 minutes. Stir in the cooked peas and allow them to heat through.

Arrange the Gougère on an attractive serving dish and fill the centre with the vegetables. Sprinkle with chopped fresh parsley or chives, if liked, and serve cut into wedges. A cheese or tomato sauce (see page 72) goes well with this dish. **Serves 4**

Aviyal (Mild Vegetable Curry)

The vegetable combination given here is a tasty one, but you can use whatever you have handy. Try, however, to include okra (better known as 'ladies fingers') as they are the ingredient that makes this curry different.

METRIC/IMPERIAL		AMERICAN	
2 carrots		2 carrots	
1 potato		1 potato	
½ small cauliflower	or about	½ small cauliflower	or about
2 tomatoes	675 g/1½ lb	2 tomatoes	1½ lb
50 g/2 oz shelled fresh or frozen peas	vegetables of your choice	⅓ cup shelled fresh or frozen peas	vegetables of your choice
100 g/4 oz fresh or canned okra		¼ lb fresh or canned okra	

1 onion

1 green pepper

4 tablespoons vegetable oil or Ghee (page 74) — American; 3 tablespoons vegetable oil or Ghee (page 74) — Metric/Imperial

METRIC/IMPERIAL	AMERICAN
1 onion	1 onion
1 green pepper	1 green pepper
3 tablespoons vegetable oil or Ghee (page 74)	4 tablespoons vegetable oil or Ghee (page 74)
1 teaspoon ground turmeric	1 teaspoon ground turmeric
2 teaspoons ground coriander	2 teaspoons ground coriander
2 teaspoons ground cumin	2 teaspoons ground cumin
1 teaspoon mustard seed	1 teaspoon mustard seed
salt and pepper	salt and pepper
50–75 g/2–3 oz fresh grated or desiccated coconut	⅔–1 cup fresh grated or shredded coconut
1 (150-g/5.3-oz) carton natural yogurt	⅔ cup plain yogurt

Wash and trim all the vegetables, peel and chop the carrots and potato and break the cauliflower into florets. Chop the tomatoes. Parboil the harder vegetables such as the peas, carrots and potato in boiling salted water for about 5 minutes, so that they will be partially cooked when added to the sauce. Drain, reserving the cooking water.

Finely chop the onion and green pepper. Heat the oil or ghee in a large heavy-based pan and put in the onion, pepper and all the spices. Sauté the mixture, stirring frequently, for 5 minutes. Add the rest of the vegetables to the pan, season with salt and pepper to taste and pour in just enough water to moisten the mixture – if you have parboiled some of the vegetables first, use the reserved cooking water for this. Cook gently, stirring occasionally and topping up the liquid if necessary, for about 10 minutes until the vegetables are tender but still crunchy. Be careful not to add too much water as the curry should be fairly dry at this stage.

Sprinkle in coconut to taste and cook for a few minutes more, then add the yogurt. Remove the curry from the heat and serve at once with plain boiled brown rice and Chapatis (see opposite). Small side dishes of sliced bananas, peanuts, mango chutney and sliced cucumber in yogurt make the meal complete. **Serves 4**

Chapatis

METRIC/IMPERIAL	AMERICAN
225 g/8 oz plain wholemeal flour	2 cups wholewheat flour
pinch of salt	pinch of salt
5–6 tablespoons water	about ½ cup water
2 tablespoons oil (optional)	3 tablespoons oil (optional)

Put the flour into a bowl with the salt and gradually mix in enough cold water to make a soft dough. Knead it well, then set it aside for 1 hour before kneading again. Divide the dough into small balls and roll them out on a floured board to make thin rounds about 10 cm/4 in across.

Pour the oil, if used, into a heavy-based pan – otherwise simply grease the pan lightly – and heat the pan until very hot. Cook the circles of dough for 15–20 seconds on each side until brown spots appear; do not overcook the Chapatis or they will be hard. Serve them as soon as possible. **Makes 4–6**

Swiss Cheese Fondue

METRIC/IMPERIAL	AMERICAN
15 g/½ oz butter	1 tablespoon butter
300 ml/½ pint dry white wine	1¼ cups dry white wine
450 g/1 lb Gruyère cheese, grated	1 lb Gruyère cheese, grated
salt and pepper	salt and pepper
2–3 tablespoons brandy or Kirsch (optional)	3–4 tablespoons brandy or Kirsch (optional)
fresh wholemeal or French bread to serve	fresh wholewheat or French bread to serve

Use the butter to grease the side and bottom of a flameproof casserole or a heavy-based pan. Pour in the wine, add the grated Gruyère and salt and pepper to taste and heat very gently, stirring occasionally, until the cheese melts and you have a thick, creamy sauce. Simmer for 5 minutes, then transfer to the table and stand the casserole over a candle-burner to keep the fondue warm and to prevent it from becoming too thick.

Stir in a little brandy or Kirsch to give the fondue extra taste. Serve cubes of fresh bread in a basket and give each diner a fork with which to dip bread into the fondue. A crisp green salad is the perfect complement to this dish, served either as an accompaniment or as a starter beforehand. **Serves 4**

VARIATION

If you like the taste of caraway, try sprinkling 1–2 teaspoons caraway seeds into the fondue with the cheese – it changes the character of the dish completely, giving it a really unusual flavour. But if you're planning this for a dinner party, check with your guests first – I usually find that if someone doesn't like caraway they loathe it!

Light Lunches and Snacks

Sandwiches with a Difference

There is nothing so easy to make as a sandwich – yet nothing quite so boring far too often. Here are some ways to make sandwiches less of a snack, more of a mouth-watering meal.

The Open Sandwich

This is best made using really firm bread – some wholemeal bread is close-textured and therefore ideal, otherwise use German pumpernickel or rye bread. Slimmers can, of course, use crispbread as a base and wholemeal crackers are also good spread with a variety of toppings.

TOPPINGS

Freshly fried mushrooms garnished with chopped fresh chives
and tomato slices.

Lettuce topped with potato salad and sliced stuffed olives and sprinkled
with a pinch of paprika.

Sliced hard-boiled egg topped with Mayonnaise (page 109)
and soya 'bacon' pieces.

Slices of tomato topped with asparagus and a little chopped fresh chervil.

Herbed Lentil Pâté (page 30) topped with watercress and capers.

Small raw or blanched cauliflower florets mixed with soured cream, topped
with flaked roasted almonds.

Avocado mashed with a little lemon juice, chilli powder and Mayonnaise
(page 109) and topped with slivers of red pepper.

Cucumber slices topped with blue cheese (Dolcelatte, Danish Blue) mixed
with Mayonnaise (page 109) and sprinkled with drained canned sweet corn.

Peanut butter sprinkled with mustard and cress and chopped onion.

Cream cheese mixed with finely chopped fresh or canned pineapple
and walnuts.

Tahini and sliced banana sprinkled with lemon juice and honey.

Cottage cheese mixed with fresh peach slices and sprinkled
with raw brown sugar.

Grated dessert apple sprinkled with lemon juice, chopped nuts and honey.

Hazelnut Butter (page 74) topped with pear slices dipped in lemon juice.

Tofu mashed with honey or maple syrup.

The Bumper Sandwich

Illustrated on page 68

METRIC/IMPERIAL	AMERICAN
5 thin slices wholemeal bread	5 thin slices wholewheat bread
butter or margarine to spread	butter or margarine to spread
salt and pepper	salt and pepper
Filling 1	*Filling 1*
a few lettuce leaves	a few lettuce leaves
¼ cucumber, finely sliced	¼ cucumber, finely sliced
2 radishes, sliced	2 radishes, sliced
¼ punnet mustard and cress	¼ punnet mustard and cress
Filling 2	*Filling 2*
cold scrambled egg (made with 2 eggs)	cold scrambled egg (made with 2 eggs)
2–3 gherkins, chopped	2–3 sweet dill pickles, chopped
2 teaspoons Mayonnaise (page 109)	2 teaspoons Mayonnaise (page 109)
Filling 3	*Filling 3*
3 tomatoes, finely sliced	3 tomatoes, finely sliced
1 onion, finely sliced	1 onion, finely sliced
Filling 4	*Filling 4*
50 g/2 oz Edam cheese, thinly sliced	2 oz Edam cheese, thinly sliced
watercress	watercress
Garnish	*Garnish*
4 black olives	4 ripe olives
4 button mushrooms	4 button mushrooms
sprig of chervil (optional)	sprig of chervil (optional)

Spread the bread with the butter or margarine and lay one piece on a plate. Arrange the lettuce, sliced cucumber and radishes and mustard and cress on top of it and cover with the second slice. Spread this with a mixture of the egg, chopped gherkins (sweet dill pickles), and the mayonnaise and sprinkle with salt and pepper to taste. Add another piece of bread and cover it with the sliced tomatoes, onion and seasoning to taste. On the fourth piece arrange the sliced cheese and watercress. Press the last slice on top of the pile and garnish the sandwich with olives, mushrooms and chervil, if used.

Cut the sandwich in half diagonally and serve – it is probably easier to eat with knives and forks than fingers. **Serves 2**

Scrambled Eggs with Tofu

Illustrated on page 65

METRIC/IMPERIAL	AMERICAN
25 g/1 oz butter or margarine	2 tablespoons butter or margarine
275 g/10 oz tofu, diced	1¼ cups diced tofu
4 eggs	4 eggs
salt and pepper	salt and pepper
pinch of paprika	pinch of paprika
chopped fresh chives to garnish	chopped fresh chives to garnish

Melt the butter or margarine in a pan. Drain the tofu and add it to the pan, mashing it with the fat to a crumb-like mixture. Sauté for a few minutes.

Beat the eggs with salt and pepper to taste and pour the mixture over the tofu. Cook gently, stirring the eggs up from the bottom, until the mixture begins to set but is still soft. Remove the pan from the heat and allow the egg to set completely for about 1 minute before serving it on toast or fresh, lightly steamed spinach. Sprinkle paprika and chopped fresh chives over the top. **Serves 4**

Avocado Omelette

Illustrated on pages 66–67

METRIC/IMPERIAL	AMERICAN
8 eggs	8 eggs
2 ripe avocados	2 ripe avocados
salt and pepper	salt and pepper
about 50 g/2 oz butter or margarine	¼ cup butter or margarine
Garnish	*Garnish*
lemon slices	lemon slices
chopped fresh chives (optional)	chopped fresh chives (optional)

Omelettes are best when small, so make four of them using 2 eggs and half an avocado for each one.

For each omelette, lightly beat the eggs. Cut the avocados in half, remove the stones and scoop out the flesh. Mash this and add one quarter of it to each portion of beaten egg. Season with salt and pepper to taste.

Gently melt 15 g/½ oz (1 tablespoon) of the fat in a large-based pan and when quite hot, pour in the first egg mixture, tilting the pan so that it spreads evenly. Continue cooking over a low heat, from time to time lifting the edge of the omelette with a spatula so that any uncooked egg runs underneath. When the omelette is nearly set but still a little creamy on top, use the spatula to fold it in half and transfer it to a warmed plate. Serve immediately, garnished with the lemon slices and chives, if used. Make the other omelettes in the same way. **Serves 4**

VARIATIONS

Instead of mashing the avocados and cooking them with the egg, cut the flesh into slices and use it as a filling.

For a real gourmet's delight, gently fry a few pistachio nuts in the pan before adding the omelette mixture, then continue cooking as above.

Hot Stuffed Tomatoes

Illustrated on pages 66–67

METRIC/IMPERIAL	AMERICAN
4 large tomatoes	4 large tomatoes
50 g/2 oz mushrooms	½ cup mushrooms
25 g/1 oz butter or margarine	2 tablespoons butter or margarine
½ clove garlic, crushed	½ clove garlic, crushed
100 g/4 oz cooked brown rice	¾ cup cooked brown rice
1 tablespoon chopped fresh parsley or basil	1 tablespoon chopped fresh parsley or basil
50 g/2 oz Cheddar cheese, grated	½ cup grated Cheddar cheese
salt and pepper	salt and pepper
about 1 tablespoon tomato purée	about 1 tablespoon tomato purée

Set the oven at moderately hot (190 C, 375 F, gas 4). Wash and dry the tomatoes. Cut a slice from the round end of each, scoop out the seeds and pulp with a teaspoon and chop these coarsely.

Finely slice the mushrooms. Melt the butter or margarine in a pan and sauté the mushrooms with the garlic until soft. Stir in the rice, chopped tomato pulp, parsley or basil, grated cheese and salt and pepper to taste. Add enough tomato purée to bind the ingredients to a moist mixture and mix well. Divide the filling between the tomato cases and arrange the tomatoes in a shallow ovenproof dish, then top each one with its own lid. Bake for 10–15 minutes or until puffed up and hot right through. Serve at once, or leave to cool and serve them cold. **Serves 4**

Deep-fried Rice Balls

Illustrated on pages 66–67

METRIC/IMPERIAL	AMERICAN
275 g/10 oz brown rice	1⅓ cups brown rice
750 ml/1¼ pints Vegetable Stock (page 22) or water	3 cups Vegetable Stock (page 22) or water
50 g/2 oz Parmesan cheese, grated	½ cup grated Parmesan cheese
50 g/2 oz butter or margarine	¼ cup butter or margarine
½ teaspoon dried oregano or thyme	½ teaspoon dried oregano or thyme
salt and pepper	salt and pepper
2 eggs, beaten	2 eggs, beaten
100 g/4 oz mozzarella cheese, diced	⅔ cup diced mozzarella cheese
about 75 g/3 oz dried wholemeal breadcrumbs	about ¾ cup dried wholewheat breadcrumbs
oil for deep-frying	oil for deep-frying

Wash the rice thoroughly under cold water and drain. Bring the vegetable stock or fresh water to the boil in a pan and add the rice; lower the heat and simmer for 30–40 minutes until the rice is soft and all the liquid has been absorbed. Turn the rice into a bowl. Allow to cool slightly, then stir in the Parmesan, butter or margarine, herbs, salt and pepper to taste and enough beaten egg to bind the mixture together; do not make it too wet or it will be difficult to shape.

Wet your hands and mould some of the rice mixture around each piece of mozzarella to make a thick, even coating. Dip each rice ball into the remaining beaten egg, then into the breadcrumbs. Heat the oil in a deep pan to 180 C/350 F and deep-fry the rice balls, a few at a time, until crisp and golden. Serve while still hot with a hot (or for a change, cold) tomato sauce (see pages 72–73). **Serves 4**

Quick Sunflower Seed Burgers

METRIC/IMPERIAL	AMERICAN
100 g/4 oz sunflower seeds, ground	1 cup sunflower seeds, ground
100 g/4 oz fresh wholemeal breadcrumbs	2 cups fresh wholewheat breadcrumbs
1 teaspoon chopped fresh or ½ teaspoon dried basil	1 teaspoon chopped fresh or ½ teaspoon dried basil
½ teaspoon fresh or ¼ teaspoon dried thyme	½ teaspoon fresh or ¼ teaspoon dried thyme
salt and pepper	salt and pepper
1 small onion, finely chopped	1 small onion, finely chopped
½ clove garlic, crushed	½ clove garlic, crushed
about 150 ml/¼ pint Vegetable Stock (page 22) or 1 large egg, lightly beaten	⅔ cup Vegetable Stock (page 22) or 1 large egg, lightly beaten
about 50 g/2 oz plain wholemeal flour	½ cup wholewheat flour
oil for frying (optional)	oil for frying (optional)

In a bowl mix together the ground sunflower seeds, breadcrumbs, herbs, a little salt and a pinch of pepper. Stir in the onion and garlic, making sure they are evenly distributed, then add the vegetable stock or beaten egg and mix well to bind the ingredients together. Using floured hands, shape the mixture into 4–6 burgers, depending on the size you prefer. Stir a little more salt and pepper into the flour and dip each burger into the mixture to coat thoroughly. Heat the oil, if used, in a frying pan and shallow fry the burgers for 2–3 minutes on each side until crisp and golden.

Alternatively, simply brush them with oil, lay them on a greased baking sheet and bake them in a moderate oven (180 C, 350 F, gas 4) for 30 minutes, turning once. **Serves 4**

Cauliflower with Pasta

METRIC/IMPERIAL	AMERICAN
1 medium cauliflower	1 medium cauliflower
350 g/12 oz wholewheat pasta shells	3 cups wholewheat pasta shells
1 tablespoon vegetable oil	1 tablespoon vegetable oil
1 clove garlic, crushed	1 clove garlic, crushed
300 ml/½ pint Tomato Sauce (page 72)	1¼ cups Tomato Sauce (page 72)
salt and pepper	salt and pepper
Garnish	*Garnish*
12 green olives	12 green olives
chopped fresh parsley	chopped fresh parsley

Break the cauliflower into florets and steam or boil them in a little salted water for about 5 minutes, until almost cooked. Bring a separate pan of salted water to the boil, add the pasta shells and cook them for 10 minutes or until just tender.

Meanwhile, heat the oil in a frying pan and sauté the garlic for a few minutes. Stir in the tomato sauce with salt and pepper to taste and heat through.

Drain the pasta and cauliflower and mix them together in an attractive serving dish. Pour the sauce over the top and garnish with olives and parsley. **Serves 4**

VARIATION
You can add protein to this dish by stirring 2–3 tablespoons tahini or natural (plain) yogurt to taste into the sauce before serving.

Mixed Grain Pilau

METRIC/IMPERIAL	AMERICAN
1 onion	1 onion
1 red pepper	1 red pepper
4 tablespoons vegetable oil	⅓ cup vegetable oil
½–1 clove garlic, crushed	½–1 clove garlic, crushed
½ teaspoon ground cardamom	½ teaspoon ground cardamom
½ teaspoon ground cumin	½ teaspoon ground cumin
½ teaspoon ground coriander	½ teaspoon ground coriander
1 bay leaf	1 bay leaf
225 g/8 oz mixed cooked grains (rice, wholewheat grains, kasha, millet)	1½ cups mixed cooked grains (rice, whole berry wheat, kasha, millet)
100 g/4 oz cooked peas	¾ cup cooked peas
50 g/2 oz sultanas	⅓ cup seedless white raisins
salt and pepper	salt and pepper
2 hard-boiled eggs	2 hard-cooked eggs
50 g/2 oz almonds (in their skins) or cooked soya beans	½ cup almonds (in their skins) or cooked soy beans

Chop the onion and red pepper. Heat the oil in a pan and gently sauté the onion, pepper and garlic for a few minutes until they begin to soften. Add the spices and bay leaf and cook for 1–2 more minutes. Stir in the grains, peas and sultanas (seedless white raisins), gently mix all the ingredients together and continue cooking over a low heat until warmed right through. Season with salt and pepper to taste and pile the pilau on to a serving dish. Coarsely chop the eggs and the almonds or soya beans and sprinkle these over the pilau. **Serves 4**

Parsnip Flan (page 69); Scrambled Egg with Tofu (page 61).

Overleaf Avocado Omelette (page 62); Deep-fried Rice Balls with Tomato Sauce (page 63); Hot Stuffed Tomatoes (page 62)

Parsnip Flan

Illustrated on page 65

METRIC/IMPERIAL	AMERICAN
Flan case	*Pie case*
1 (198-g/7-oz) packet wholemeal crackers or crispbread	1 (7-oz) packet wholemeal crackers or crispbread
about 75 g/3 oz butter or margarine	about ⅓ cup butter or margarine
50 g/2 oz Cheddar cheese, grated	½ cup grated Cheddar cheese
salt and pepper	salt and pepper
Filling	*Filling*
450 g/1 lb parsnips	1 lb parsnips
2 eggs, beaten	2 eggs, beaten
50 g/2 oz Cheddar cheese, grated	½ cup grated Cheddar cheese
pinch of freshly grated nutmeg	pinch of freshly grated nutmeg
salt and pepper	salt and pepper
2 large tomatoes, sliced	2 large tomatoes, sliced

Set the oven at moderately hot (190 C, 375 F, gas 5). Put the crackers or crispbread into a plastic bag and crush them to fine, even-sized crumbs with a rolling pin. Melt the butter or margarine in a pan and stir in the crumbs, adding a little more fat if the mixture seems dry. Stir well, add the grated Cheddar and salt and pepper to taste and remove the pan from the heat. Grease a 20-cm/8-in flan tin or pie pan and line it with the mixture. Stand in a cool place to firm up.

Peel and chop the parsnips and cook them in boiling salted water for 15–20 minutes until tender. Mash them to a purée and leave to cool slightly. Mix in the beaten egg, grated Cheddar, nutmeg and salt and pepper to taste, spoon the mixture into the flan case and arrange the sliced tomatoes on top. Bake for 20–30 minutes until the filling is cooked and the flan case crisp. **Serves 4**

Black-eye Bean Casserole

METRIC/IMPERIAL	AMERICAN
225 g/8 oz black-eye beans, soaked in water overnight	1¼ cups black-eyed peas, soaked in water overnight
2 tablespoons vegetable oil	3 tablespoons vegetable oil
1 large carrot, sliced	1 large carrot, sliced
1 large leek, sliced	1 large leek, sliced
2 large onions, chopped	2 large onions, chopped
50 g/2 oz canned sweet corn	⅓ cup canned corn
½–1 teaspoon dried thyme or savory	½–1 teaspoon dried thyme or savory
1 teaspoon yeast extract or to taste	1 teaspoon yeast extract or to taste
salt and pepper	salt and pepper
about 200 ml/7 fl oz Vegetable Stock (page 22)	about ¾ cup Vegetable Stock (page 22)

Drain the black-eye beans, put them into a pan with fresh water to cover and bring to the boil. Simmer for 45–60 minutes, until tender, drain and leave on one side.

Set the oven at moderately hot (200 C, 400 F, gas 6). Heat the oil in a pan and sauté the chopped carrot, leek and onions for 5–10 minutes. Drain the sweet corn and add it to the pan, followed by the black-eye beans, then turn all the ingredients into an ovenproof casserole. Mix the herbs, yeast extract and salt and pepper to taste into the stock and pour this into the casserole. Cover and bake for about 30 minutes. Serve in individual soup bowls with Wholemeal Baps (see page 120), brown rice or any other kind of grain and a small salad. **Serves 4**

Bumper Sandwich (page 60).

Baked Vegetables with Nut Topping

METRIC/IMPERIAL	AMERICAN
2 onions	2 onions
2 leeks	2 leeks
2 large carrots	2 large carrots
$\frac{1}{2}$ small cabbage	$\frac{1}{2}$ small cabbage
2 tablespoons oil	3 tablespoons oil
1 teaspoon fresh or $\frac{1}{2}$ teaspoon dried thyme	1 teaspoon fresh or $\frac{1}{2}$ teaspoon dried thyme
dash of soy sauce	dash of soy sauce
salt and pepper	salt and pepper
75 g/3 oz raw or roasted peanuts	$\frac{3}{4}$ cup raw or roasted peanuts
75 g/3 oz dried wholemeal breadcrumbs	$\frac{3}{4}$ cup dried wholewheat breadcrumbs

Set the oven at moderate (180 C, 350 F, gas 4). Slice the onions and leeks. Chop the carrots and cabbage. Heat the oil in a large pan and sauté the onion gently for 5 minutes. Stir in the carrots, coating them well with oil and cook for 5 minutes more. Add the leeks and cabbage and cook for a further 5 minutes. If you like your vegetables crunchy, take the pan off the heat now as they are ready. If you prefer them well cooked, sprinkle them with a little water, cover the pan and continue cooking for 5–10 minutes until soft.

Transfer the vegetables to a shallow ovenproof dish and sprinkle in the thyme, soy sauce and salt and pepper to taste. Chop the peanuts coarsely, mix them with the breadcrumbs and spread the mixture evenly over the vegetables. Bake for 20 minutes or until the topping is golden and crunchy. Serve with a cheese or peanut sauce, if liked (see pages 72–73). **Serves 4**

Onion and Tomato Bake

I'm mad about the taste of basil and usually put in even more than suggested here. It's the ideal herb to go with tomatoes and onions.

METRIC/IMPERIAL	AMERICAN
275 g/10 oz broad beans	10 oz fresh lima beans
3 large onions	3 large onions
450 g/1 lb tomatoes	1 lb tomatoes
1 tablespoon oil	1 tablespoon oil
50 g/2 oz butter or margarine	$\frac{1}{4}$ cup butter or margarine
1–2 tablespoons chopped fresh or 2–3 teaspoons dried basil	1–2 tablespoons chopped fresh or 2–3 teaspoons dried basil
salt and pepper	salt and pepper
50 g/2 oz dried wholemeal breadcrumbs	$\frac{1}{2}$ cup dried wholewheat breadcrumbs

Set the oven at moderately hot (200 C, 400 F, gas 6). Shell the broad (lima) beans and cook them in boiling salted water for about 20 minutes or until tender. Drain and leave on one side.

Slice the onions and tomatoes. Heat the oil in a pan and lightly sauté the onion until it begins to soften. Arrange half of it in the base of a shallow ovenproof dish, cover with half the beans and top with half the sliced tomatoes. Divide the butter or margarine into three portions and cut each into small pieces. Sprinkle one portion over the layer of tomatoes followed by half the basil and salt and pepper to taste. Repeat these layers, using up the rest of the onion, beans, tomatoes, basil and a second portion of butter or margarine. Spread the breadcrumbs evenly over the top of the dish and dot with the remaining fat. Bake for 20 minutes or until nicely browned. **Serves 4**

Fennel au Gratin

METRIC/IMPERIAL	AMERICAN
450 g/1 lb fennel	1 lb fennel
25 g/1 oz butter or margarine	2 tablespoons butter or margarine
15 g/½ oz plain wholemeal flour	2 tablespoons wholewheat flour
300 ml/½ pint milk	1¼ cups milk
50 g/2 oz Gruyère cheese, grated	½ cup grated Gruyère cheese
50 g/2 oz Parmesan cheese, grated	½ cup grated Parmesan cheese
salt and pepper	salt and pepper
25 g/1 oz dried wholemeal breadcrumbs	¼ cup dried wholewheat breadcrumbs

Trim the fennel bulbs, removing the hard stalks. Cut off the feathery leaves, reserving these on one side, and slice the bulbs into halves or quarters, depending on their size. Bring some salted water to the boil in a pan, add the fennel and simmer for 15–20 minutes until tender.

Make a white sauce (see page 72) with the butter or margarine, the flour and milk, remove the pan from the heat and beat in the grated Gruyère with all but 15 g/½ oz Parmesan. If the sauce is too thick, add a little more milk or water. Season with salt and pepper to taste.

Drain the fennel and arrange it in a shallow flameproof dish. Pour the sauce on top to cover completely. Mix the remaining Parmesan with the breadcrumbs, sprinkle the mixture over the fennel and grill the dish for just a few minutes, until lightly browned. Serve garnished with the reserved fennel leaves. **Serves 4**

Jacket Parsnips

METRIC/IMPERIAL	AMERICAN
4 medium parsnips	4 medium parsnips
75 g/3 oz ham-flavoured soya chunks (optional)	½ cup textured vegetable protein 'ham' chunks (optional)
175 ml/6 fl oz water (optional)	¾ cup water (optional)
2 tablespoons oil	3 tablespoons oil
15 g/½ oz butter or margarine	1 tablespoon butter or margarine
1 large onion, chopped	1 large onion, chopped
50 g/2 oz canned sweet corn	⅓ cup canned corn
salt and pepper	salt and pepper
chopped fresh parsley to garnish	chopped fresh parsley to garnish

Try to pick plump, fairly unblemished parsnips and chop off the long, thin ends so that they will stand firmly. Scrub the skins, remove the tops and arrange the parsnips on a baking sheet. Bake them in a moderately hot oven (190 C, 375 F, gas 5) for about 1 hour, until tender – the exact cooking time depends on the size and age of the vegetables.

While the parsnips are cooking, prepare the filling. Hydrate the ham-flavoured chunks, if used, by putting them in a pan with the water, bringing to the boil and simmering them over a low heat for 20–30 minutes, following the instructions on the packet. Drain the chunks and leave on one side.

Heat the oil with the butter or margarine in a pan. Add the chopped onion and cook gently for 10 minutes, stirring occasionally to prevent it from colouring. Mix in the ham-flavoured chunks, coating them in fat and cook for a further 5 minutes, still stirring. Drain the sweet corn, add it to the pan and heat it through for 1–2 minutes. Season the mixture with salt and pepper.

When the parsnips are soft, put one on each plate and pile the filling on top. You may need to add a little more butter or margarine if it has all been absorbed in the cooking process. Sprinkle with chopped fresh parsley and serve at once. **Serves 4**

Sauces, Butters and Spreads

White Sauce

Once you know how to make a simple white sauce you will find you can adapt it in countless ways so as to add interest, texture and protein to basic ingredients. Below are some of the better known sauces. Try also adding herbs (parsley being an obvious choice), finely chopped mushrooms or celery, fennel, French mustard, chopped gherkins and capers and so on.

METRIC/IMPERIAL	AMERICAN
25 g/1 oz butter or margarine	2 tablespoons butter or margarine
25 g/1 oz plain wholemeal flour	$\frac{1}{4}$ cup wholewheat flour
300 ml/$\frac{1}{2}$ pint milk	$1\frac{1}{4}$ cups milk
salt and pepper	salt and pepper

Melt the fat over a low heat and sprinkle in the flour, then cook gently for a few minutes to make a roux. Gradually pour in the milk, stirring continuously, and bring the mixture to the boil. Cook for about 1 minute, stirring until the sauce thickens. Season with salt and pepper to taste and use as required.

  This makes a fairly thick sauce; if you prefer it to be thinner, just add a little more milk. **Makes 300 ml/$\frac{1}{2}$ pint ($1\frac{1}{4}$ cups)**

VARIATIONS

Cream Sauce Make the sauce as above but using half milk and half single (light) cream for a much richer tasting sauce.

Cheese Sauce Mix 75–100 g/3–4 oz ($\frac{3}{4}$–1 cup) grated Cheddar cheese and a pinch of dry mustard into the finished sauce. Stir well so that the cheese melts completely.

Yogurt Cheese Sauce Make the sauce following the basic recipe and let it cool slightly, stirring to prevent a skin from forming. Mix in about 150 g/5 oz ($\frac{2}{3}$ cup) natural (plain) yogurt and 100 g/4 oz (1 cup) grated Cheddar cheese. Season with a pinch of paprika and salt and pepper to taste.

Onion Sauce Melt the fat as for basic White Sauce and add a finely chopped onion to the pan. Sauté it gently for a few minutes before sprinkling in the flour and proceeding as above.

Tomato Sauce (hot)

METRIC/IMPERIAL	AMERICAN
2 tablespoons oil	3 tablespoons oil
2 cloves garlic, crushed	2 cloves garlic, crushed
450 g/1 lb ripe tomatoes or 2 (227-g/8-oz) cans tomatoes	1 lb ripe tomatoes or 2 (8-oz) cans tomatoes
1 teaspoon dried oregano	1 teaspoon dried oregano
pinch of raw brown sugar	pinch of raw brown sugar
salt and pepper	salt and pepper

Heat the oil in a pan and gently sauté the crushed garlic for a few moments. Add the tomatoes, oregano, sugar and salt and pepper to taste and cook over a medium heat, stirring frequently, until the tomatoes are reduced to a pulp (add a drop of water if it seems too dry). Taste and adjust seasoning and serve. **Serves 4**

Blender Tomato Sauce (cold)

METRIC/IMPERIAL
450 g/1 lb tomatoes
2 onions
1–2 cloves garlic, crushed
1 tablespoon fresh or 2 teaspoons dried
marjoram
salt and pepper
pinch of raw brown sugar (optional)
a little tomato purée (optional)

AMERICAN
1 lb tomatoes
2 onions
1–2 cloves garlic, crushed
1 tablespoon fresh or 2 teaspoons dried
marjoram
salt and pepper
pinch of raw brown sugar (optional)
a little tomato purée (optional)

Cut crosses in the bases of the tomatoes, plunge the tomatoes briefly into hot water, then into cold water and peel away the skins. Chop the flesh into small pieces. Finely chop the onions. Combine all the ingredients in a liquidiser or blender and blend them together until you have a thick, smooth sauce. You may need to add a little tomato purée if the tomatoes you are using are not very strong in flavour.

Chill the sauce in the refrigerator and adjust the seasoning just before serving. **Serves 4**

Peanut Sauce

METRIC/IMPERIAL
300 ml/½ pint Vegetable Stock (page 22)
2 tablespoons dried skimmed milk
100 g/4 oz peanut butter
1 teaspoon molasses or to taste
1 clove garlic, crushed
sprinkling of paprika

AMERICAN
1¼ cups Vegetable Stock (page 22)
3 tablespoons dried skimmed milk solids
½ cup peanut butter
1 teaspoon molasses or to taste
1 clove garlic, crushed
sprinkling of paprika

Combine the stock with the dried milk in a saucepan and bring the mixture to the boil. Dissolve the peanut butter and molasses in the mixture, add the garlic and simmer over a low heat for 15 minutes, stirring frequently. Sprinkle the sauce with paprika to taste and serve at once. **Makes about 300 ml/½ pint (1¼ cups)**

Almond Butter Sauce

METRIC/IMPERIAL
75 g/3 oz butter
25 g/1 oz ground almonds

AMERICAN
½ cup butter
2 tablespoons ground almonds

Melt the butter in a saucepan and continue cooking it gently until it begins to brown. Stir in the nuts and blend well to make a smooth sauce. Serve over vegetables for a very special topping. **Serves 4**

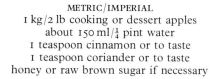

Apple Sauce

Apple sauce can be made with any kind of apples, but if you use dessert apples you won't need to add any sweetening – a great advantage if you're watching your waistline.

METRIC/IMPERIAL	AMERICAN
1 kg/2 lb cooking or dessert apples	2 lb baking or dessert apples
about 150 ml/¼ pint water	about ⅔ cup water
1 teaspoon cinnamon or to taste	1 teaspoon cinnamon or to taste
1 teaspoon coriander or to taste	1 teaspoon coriander or to taste
honey or raw brown sugar if necessary	honey or raw brown sugar if necessary

Peel, core and slice the apples, place them in a heavy-based pan with a little water and cook them over a gentle heat for about 20 minutes until the apples have broken down to make a thick purée. Stir frequently with a wooden spoon to make the sauce as smooth as possible, and add more water if it looks too dry. Add the spices and sweeten to taste.

You can use this sauce on waffles and pancakes – or eat it as a dessert on its own with a little natural (plain) yogurt and a few chopped nuts. **Serves 4**

Tofu and Banana Sauce

METRIC/IMPERIAL	AMERICAN
225 g/8 oz tofu	1 cup diced tofu
1 large ripe banana	1 large ripe banana
1–2 tablespoons maple syrup or clear honey	2–3 tablespoons maple syrup or clear honey
1 tablespoon tahini	1 tablespoon tahini
a little milk to mix	a little milk to mix

Drain the tofu, mash it to a thick cream and mix it with all the remaining ingredients. Add enough milk to give the mixture a creamy consistency and serve.

This sauce is unusually good served with Oat and Nut Waffles (see page 81), especially if you have made the waffles themselves with sesame seeds – they contrast with the creamy sauce in texture, yet have a complementary taste. **Serves 4**

Ghee (Clarified Butter)

METRIC/IMPERIAL	AMERICAN
1 kg/2 lb butter	2 lb butter

Melt the butter in a pan and bring it to the boil, stirring continuously. Lower the heat and simmer gently for 30 minutes. Take the pan off the heat, skim the froth from the top with a slotted spoon and leave the butter to cool for about 2 hours. Strain it into a jar through a piece of muslin (cheese cloth) or a sieve lined with absorbent kitchen paper and store it in the refrigerator. It will keep for up to a year. **Makes about 725 g/1 lb 10 oz (3¼ cups)**

Peanut Butter

METRIC/IMPERIAL	AMERICAN
100 g/4 oz raw peanuts	1 cup raw peanuts
1–2 tablespoons vegetable oil	2–3 tablespoons vegetable oil
salt or honey	salt or honey

Roast the peanuts first, if liked, in a very cool oven (120 C, 250 F, gas $\frac{1}{2}$) for 10–15 minutes, until just beginning to colour. Remove the outer skin if you do roast them, as this can be rather tough. Grind the nuts to a powder and mix the powder with enough oil to give a buttery texture (you will find that roast nuts need far less oil than raw ones). Add a little salt or honey to taste and store the peanut butter in a screw-top jar. Eat while still fresh. **Makes 100 g/4 oz ($\frac{1}{2}$ cup)**

VARIATIONS
Substitute hazelnuts, cashew nuts, almonds or any other kind of nut for the peanuts and make the butter as above.

Apple Spread

Follow the recipe for Apple Sauce (see opposite), but continue cooking past the point where the apples have become a soft purée. Check frequently that the apple isn't sticking to the pan and stir it often. After about 20–30 minutes the mixture will go golden brown and thicken to a buttery sauce. Add spices and sweetening once the apple has reached the desired consistency, cook for a few more minutes and spoon the mixture into a clean, warmed screw-top jar.

You can eat this spread with bread, biscuits and cakes; or use it to sweeten your breakfast porridge. Eat it within a week. **Makes about 225 g/8 oz (1 cup)**

Date and Walnut Spread

METRIC/IMPERIAL	AMERICAN
225 g/8 oz stoned dates	1$\frac{1}{4}$ cups pitted dates
2–3 teaspoons lemon juice	2–3 teaspoons lemon juice
50 g/2 oz chopped walnuts	$\frac{1}{3}$ cup chopped walnuts

Chop the dates as finely as possible and put them in a saucepan with 150 ml/$\frac{1}{4}$ pint ($\frac{2}{3}$ cup) water and the lemon juice. Heat gently, pressing continually with a wooden spoon, until the mixture is thick. Cool slightly, add the nuts and store in a screw-top jar. **Makes 400 g/14 oz (2 cups)**

Ricotta Spread

METRIC/IMPERIAL	AMERICAN
175 g/6 oz ricotta cheese	$\frac{3}{4}$ cup ricotta cheese
50 g/2 oz Parmesan cheese, grated	$\frac{1}{2}$ cup grated Parmesan cheese
generous pinch of grated nutmeg	generous pinch of grated nutmeg
salt and pepper	salt and pepper

Mix all the ingredients thoroughly together until smooth. Spread it on slices of bread; it is also delicious served with vegetables or pasta. **Serves 4**

For Growing Appetites

Banana Nut Risotto

Illustrated on pages 86–87

METRIC/IMPERIAL	AMERICAN
225 g/8 oz brown rice	1 cup brown rice
2 tablespoons vegetable oil	3 tablespoons vegetable oil
1 large onion, sliced	1 large onion, sliced
generous 600 ml/1 pint water	generous $2\frac{1}{2}$ cups water
2 large bananas	2 large bananas
2 firm tomatoes or $\frac{1}{2}$ red pepper, deseeded	2 firm tomatoes or $\frac{1}{2}$ red pepper, deseeded
100 g/4 oz cooked peas	$\frac{3}{4}$ cup cooked peas
50 g/2 oz raisins	$\frac{1}{3}$ cup raisins
salt and pepper	salt and pepper
50 g/2 oz walnut pieces or pine nuts	$\frac{1}{2}$ cup walnut pieces or pine nuts

Wash the rice thoroughly in cold water and leave to drain. Heat the oil in a saucepan and gently sauté the sliced onion for 5 minutes. Add the rice and continue cooking for a few minutes, then pour in the cold water. Cook gently, covered, for 30–40 minutes, until all the water has been absorbed and the rice is light and fluffy – you may need to add a drop more water, but do not stir the rice.

Slice the bananas and tomatoes or red pepper and mix them into the rice with the peas and raisins. Heat the risotto through for 1 minute, season to taste with salt and pepper and serve sprinkled with walnuts – or for a more delicate taste, pine nuts. **Serves 4**

Vegetable Stew with Dumplings

Illustrated on page 85

METRIC/IMPERIAL	AMERICAN
Stew	*Stew*
2 medium leeks	2 medium leeks
1 large onion	1 large onion
2 medium carrots	2 medium carrots
$\frac{1}{2}$ small cauliflower	$\frac{1}{2}$ small cauliflower
2 tablespoons oil	3 tablespoons oil
about 300 ml/$\frac{1}{2}$ pint Vegetable Stock (page 22)	about $1\frac{1}{4}$ cups Vegetable Stock (page 22)
1 teaspoon chopped fresh mixed herbs or	1 teaspoon chopped fresh mixed herbs or
$\frac{1}{2}$ teaspoon dried mixed herbs	$\frac{1}{2}$ teaspoon dried mixed herbs
50 g/2 oz mushrooms	$\frac{1}{2}$ cup mushrooms
salt and pepper	salt and pepper
chopped fresh chives to garnish	chopped fresh chives to garnish
Dumplings	*Dumplings*
25 g/1 oz butter or margarine	2 tablespoons butter or margarine
2 eggs	2 eggs
50 g/2 oz wholewheat semolina	$\frac{1}{3}$ cup wholewheat semolina
$\frac{1}{2}$ teaspoon chopped fresh mixed herbs or	$\frac{1}{2}$ teaspoon chopped fresh mixed herbs or
$\frac{1}{4}$ teaspoon dried mixed herbs	$\frac{1}{4}$ teaspoon dried mixed herbs
salt and pepper	salt and pepper

Wash the leeks thoroughly and cut them into slices. Slice the onion. Scrub and chop the carrots and break the cauliflower into florets. Heat the oil in a pan and sauté the leeks and onion for 5 minutes. Pour in the stock, add the carrots, cauliflower florets and herbs and bring the mixture to the boil. Cover the pan and simmer for 10 minutes. Slice the mushrooms, put them in the pan and cook for a further 10 minutes or until the vegetables are almost tender. Season with salt and pepper to taste.

Meanwhile, make the dumplings. Soften the butter or margarine and beat it with the eggs. Add the semolina and mix well. Sprinkle with herbs and salt and pepper to taste and divide the mixture into small balls. Return the stew to the boil, adding a little more vegetable stock, if necessary, and drop the balls carefully into the pan. Cook the dumplings for 5 minutes. Take the pan off the heat, sprinkle the stew with chopped chives and serve piping hot. **Serves 4**

Toad-in-the-hole

METRIC/IMPERIAL	AMERICAN
100 g/4 oz plain wholemeal flour	1 cup wholewheat flour
pinch of salt	pinch of salt
1 egg	1 egg
300 ml/½ pint milk	1¼ cups milk
1 (425-g/15-oz) can soya or wheat protein 'sausages'	1 (15-oz) can textured vegetable protein 'sausages'
15 g/½ oz butter or margarine	1 tablespoon butter or margarine

Set the oven at hot (220 C, 425 F, gas 7). Mix the flour and salt together in a bowl. Stir in the egg with a wooden spoon, then gradually add the milk, beating continuously to make a smooth, creamy mixture. Use a whisk to lighten the batter and let it stand in a cool place for a while.

Rinse and drain the 'sausages'. Put the butter or margarine into a baking tin or pan and place it in the oven for a few minutes so that the fat melts. Arrange the 'sausages' in the tin and return it to the heat for 5–10 minutes. Stir the batter briefly and pour it into the tin so that it spreads evenly.

Bake the dish for 10 minutes or until the batter has begun to rise, then reduce the oven temperature to moderate (180 C, 350 F, gas 4) and continue baking for about 30 minutes, until golden brown. Serve at once. **Serves 4**

Hot Cabbage Salad

METRIC/IMPERIAL	AMERICAN
½ white cabbage	½ white cabbage
3 carrots	3 carrots
1 onion	1 onion
2 tablespoons vegetable oil	3 tablespoons vegetable oil
2 tablespoons raisins	3 tablespoons raisins
1 teaspoon fresh or ½ teaspoon dried marjoram	1 teaspoon fresh or ½ teaspoon dried marjoram
pinch of raw brown sugar	pinch of raw brown sugar
salt and pepper	salt and pepper
1 (150-g/5.3-oz) carton natural yogurt	⅔ cup plain yogurt
50 g/2 oz chopped nuts (optional)	⅓ cup chopped nuts (optional)

Shred the cabbage. Slice the carrots and onion as finely as possible. Heat the oil in a pan and gently fry the vegetables and raisins for 3–4 minutes, stirring continually. Mix the herbs, sugar and salt and pepper to taste into the yogurt and stir the mixture into the vegetables with the chopped nuts, if used. Heat through very gently for a minute, then serve at once. **Serves 4**

Pea and Potato Pancakes

Illustrated on page 88

METRIC/IMPERIAL	AMERICAN
15 g/½ oz butter or margarine	1 tablespoon butter or margarine
1 onion, chopped	1 onion, chopped
50 g/2 oz cooked peas	⅓ cup cooked peas
675 g/1½ lb potatoes	1½ lb potatoes
2 eggs	2 eggs
25 g/1 oz plain wholemeal flour	¼ cup wholewheat flour
50 g/2 oz Cheddar cheese, grated	½ cup grated Cheddar cheese
about 150 ml/¼ pint milk	⅔ cup milk
salt and pepper	salt and pepper
2 tablespoons oil	3 tablespoons oil

Melt the butter or margarine in a saucepan and gently sauté the chopped onion until soft. Chop the peas, if liked. Peel and grate the potatoes. Combine these with the eggs, flour, cheese and enough milk to make a thick, batter-like mixture and season generously with salt and pepper.

Heat the oil in a heavy-based frying pan and spoon in some of the pea and potato mixture. Cook it for a few minutes until it begins to brown underneath, then use a spatula to flip the pancake over and cook it on the other side. Use the rest of the mixture in the same way and serve the pancakes with stewed or fresh tomatoes, baked beans, a poached egg, or whatever you (or your children) fancy. **Serves 4**

Little Pizza

Illustrated on pages 86–87

METRIC/IMPERIAL	AMERICAN
Pizza	*Pizza*
100 g/4 oz self-raising wholemeal flour	1 cup wholewheat flour mixed with
pinch of salt	1 teaspoon baking powder
2–3 tablespoons cold water	pinch of salt
3 tablespoons vegetable oil	3–4 tablespoons cold water
Topping	4 tablespoons vegetable oil
1–2 fresh tomatoes, sliced	*Topping*
1 tablespoon canned sweet corn	1–2 fresh tomatoes, sliced
50 g/2 oz Cheddar cheese, grated	1 tablespoon canned corn
½ teaspoon chopped fresh marjoram or ¼	½ cup grated Cheddar cheese
teaspoon dried oregano	½ teaspoon chopped fresh marjoram or ¼
salt and pepper	teaspoon dried oregano
	salt and pepper

Mix the flour and salt together in a bowl. Combine the water with 1 tablespoon oil, stir into the dry ingredients and knead to a smooth dough. Add a little more water if it is too dry.

Roll the dough out on a floured board and form it into a 15-cm/6-in round. Heat the remaining oil in a heavy-based frying pan and, when hot, carefully slide the dough into the pan. Cook for a few minutes until the underside begins to brown, then turn the pizza and cook the other side. Transfer it to a flat dish and top with the sliced tomatoes, the sweet corn, grated cheese and finally a sprinkling of marjoram or oregano and salt and pepper to taste. Heat the pizza under a gentle grill for just a few minutes and serve immediately. **Serves 2**

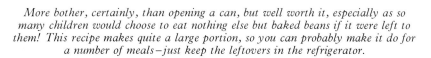

Boston Baked Beans

Illustrated on page 88

More bother, certainly, than opening a can, but well worth it, especially as so
many children would choose to eat nothing else but baked beans if it were left to
them! This recipe makes quite a large portion, so you can probably make it do for
a number of meals – just keep the leftovers in the refrigerator.

METRIC/IMPERIAL	AMERICAN
450 g/1 lb dried haricot beans, soaked in water overnight	2 cups dried navy beans, soaked in water overnight
2 onions	2 onions
450 g/1 lb tomatoes	1 lb tomatoes
3 tablespoons molasses	4 tablespoons molasses
2 teaspoons raw brown sugar	2 teaspoons raw brown sugar
1–2 teaspoons mustard powder	1–2 teaspoons mustard powder
1 teaspoon chopped fresh mixed herbs or ½ teaspoon dried mixed herbs	1 teaspoon chopped fresh mixed herbs or ½ teaspoon dried mixed herbs
2 tablespoons tomato purée	3 tablespoons tomato purée
salt and pepper	salt and pepper

Drain the beans, put them into a pan with plenty of fresh water and bring to the
boil. Cover the pan and simmer the beans for 35–40 minutes, until almost cooked,
then drain again, this time reserving the water.

Set the oven at moderate (165 C, 325 F, gas 3). Chop the onions and tomatoes. Tip
the beans into a casserole and mix in the onion, tomato, molasses, sugar, mustard,
herbs, tomato purée and salt and pepper to taste. Pour 200 ml/7 fl oz (¾ cup) of the
water in which the beans have been cooked into the casserole and stir well. Cover
and bake the beans for 3 hours or until the beans are soft and have absorbed all the
flavours. Stir them every now and again, adding a drop more of the cooking water
if necessary. Adjust the seasoning and serve. **Serves 8**

Cheese and Onion Bread Pudding

A savoury version of every youngster's favourite sweet!

METRIC/IMPERIAL	AMERICAN
2 tablespoons vegetable oil	3 tablespoons vegetable oil
2 large onions, sliced	2 large onions, sliced
6 thin slices wholemeal bread	6 thin slices wholewheat bread
175 g/6 oz Cheddar cheese, grated	1½ cups grated Cheddar cheese
2 eggs	2 eggs
300 ml/½ pint milk	1¼ cups milk
salt and pepper	salt and pepper
50 g/2 oz soya 'bacon' pieces (optional)	⅓ cup textured vegetable protein 'bacon-flavoured' pieces (optional)

Set the oven at moderate (180 C, 350 F, gas 4). Heat the oil in a pan and cook the
sliced onion gently until it softens.

Trim the crusts from the bread and cut each slice in half. Lay some of the bread
across the base of a small ovenproof casserole and cover with a layer of grated
cheese, then with a layer of onion. Repeat the layers, reserving a little cheese on
one side, until all the ingredients have been used. Beat together the eggs and milk,
season well with salt and pepper and pour the mixture over the casserole. Sprinkle
the top with the remaining cheese and the soya 'bacon' pieces, if used.

Bake the pudding for 40–50 minutes until set. Serve hot with a green vegetable or
a crisp salad. **Serves 4**

Crispy Nut Croquettes

Illustrated on page 85

METRIC/IMPERIAL	AMERICAN
350 g/12 oz cooked peas	2 cups cooked peas
100 g/4 oz brazil nuts	1 cup brazil nuts
100 g/4 oz fresh wholemeal breadcrumbs	2 cups fresh wholewheat breadcrumbs
2 eggs	2 eggs
1 teaspoon chopped fresh mixed herbs	1 teaspoon chopped fresh mixed herbs
salt and pepper	salt and pepper
about 50 g/2 oz oat flakes	about ½ cup rolled oats
oil for deep-frying	oil for deep-frying
dill sprig to garnish (optional)	dill sprig to garnish (optional)

Mash the cooked peas to a purée. Grind the brazil nuts and mix them with the pea purée, breadcrumbs, one egg, the herbs and salt and pepper to taste to make a fairly stiff paste. Shape into croquettes about 2.5 cm/1 in. in diameter and 7.5 cm/3 in long. Beat the remaining egg and dip the croquettes first into beaten egg, then into the oat flakes. Heat the oil for deep-frying to 190 C/375 F and deep-fry the croquettes quickly until crisp and golden. Serve hot or cold. **Serves 4**

Baked Potato Surprises

METRIC/IMPERIAL	AMERICAN
4 medium potatoes	4 medium potatoes
25 g/1 oz butter or margarine	2 tablespoons butter or margarine
4 eggs	4 eggs
salt and pepper	salt and pepper
50 g/2 oz Cheddar cheese, grated	½ cup grated Cheddar cheese

Clean and prick the potatoes and bake them in a moderately hot oven (200 C, 400 F, gas 6) for 1 hour or until just cooked.

When they are cool enough to handle, cut a 'lid' out of the top of each – not quite cutting through on one side, so that the lid remains attached – and scoop out some of the potato. Drop a knob of butter or margarine into each one, followed by an egg, taking care not to break the yolk. Season with salt and pepper, sprinkle with grated cheese and stand the potatoes side by side in an ovenproof dish. Return them to the oven for 15 minutes or until the eggs are set. **Serves 4**

VARIATIONS

Baked potatoes are always popular with children and are exceptionally easy to prepare. Follow the recipe given above for cooking the potatoes, then cut and fill them with any of a variety of fillings (see also Foil-baked Potatoes, page 92):

Cottage cheese mixed with grated Cheddar cheese

Baked beans, either canned or home-made (page 79)

Fried mushrooms, tomatoes and onions

Natural (plain) yogurt or soured cream

Any left-over vegetable dishes such as Cauliflower Cheese (page 43),
Vegetable Stew (page 76), Aviyal (page 58)

Top with breadcrumbs, if liked, grill for a few minutes and serve immediately.

Peanut Butter Waffles

Illustrated on pages 86–87

Children find waffles fun to eat and if you use wholesome ingredients, there's no reason why you shouldn't dish them up often. Since peanut butter is also popular with most children, try this for a start.

METRIC/IMPERIAL	AMERICAN
100 g/4 oz plain wholemeal flour	1 cup wholewheat flour
$\frac{1}{2}$ teaspoon baking powder	$\frac{1}{2}$ teaspoon baking powder
pinch of salt	pinch of salt
$\frac{1}{2}$–1 teaspoon mixed spice	$\frac{1}{2}$–1 teaspoon mixed spice
2 eggs	2 eggs
450 ml/$\frac{3}{4}$ pint milk	scant 2 cups milk
75 g/3 oz clear honey	$\frac{1}{4}$ cup clear honey
100 g/4 oz crunchy peanut butter	$\frac{1}{2}$ cup crunchy peanut butter
1 dessert apple	1 dessert apple

Mix together the flour, baking powder, salt and spice. In another bowl, lightly beat the eggs with the milk and honey, add the peanut butter and blend thoroughly. Core and grate the apple and add it to the mixture. Gradually stir the mixture into the dry ingredients and continue mixing until smooth.

Use the batter to make the waffles, following the instructions that come with your particular waffle iron. In general, you simply pour the batter into the greased iron, close it firmly and cook for a few minutes until the waffle is crisp. Serve at once. Apple Sauce (see page 74) goes well with Peanut Butter Waffles. **Makes 10–12**

Oat and Nut Waffles

METRIC/IMPERIAL	AMERICAN
100 g/4 oz plain wholemeal flour	1 cup wholewheat flour
2 teaspoons baking powder	2 teaspoons baking powder
pinch of salt	pinch of salt
50 g/2 oz fine oat flakes	$\frac{1}{2}$ cup fine rolled oats
50 g/2 oz chopped roasted hazelnuts	$\frac{1}{3}$ cup chopped roasted hazelnuts
50 g/2 oz butter or margarine	$\frac{1}{4}$ cup butter or margarine
2 eggs	2 eggs
1–2 tablespoons clear honey	2–3 tablespoons clear honey
300 ml/$\frac{1}{2}$ pint milk	$1\frac{1}{4}$ cups milk

Mix together the flour, baking powder and salt and stir in the oats and chopped hazelnuts. Melt the butter or margarine. Separate the eggs and combine the yolks with honey to taste, the butter or margarine and the milk, blending well. Make a well in the dry ingredients, pour in the milk mixture and beat until well blended. Whisk the egg whites until stiff and fold them into the batter.

Prepare your waffle iron following the manufacturer's instructions. Pour in just enough batter to cover the plates, close the iron and cook quickly for 2 minutes or until the waffle is golden and crisp. Use the rest of the batter in the same way.

Serve with Tofu and Banana Sauce (see page 74). Honey, maple syrup, raw sugar jam or just knobs of butter are also good with waffles. **Makes 10–12**

VARIATION
For a change, replace the nuts with sesame seeds.

Vegan Fare

If you're giving up meat for moral reasons, you may come to the point where you feel it wrong to exploit animals at all. In that case you could opt for a vegan diet, one that excludes animal by-products such as milk, cheese, butter, yogurt, eggs, even honey. Obviously a vegan diet is going to be more restricted than a vegetarian one, but that doesn't mean it has to be boring. Use a wide variety of ingredients, be imaginative in the way you present and combine them, and you can eat as well as any omnivore – and for less money.

Vegans get the bulk of their protein from nuts, pulses, beans (and bean products, soya in particular), tahini and sesame paste. Grains in all forms provide an additional source of protein, as well as many other valuable nutrients, wholemeal flour being the easiest form to use. Salads and fruits can, of course, be eaten in any amount. Combine all these basic ingredients and you can produce countless meals with which to delight not just other vegans, but meat-eaters too.

Although basic ingredients present no problem, many new vegans are stumped by the little details. Is margarine all right to use instead of butter? What about an alternative binding ingredient to eggs? Or to milk in a sauce? In fact, there are now a wide variety of products on the market that are made specifically to help solve these problems. Although most margarines are not vegan (if they don't contain animal fat – which many of them do! – they contain whey), there are two or three that are guaranteed vegan. Soya flour can be used to bind a dish instead of eggs. Soya milk will make a white sauce just as creamy as cow's milk and it can also be used in rice dishes and drinks.

The following chapter contains a variety of recipes devised specially for vegans, but there are many more scattered throughout the book that can easily be adapted to be suitable for vegans if they are not so already. Here are some examples:

Soups and Starters Most of the soups can be used if you replace the cow's milk with soya milk and the butter with vegan margarine or vegetable oil. Starters such as Grapefruit Brulée (page 34), Guacamole (page 37), Bazargan (page 32) and Herbed Lentil Pâté (page 30) are fine as they stand and you could make Nut and Pasta Salad (page 32) with Vegan Salad Cream (page 110) instead of mayonnaise.

Main dishes Fruit and Vegetable Kebabs (page 40) and Chestnut Roll (page 54) would be suitable. You can also adapt Courgettes Provençale with Haricot Beans (page 41) and Aviyal (page 58) by omitting the yogurt; Lentil-stuffed Courgettes (page 41) by topping the courgettes with nuts instead of cheese; Aduki and Celery Casserole (page 44) by leaving out the hard-boiled eggs and Sweet and Sour Cabbage (page 56) by sweetening with raw brown sugar instead of honey.

Light Lunches and Snacks Quick Sunflower Seed Burgers (page 63), Cauli-flower with Pasta (page 64), Black-eye Bean Casserole (page 69), Baked Vegetables with Nut Topping (page 70), Onion and Tomato Bake (page 70) and Jacket Parsnips (page 71) will all fit in with a vegan diet.

Once you get the idea you'll find it easy – and fun – to adapt other recipes.

Winter Vegetable Stew

METRIC/IMPERIAL	AMERICAN
1 large turnip	1 large turnip
1 large parsnip	1 large parsnip
2 carrots	2 carrots
2 leeks	2 leeks
¼ medium cabbage	¼ medium cabbage
1 onion	1 onion
75 g/3 oz pearl barley or pot barley, soaked in water overnight and drained	½ cup pearl barley or pot barley, soaked in water overnight and drained
1 teaspoon fresh or ½ teaspoon dried thyme	1 teaspoon fresh or ½ teaspoon dried thyme
1–2 teaspoons miso	1–2 teaspoons miso
salt and pepper	salt and pepper
about 1.15 litres/2 pints water	5 cups water

Peel and dice the turnip, parsnip and carrots. Wash and slice the leeks and cabbage. Chop the onion. Put all the ingredients except the miso with salt and pepper to taste into a large saucepan and pour in just enough water to cover. Bring to the boil, cover and simmer gently over a low heat for about 1–1½ hours (or 2–3 hours, if you are using pot barley), until the grain is tender.

Dilute the miso with a little cold water. Add to the stew and continue cooking for just 1 minute. Serve with fresh-from-the-oven Wholemeal Baps (page 120), if liked. **Serves 4**

Chop Suey with Tofu

METRIC/IMPERIAL	AMERICAN
1 onion	1 onion
1 green pepper	1 green pepper
¼ medium white cabbage	¼ medium white cabbage
100 g/4 oz mushrooms	1 cup mushrooms
½ bunch watercress	½ bunch watercress
1 tablespoon arrowroot	1 tablespoon arrowroot
1 tablespoon soy sauce or to taste	1 tablespoon soy sauce or to taste
pinch of sugar	pinch of sugar
3–4 tablespoons water	4–5 tablespoons water
2 tablespoons oil	3 tablespoons oil
100 g/4 oz tofu	½ cup tofu
100 g/4 oz bean sprouts	2 cups bean sprouts

Chop the onion and green pepper; shred the cabbage; slice the mushrooms; wash and remove any coarse stems from the watercress. In a cup or small bowl, mix the arrowroot with the soy sauce, sugar and enough water to give a liquid consistency.

Heat the oil in a large pan and sauté the onion and pepper for 5 minutes or until they begin to soften. Drain the tofu, chop it coarsely and add it to the pan, mixing well. Continue cooking for 2 more minutes.

Now add the cabbage, watercress and mushrooms and sauté for a further 2 minutes, stirring frequently. Add the bean sprouts and the arrowroot solution and simmer all the ingredients for a few minutes until the sauce begins to thicken. Pour in a little water to give a more liquid sauce, stir and heat through. Serve immediately with rice, putting soy sauce on the table for anyone who needs it. **Serves 4**

VARIATION
Whole blanched almonds can be substituted for the tofu as a source of protein.

Chickpeas and Pasta

METRIC/IMPERIAL	AMERICAN
2 tablespoons olive oil	3 tablespoons olive oil
1 clove garlic, crushed	1 clove garlic, crushed
225 g/8 oz chickpeas, soaked in water overnight	1 cup garbanzos beans, soaked in water overnight
175 g/6 oz wholewheat tagliatelle	1½ cups wholewheat tagliatelle
salt and pepper	salt and pepper
chopped fresh parsley	chopped fresh parsley

Heat the oil in a large saucepan and gently sauté the garlic for a few minutes. Drain the chickpeas (garbanzos), add them to the pan with enough fresh water to cover and bring to the boil. Cover the pan and simmer for 1–2 hours until the chickpeas are cooked but still firm. You may need to add a little more water during the cooking process.

Now bring the liquid to a fast boil and plunge the tagliatelle into it. Continue boiling for about 10 minutes or until the pasta is cooked. Season the mixture with salt and pepper to taste and sprinkle it generously with chopped parsley. Serve immediately, with fresh brown bread and a salad. **Serves 4**

Sweet Corn Ratatouille

Illustrated on pages 106–107

METRIC/IMPERIAL	AMERICAN
1 large aubergine	1 large eggplant
salt and pepper	salt and pepper
1 large red or green pepper, deseeded	1 large red or green pepper, deseeded
1 large onion	1 large onion
2 courgettes	2 zucchini
3 large tomatoes	3 large tomatoes
3 tablespoons oil	4 tablespoons oil
1 clove garlic, crushed	1 clove garlic, crushed
100 g/4 oz canned sweet corn	⅔ cup canned corn
1 bay leaf	1 bay leaf
50 g/2 oz walnut pieces	½ cup walnut pieces
chopped fresh parsley to garnish	chopped fresh parsley to garnish

Dice the aubergine (eggplant), sprinkle it with salt and set it aside for 30 minutes. Slice the pepper and onion into thick strips and the courgettes into 1-cm/½-in chunks. Chop the tomatoes coarsely.

Heat the oil in a pan and add the garlic, onion and pepper slices. Fry gently for 5 minutes, stirring frequently. Rinse and pat dry the aubergine and add it to the pan with the courgettes; cook for 10 minutes more.

Now add the tomatoes, drained sweet corn, bay leaf and salt and pepper to taste, cover the pan and simmer for about 10 minutes or until the vegetables are just cooked. Remove the bay leaf. Stir the walnut pieces through the ratatouille, taste and adjust the seasoning and sprinkle with parsley. Serve with jacket potatoes, pasta, rice or millet. **Serves 4**

Vegetable Stew with Dumplings (page 76); Crispy Nut Croquettes (page 80).

Overleaf *Banana Nut Risotto (page 76); Little Pizza (page 78); Peanut Butter Waffles (page 81) with honey, melted butter and Apple Sauce (page 74).*

Peter ran straight away to Mr. McGregor's garden, and squeezed under the gate!
he ate s
tuces and some French beans; and then he ate some radishes;

Country Flan

METRIC/IMPERIAL	AMERICAN
Pastry	*Dough*
175 g/6 oz plain wholemeal flour	1½ cups wholewheat flour
pinch of salt	pinch of salt
1 teaspoon baking powder	1 teaspoon baking powder
25 g/1 oz sesame seeds	¼ cup sesame seeds
75 g/3 oz vegan margarine	⅓ cup vegan margarine
about 3 tablespoons water	about 4 tablespoons water
Filling	*Filling*
225 g/8 oz potatoes	½ lb potatoes
2 large carrots	2 large carrots
100 g/4 oz shelled fresh or frozen peas	¾ cup shelled fresh or frozen peas
2 large onions	2 large onions
25 g/1 oz vegan margarine or oil	2 tablespoons vegan margarine or oil
25 g/1 oz plain wholemeal flour	¼ cup wholewheat flour
25 g/1 oz soya flour ⎫ or 300 ml/½	¼ cup soy flour ⎫ or 1¼ cups
300 ml/½ pint Vegetable ⎬ pint soya	1¼ cups Vegetable Stock ⎬ soy milk
Stock (page 22) ⎭ milk	(page 22) ⎭
salt and pepper	salt and pepper
2 tablespoons chopped fresh parsley	3 tablespoons chopped fresh parsley
100 g/4 oz canned sweet corn	⅔ cup canned corn
parsley sprigs to garnish	parsley sprigs to garnish

Sift the flour, salt and baking powder into a mixing bowl. Stir in any bran left in the sieve, followed by the sesame seeds. Cut the margarine into flakes and rub it into the dry ingredients with your fingertips until the mixture resembles coarse breadcrumbs. Pour in just enough water to bind the ingredients together and knead lightly to make a dough. Leave to stand in a cool place while you prepare the filling.

Set the oven at moderately hot (200 C, 400 F, gas 6). Place a baking sheet in the oven to warm up. Peel and dice the potatoes and carrots and cook them in boiling salted water for 10–12 minutes, until just tender. Simmer fresh peas, if used, for 10–15 minutes and frozen peas for 5 minutes, until cooked. Drain all the vegetables and leave them on one side.

Slice the onions. Heat the margarine or oil in a pan and sauté the onion until soft but not browned. Sprinkle in the flour, stir and cook for a few minutes. Whisk the soya flour, if used, into the vegetable stock and pour this mixture or the soya milk into the pan, stirring continuously. Bring to the boil and simmer for a few minutes until the sauce is thick and creamy. Season with salt and pepper to taste and stir in the chopped parsley.

Roll the pastry out to a round on a lightly floured surface and use it to line an 18-cm/7-in or 20-cm/8-in flan tin or pie pan. Drain the sweet corn. Mix the potatoes, carrots, peas and sweet corn into the creamed sauce and spoon the mixture into the flan case. Smooth the top, place the flan on the warmed baking sheet and bake for 20–30 minutes, until the pastry is cooked. Serve hot, garnished with plenty of parsley sprigs. **Serves 4**

NOTE If you prefer, you can make the pastry with oil instead of vegan margarine. Sift the dry ingredients together into a bowl as above, stir the oil into half the water and pour this liquid into the mixing bowl. Mix lightly but thoroughly, adding the remaining water, to make a dough. Leave to stand in a cool place for about 30 minutes and continue as above.

Pea and Potato Pancakes (page 78) with Boston Baked Beans (page 79).

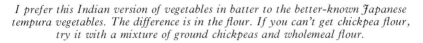

Pakora (Deep-fried Vegetables)

Illustrated on pages 106–107

I prefer this Indian version of vegetables in batter to the better-known Japanese tempura vegetables. The difference is in the flour. If you can't get chickpea flour, try it with a mixture of ground chickpeas and wholemeal flour.

METRIC/IMPERIAL	AMERICAN
225 g/8 oz gram (chickpea) flour	2 cups gram (garbanzos bean) flour
2 teaspoons ground cumin	2 teaspoons ground cumin
generous pinch of cayenne	generous pinch of cayenne
pinch each of salt and pepper	pinch each of salt and pepper
a little cold water to mix	a little cold water to mix
1 kg/2 lb vegetables in season (carrots, broccoli, small Brussels sprouts, cauliflower, courgettes, aubergine, mushrooms, parsnips, okra)	2 lb vegetables in season (carrots, broccoli, small Brussels sprouts, cauliflower, zucchini, eggplant, mushrooms, parsnips, okra)
oil for deep-frying	oil for deep-frying

Beat together the flour, spices, salt and pepper and add just enough water to give the batter the consistency of a smooth, thin white sauce. The consistency is very important as it must be thin enough to let the vegetables cook, yet thick enough to seal in the goodness. Chill the batter for at least 1 hour, if possible.

Prepare all the vegetables by trimming and peeling them, if necessary, and cutting them into small strips and slices or breaking them into florets as appropriate. Heat the oil in a deep pan to 190 C/375 F, until it spits as soon as you drop a piece of batter into it. Dip the vegetables one at a time into the batter, making sure they are well coated, then drop them into the fat and deep-fry until golden and crisp. Allow more time for the longer-cooking vegetables such as the carrots and parsnips. Drain thoroughly and keep the cooked vegetables warm while you deep-fry the rest.

Nicest eaten just sprinkled with soy sauce, but mango, tomato and green chilli chutneys and Apple Sauce (page 74) also go well. **Serves 4**

Brussels and Butter Bean Bake

METRIC/IMPERIAL	AMERICAN
225 g/8 oz butter beans, soaked in water overnight	1 cup dried lima beans, soaked in water overnight
3 medium tomatoes	3 medium tomatoes
1 onion	1 onion
1 stick celery	1 stalk celery
about 300 ml/½ pint Vegetable Stock (page 22) or water	about 1¼ cups Vegetable Stock (page 22) or water
225 g/8 oz Brussels sprouts	½ lb Brussels sprouts
1 teaspoon chopped fresh or ½ teaspoon dried sage	1 teaspoon chopped fresh or ½ teaspoon dried sage
salt and pepper	salt and pepper
1 tablespoon oil	1 tablespoon oil
25 g/1 oz wholemeal flour	¼ cup wholewheat flour
25 g/1 oz soya flour 300 ml/½ pint water } or 300 ml/ ½ pint soya milk	¼ cup soy flour 1¼ cups water } or 1¼ cups soy milk
50 g/2 oz dried wholemeal breadcrumbs	½ cup dried wholewheat breadcrumbs
generous pinch of grated nutmeg	generous pinch of grated nutmeg
25 g/1 oz vegan margarine	2 tablespoons vegan margarine

Drain the butter beans and put them into a pan. Chop the tomatoes. Finely slice

the onion and celery. Add these vegetables to the pan, pour in enough vegetable stock or water to cover and bring to the boil. Cover the pan and simmer the beans and vegetables over a low heat for about 30 minutes.

Set the oven at moderately hot (190 C, 375 F, gas 5). Trim the Brussels sprouts and cut the larger ones in half. Put them into the pan with the sage and salt and pepper to taste. Add more liquid if necessary and simmer for a further 20–30 minutes or until the beans are just cooked and all the liquid has been absorbed.

Meanwhile, heat the oil in another pan, blend in the flour and cook for 1 minute. Whisk the soya flour if used, into the water. Pour this mixture or the soya milk into the pan and bring to the boil, stirring continuously. Simmer for 1 minute, until the sauce thickens, and season well with salt and pepper.

Arrange the bean and vegetable mixture in a shallow ovenproof dish and spoon the sauce over them. Mix the breadcrumbs with the nutmeg, sprinkle the mixture over the dish and dot with the margarine. Bake for 20 minutes or until golden brown. **Serves 4**

Nut-stuffed Aubergines

Illustrated on pages 106–107

METRIC/IMPERIAL	AMERICAN
2 large aubergines	2 large eggplants
100 g/4 oz mushrooms	1 cup mushrooms
2 tablespoons oil	3 tablespoons oil
1 onion, sliced	1 onion, sliced
100 g/4 oz chopped mixed nuts	$\frac{2}{3}$ cup chopped mixed nuts
100 g/4 oz dried wholemeal breadcrumbs	1 cup dried wholewheat breadcrumbs
1 tablespoon wheatgerm	1 tablespoon wheatgerm
1 teaspoon fresh or $\frac{1}{2}$ teaspoon dried marjoram	1 teaspoon fresh or $\frac{1}{2}$ teaspoon dried marjoram
salt and pepper	salt and pepper
15 g/$\frac{1}{2}$ oz vegan margarine	1 tablespoon vegan margarine
chopped fresh chives or thyme to garnish (optional)	chopped fresh chives or thyme to garnish (optional)

Set the oven at moderately hot (190 C, 375 F, gas 5). Bring a large pan of water to the boil, add the aubergines (eggplants) and parboil them for about 10 minutes. Drain, allow them to cool slightly and cut them in half lengthways. Scoop out as much of the flesh as possible without damaging the skin and put it on one side.

Chop the mushrooms. Heat the oil in a saucepan and fry the sliced onion until it begins to brown. Add the nuts and 75 g/3 oz ($\frac{3}{4}$ cup) breadcrumbs and cook until the breadcrumbs are crisp. Stir in the mushroom and wheatgerm and continue cooking for 5 more minutes. Combine the chopped aubergine flesh with the breadcrumbs and nut mixture. Add the marjoram and season well with salt and pepper.

Arrange the four aubergine shells close together in a shallow ovenproof dish and divide the filling between them. Sprinkle with the remaining breadcrumbs and dot with the margarine. Bake the aubergines for 20 minutes and serve garnished with chives or thyme, if liked. **Serves 4**

VARIATIONS

Use the same method to stuff other vegetables such as onions, courgettes (zucchini) and marrow (summer squash). Green and red peppers can simply be parboiled and filled with the aubergine mixture given above.

Foil-baked Potatoes

Illustrated on pages 106–107

I find this the best way to bake potatoes, as the foil helps them to cook more evenly, taste more wholesome, prevents them from drying out (so you can eat that nutrient-packed peel!) – and there's no washing up.

METRIC/IMPERIAL	AMERICAN
4 large even-sized potatoes	4 large even-sized potatoes
oil	oil
salt	salt

Try to choose potatoes that have unblemished skin and a good shape. Scrub them thoroughly and leave them to dry. Rub a little oil over the skins, sprinkle them liberally with salt and wrap each one in its own piece of cooking foil. Bake the potatoes in a moderately hot oven (200 C, 400 F, gas 6) for 1–1½ hours until cooked, when they should feel soft to the touch.

You can serve your potatoes just as they are, topped with a chunk of vegan margarine, sea salt, freshly ground black pepper and a sprinkling of chopped fresh chives. With a nutty salad you have a perfectly balanced meal. However, if you wish to be more adventurous, here are some alternative ideas:

Mushroom and Olive Filling

METRIC/IMPERIAL	AMERICAN
100 g/4 oz mushrooms	1 cup mushrooms
25 g/1 oz vegan margarine	2 tablespoons vegan margarine
12 stuffed olives	12 stuffed olives
salt and pepper	salt and pepper

Clean and chop the mushrooms. Melt the margarine in a pan, add the mushroom and sauté until just tender. Slice the olives, mix them into the mushroom and season with salt and pepper. Cut slits into the cooked potatoes, put a spoonful or two of filling inside each and either serve at once or return to the oven, lowering the heat slightly to 190 C (375 F, gas 5), for 5 minutes. **Serves 4**

Kidney Bean and Tomato Filling

METRIC/IMPERIAL	AMERICAN
1 onion	1 onion
1 green pepper, deseeded	1 green pepper, deseeded
1 stick celery	1 stalk celery
1 tablespoon oil	1 tablespoon oil
4 medium tomatoes or 1 (396-g/14-oz) can tomatoes	4 medium tomatoes or 1 (14-oz) can tomatoes
275 g/10 oz cooked kidney beans	2 cups cooked kidney beans
1–2 teaspoons chilli powder or to taste	1–2 teaspoons chilli pepper or to taste
salt and pepper	salt and pepper

Trim and chop the onion, pepper and celery. Heat the oil in a pan and sauté the chopped vegetables until tender. Drain the canned tomatoes, if used, reserving the juice. Dice the canned or fresh tomatoes and stir them into the mixture with the cooked beans, chilli powder and salt and pepper to taste. Add a little water or tomato juice and simmer for 30 minutes until reduced to a fairly thick sauce.

Split the potato skins, arrange the potatoes on individual plates and pour over the sauce. **Serves 4**

Tofu and Spinach Filling

METRIC/IMPERIAL	AMERICAN
225 g/8 oz fresh spinach	½ lb fresh spinach
salt and pepper	salt and pepper
1 tablespoon oil	1 tablespoon oil
1 onion, sliced	1 onion, sliced
100 g/4 oz tofu	½ cup diced tofu
2 tomatoes	2 tomatoes
25 g/1 oz sesame seeds	¼ cup sesame seeds
25 g/1 oz vegan margarine (optional)	2 tablespoons vegan margarine (optional)

Wash the spinach, put it wet into a pan with a little salt and steam it over a high heat for about 15 minutes or until tender. Drain, chop it finely and set it on one side.

Heat the oil in a pan and sauté the sliced onion until just beginning to colour. Drain the tofu, add it to the pan and mash it with the onion; continue cooking for 5 minutes. Chop the tomatoes coarsely and put them in the pan followed by the spinach, sesame seeds and salt and pepper to taste. Mix all the ingredients thoroughly together and heat through.

Split open the baked potatoes, pile some of the filling into each and serve. Alternatively, scoop out some of the potato flesh and mash it with the filling; put the filling into the potatoes, top with knobs of margarine and return the potatoes to a moderately hot oven (190 C, 375 F, gas 5) for 5 minutes. **Serves 4**

Carrot and Almond Filling

METRIC/IMPERIAL	AMERICAN
2 large carrots	2 large carrots
25 g/1 oz vegan margarine	2 tablespoons vegan margarine
50 g/2 oz slivered almonds	½ cup slivered almonds
1 teaspoon grated orange rind	1 teaspoon grated orange rind
generous pinch of raw brown sugar	generous pinch of raw brown sugar
salt and pepper	salt and pepper

Trim, peel and slice the carrots and parboil them in a little boiling salted water for about 10 minutes until almost tender.

In a separate pan, melt the margarine and add the slivered almonds, orange rind, sugar and salt and pepper to taste. Cook for a few minutes over a low heat, stirring frequently. Drain the carrots, put them in the pan and continue cooking gently for 5–10 minutes more, basting the carrots frequently with the sauce.

Split open the cooked potatoes, place each on an individual plate and pour over the hot sauce. **Serves 4**

Onion and 'Bacon' Filling

METRIC/IMPERIAL	AMERICAN
2 tablespoons oil	3 tablespoons oil
2 onions, sliced	2 onions, sliced
2 tablespoons soya 'bacon' pieces	3 tablespoons textured vegetable protein
salt and pepper	'bacon-flavoured' pieces
	salt and pepper

Heat the oil in a pan and fry the sliced onion and 'bacon' pieces until the onion is soft but not browned and the 'bacon' is crisp. Season with salt and pepper to taste.

Split open the baked potatoes, arrange them on individual plates and top each with a little onion and 'bacon'. **Serves 4**

Sesame Vegetable Crumble

METRIC/IMPERIAL	AMERICAN
Vegetable Base	*Vegetable Base*
2 tablespoons oil	3 tablespoons oil
1 onion, sliced	1 onion, sliced
2 sticks celery, chopped	2 stalks celery, chopped
2 carrots, chopped	2 carrots, chopped
25 g/1 oz plain wholemeal flour	$\frac{1}{4}$ cup wholewheat flour
about 300 ml/$\frac{1}{2}$ pint water	$1\frac{1}{4}$ cups water
$\frac{1}{2}$ small cauliflower	$\frac{1}{2}$ small cauliflower
100 g/4 oz cooked peas	$\frac{3}{4}$ cup cooked peas
2 tablespoons tahini or to taste	3 tablespoons tahini or to taste
salt and pepper	salt and pepper
Crumble Topping	*Crumble Topping*
50 g/2 oz vegan margarine or	4 tablespoons vegan margarine or oil
3 tablespoons oil	1 cup wholewheat flour
100 g/4 oz plain wholemeal flour	$\frac{1}{4}$ cup sesame seeds
25 g/1 oz sesame seeds	pinch of salt
pinch of salt	

Set the oven at moderately hot (200 C, 400 F, gas 6). Heat the oil in a pan and sauté the sliced onion, celery and carrots for 5 minutes. Sprinkle in the flour and continue cooking gently until the flour begins to brown. Stir in the water, bring the mixture to the boil, stirring continuously, and boil for about 1 minute, until the sauce thickens. Add more water if necessary to give a fairly liquid consistency.

   Break the cauliflower into florets and put it in the pan. Simmer for 5 minutes, stirring frequently. Add the peas, tahini, and salt and pepper to taste and stir well. Transfer it to a shallow ovenproof dish.

   Make the crumble by rubbing the margarine or oil into the flour until well mixed, then stirring in the sesame seeds and salt. Sprinkle the mixture evenly over the vegetables and bake for 20 minutes or until golden brown. **Serves 4**

Buckwheat Burgers

METRIC/IMPERIAL	AMERICAN
225 g/8 oz buckwheat or kasha (roasted buckwheat)	$1\frac{3}{4}$ cups buckwheat or kasha (roasted buckwheat)
1 onion	1 onion
1 carrot	1 carrot
3 tablespoons oil	4 tablespoons oil
about 750 ml/$1\frac{1}{4}$ pints water or Vegetable Stock (page 22)	3 cups water or Vegetable Stock (page 22)
salt and pepper	salt and pepper
50 g/2 oz any cooked beans	$\frac{1}{2}$ cup any cooked beans
1–2 tablespoons chopped fresh parsley	2–3 tablespoons chopped fresh parsley
25 g/1 oz plain wholemeal flour or soya flour	$\frac{1}{4}$ cup wholewheat flour or soy flour
4 Wholemeal Baps (page 120)	4 Wholemeal Baps (page 120)

Put the buckwheat, if used, in a dry pan over a medium heat and dry roast it for about 5 minutes, moving the pan continuously, until it begins to brown.

   Finely chop the onion. Grate the carrot. Heat 1 tablespoon oil in a pan and sauté the onion and carrot for a few minutes; add the roasted buckwheat or kasha and cook a few minutes longer. Pour in the water or stock and bring the mixture to the boil. Add salt to taste, lower the heat and simmer gently for 15–25 minutes until the grain is tender. The mixture should be moist; add more liquid if necessary.

   Mash the cooked beans and stir them into the buckwheat with the parsley and

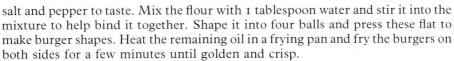

salt and pepper to taste. Mix the flour with 1 tablespoon water and stir it into the mixture to help bind it together. Shape it into four balls and press these flat to make burger shapes. Heat the remaining oil in a frying pan and fry the burgers on both sides for a few minutes until golden and crisp.

Slice the wholemeal baps in half and lightly toast each cut side. Sandwich the buckwheat burgers inside the baps and serve. **Serves 4**

Split Pea and Tomato Pizza

A crisp, crunchy dough base with a creamy topping.

METRIC/IMPERIAL	AMERICAN
Dough	*Dough*
½ teaspoon dried yeast	½ teaspoon active dry yeast
150 ml/¼ pint warm water	⅔ cup warm water
225 g/8 oz plain wholemeal flour	2 cups wholewheat flour
1 tablespoon oil	1 tablespoon oil
Topping	*Topping*
225 g/8 oz yellow split peas, soaked in water overnight	1 cup yellow split peas, soaked in water overnight
4 large tomatoes } or 1 (396-g/ 14-oz) can tomatoes 2 tablespoons tomato purée }	4 large tomatoes } or 1 (14-oz) can tomatoes 3 tablespoons tomato purée }
2 tablespoons oil	3 tablespoons oil
1 clove garlic, crushed	1 clove garlic, crushed
squeeze of lemon	squeeze of lemon
salt and pepper	salt and pepper
1 green pepper	1 green pepper
12 black olives	12 ripe olives
1 teaspoon dried oregano or basil	1 teaspoon dried oregano or basil
sprinkling of cayenne	sprinkling of cayenne

Prepare the topping first. Drain the split peas, put them in a pan with fresh water to cover, bring to the boil and simmer them for 20–30 minutes, until soft.

Set the oven at moderately hot (200 C, 400 F, gas 6). Peel the fresh tomatoes, if used (see Tomato Soup with Tofu, page 23), mash the flesh and put it in a separate pan with the purée and 1–2 tablespoons of water. Alternatively, empty the can of tomatoes into the pan. Bring to the boil, lower the heat and simmer for about 20 minutes until you have a thick sauce.

Drain the cooked peas and beat them with the tomato sauce, the oil, crushed garlic and lemon juice. Season well with salt and pepper.

To make the pizza base, sprinkle the yeast on to the warm water, stir and leave to stand in a warm place for a few minutes until frothy. Put the flour into a warmed bowl, make a well in the centre and pour in the yeast mixture. Mix the liquid gradually into the flour, add the oil and knead all the ingredients well together to form a smooth dough. Turn out on to a floured board and knead gently for at least 5 minutes.

Break the mixture into four even-sized pieces and roll them out to thin, 20-cm/ 8-in rounds. Arrange these rounds on lightly greased baking sheets and bake them for 5 minutes. Remove them from the oven and spread each one with some of the split pea mixture. Slice the green pepper into thin rings, remove the seeds and arrange the rings on top of the pizzas, together with the olives. Sprinkle the pizzas with oregano or basil and a little cayenne and return them to the oven for a further 15 minutes or until the dough is cooked and golden. Serve at once. **Serves 4**

Raw Deal

If salads have a bad name with people who claim to love their food, it's because many people are not adventurous enough with the ingredients they use – nor fussy enough about how fresh they are! Young vegetables taste delicious raw; in fact, it's almost a shame to cook them. Try whatever varieties are in season, mix them with fruits and nuts, and pour over them simple or exotic dressings.

Fennel Salad

METRIC/IMPERIAL	AMERICAN
1 large grapefruit	1 large grapefruit
1 large fennel	1 large fennel
1 cucumber	1 cucumber
6 radishes	6 radishes
1 head chicory	1 head Belgian endive
1 tablespoon chopped fresh mint	1 tablespoon chopped fresh mint
1 (150-g/5.3-oz) carton natural yogurt	⅔ cup plain yogurt
salt and black pepper	salt and black pepper

Finely grate the grapefruit peel and reserve it on one side. Peel the fruit, divide it into segments and remove the skin from each segment. Cut the base and coarse outer leaves from the fennel and slice the fennel finely. Cut the cucumber into small chunks. Remove the stalks from the radishes and slice them, together with the chicory. Combine all these ingredients in a bowl. Mix the mint into the yogurt, add salt and pepper to taste and pour the dressing over the salad. Sprinkle a little grapefruit peel over the top and serve. **Serves 4**

Three Bean Salad

Illustrated on page 105

METRIC/IMPERIAL	AMERICAN
100 g/4 oz French beans	1 cup French beans
1 large onion	1 large onion
100 g/4 oz cooked kidney beans	1 cup cooked kidney beans
100 g/4 oz cooked chickpeas	1 cup cooked garbanzos beans
1 small clove garlic, finely chopped	1 small clove garlic, finely chopped
6 tablespoons French Dressing (page 104)	½ cup French Dressing (page 104)
¼ leek or 1 small green pepper	¼ leek or 1 small green pepper
salt and pepper	salt and pepper

Top and tail the French beans and cut them into 2.5-cm/1-in pieces. Cook them in a little boiling salted water for 10–15 minutes, until just tender, drain and leave to cool. Slice the onion. Mix the French beans, kidney beans, chickpeas, onion and the garlic together in a bowl, pour the French dressing over the mixture and toss well. Leave the salad in a cool place to marinate for at least a few hours, preferably 1–2 days, so that the beans can absorb all the flavours. Just before serving, finely shred the leek or green pepper, removing the seeds from the pepper. Season the salad with salt and pepper and sprinkle the shredded leek or pepper over the top. **Serves 4**

California Salad

Illustrated on page 108

METRIC/IMPERIAL	AMERICAN
1 large peach	1 large peach
2 sticks celery	2 stalks celery
50 g/2 oz mushrooms	½ cup mushrooms
½ cucumber	½ cucumber
1 small red pepper	1 small red pepper
2 tomatoes	2 tomatoes
1 large orange	1 large orange
1 large banana	1 large banana
½ lettuce (optional)	½ lettuce (optional)
150 ml/¼ pint Lemon and Honey Dressing (page 104)	⅔ cup Lemon and Honey Dressing (page 104)
225 g/8 oz cottage cheese	1 cup cottage cheese
watercress to garnish	watercress to garnish

Wash and slice the peach, removing the stone. Chop the celery. Clean and finely slice the mushrooms, together with the cucumber. Dice the red pepper, removing the seeds, and quarter the tomatoes. Peel the orange, removing as much of the pith as possible, and slice the flesh into very thin circles. Slice the banana.

Wash, drain and shred the lettuce, if used, and arrange it on a serving plate. Lightly mix all the prepared vegetables and fruits together, pour over the dressing and toss. Serve the salad in a bowl or on the bed of lettuce and pile the cottage cheese on top. Garnish with the watercress. **Serves 4**

Spinach Salad

METRIC/IMPERIAL	AMERICAN
225 g/8 oz young, fresh spinach	½ lb young, fresh spinach
3 tomatoes	3 tomatoes
3 sticks celery	3 stalks celery
10 black olives	10 ripe olives
6 tablespoons Italian Dressing (page 109)	½ cup Italian Dressing (page 109)
75 g/3 oz pine nuts	¾ cup pine nuts

Wash, drain and shred or chop the spinach. Slice the tomatoes. Chop the celery and olives, removing the stones. Toss all the vegetables in the dressing and serve with the olives and pine nuts scattered on top. **Serves 4**

Wholewheat and Carrot Salad

METRIC/IMPERIAL	AMERICAN
4 medium carrots	4 medium carrots
175 g/6 oz cooked wheat grains	1¼ cups cooked whole berry wheat
75 g/3 oz raisins	½ cup raisins
3–4 tablespoons Tahini Garlic Dressing (page 111)	4–5 tablespoons Tahini Garlic Dressing (page 111)

Scrape and grate the carrots and mix them in a bowl with the wheat grains and raisins. Add just enough dressing to moisten the salad, toss lightly and serve. **Serves 4**

French Beans Niçoise

METRIC/IMPERIAL	AMERICAN
450 g/1 lb French beans	1 lb French beans
4 tomatoes	4 tomatoes
10 green olives	10 green olives
½ clove garlic, crushed	½ clove garlic, crushed
6 tablespoons Vinaigrette Dressing (page 104)	½ cup Vinaigrette Dressing (page 104)
2 hard-boiled eggs, chopped	2 hard-cooked eggs, chopped

Top and tail the French beans, cut them into large pieces and cook them in boiling salted water for 10–15 minutes, until just tender. Drain and leave to cool.
  Quarter the tomatoes. Mix the beans, olives, tomatoes and garlic together in a bowl, add the dressing and let the salad stand for a short time. Serve topped with the chopped eggs. **Serves 4**

Chinese Leaves and Avocado Salad

Illustrated on page 105

METRIC/IMPERIAL	AMERICAN
1 small head Chinese leaves	1 small head Chinese leaves
1 small green pepper, deseeded	1 small green pepper, deseeded
2 sticks celery	2 stalks celery
½ small red cabbage	½ small red cabbage
2 tomatoes	2 tomatoes
1 large avocado	1 large avocado
50 g/2 oz raisins	⅓ cup raisins
150 ml/¼ pint Tofu Dressing (page 110)	⅔ cup Tofu Dressing (page 110)
50 g/2 oz flaked almonds, toasted	¼ cup flaked almonds, toasted
squeeze of lemon	squeeze of lemon

Chop the Chinese leaves, pepper, celery and red cabbage. Quarter the tomatoes. Peel and halve the avocado, remove the stone and slice the flesh. Mix all the prepared ingredients together in a bowl, keeping some avocado on one side for garnishing, if liked, add the raisins and stir in the dressing. Sprinkle the nuts over the top. Dip the reserved avocado slices in a little lemon juice to prevent discoloration and arrange them on the salad. **Serves 4**

Macaroni Salad

METRIC/IMPERIAL	AMERICAN
100 g/4 oz wholewheat macaroni	1 cup wholewheat macaroni
50 g/2 oz shelled fresh or frozen peas	⅓ cup shelled fresh or frozen peas
100 g/4 oz mushrooms	1 cup mushrooms
1 small onion	1 small onion
½ small red pepper, deseeded	½ small red pepper, deseeded
4 tablespoons French Dressing (page 104)	⅓ cup French Dressing (page 104)
1–2 teaspoons grated Parmesan cheese	1–2 teaspoons grated Parmesan cheese

Cook the macaroni in boiling salted water for about 10 minutes, until just tender, drain and rinse through with cold water. Cook fresh peas in boiling water for 10–15 minutes, frozen peas for 5 minutes and drain. Clean and slice the mushrooms. Finely chop the onion and pepper. Mix the macaroni, peas, mushroom, onion and pepper together in a bowl, stir in the dressing and sprinkle with Parmesan. **Serves 4**

Chef's Salad

METRIC/IMPERIAL	AMERICAN
I crisp lettuce	I crisp lettuce
4 large tomatoes	4 large tomatoes
10 radishes	10 radishes
½ small onion	½ small onion
4 hard-boiled eggs	4 hard-cooked eggs
225 g/8 oz Emmental cheese	½ lb Emmental cheese
about 150 ml/¼ pint Thousand Island Dressing (page 109)	about ⅔ cup Thousand Island Dressing (page 109)
100 g/4 oz bean sprouts	2 cups bean sprouts
50 g/2 oz chopped walnuts	⅓ cup chopped walnuts

Wash, drain and shred the lettuce. Quarter the tomatoes. Trim and finely slice the radishes, together with the onion. Combine these vegetables in a bowl and mix gently. Quarter the eggs, dice the Emmental and add these ingredients to the salad. Stir in the dressing just before serving and sprinkle the bean sprouts and chopped walnuts on top. **Serves 4**

Lentil and Mung Bean Salad

METRIC/IMPERIAL	AMERICAN
I small onion	I small onion
I small green pepper, deseeded	I small green pepper, deseeded
¼ cucumber	¼ cucumber
100 g/4 oz cooked brown lentils	I cup cooked brown lentils
100 g/4 oz cooked mung beans	I cup cooked mung beans
1–2 tablespoons Lemon and Honey Dressing (page 104)	2–3 tablespoons Lemon and Honey Dressing (page 104)
4 tablespoons natural yogurt or to taste	5 tablespoons plain yogurt or to taste

Chop the onion, green pepper and cucumber and mix them in a bowl with the lentils and mung beans. Pour on just a little dressing and leave the salad to marinate for 1–2 hours.

Stir in enough yogurt to give the beans a creamy coating and serve the salad on a bed of shredded cabbage, if liked. **Serves 4**

Chickpea Salad

METRIC/IMPERIAL	AMERICAN
350 g/12 oz cooked chickpeas	3½ cups cooked garbanzos beans
about 6 tablespoons Italian Dressing (page 109)	about ½ cup Italian Dressing (page 109)
¼ lettuce	¼ lettuce
I stick celery, chopped	I stalk celery, chopped
2 carrots, sliced	2 carrots, sliced
10 stuffed olives	10 stuffed olives
chopped fresh parsley or chives	chopped fresh parsley or chives

Toss the chickpeas (garbanzos beans) in the dressing and leave them to marinate for at least 1 hour.

Separate the lettuce into leaves and arrange them on a serving plate. Mix the chopped celery and carrots with the chickpeas, pile the mixture on to the lettuce and sprinkle with the olives and herbs. **Serves 4**

Creamy Cumin Cucumber

METRIC/IMPERIAL	AMERICAN
4 tablespoons cottage cheese	5 tablespoons cottage cheese
a little milk (optional)	a little milk (optional)
½–1 teaspoon ground cumin	½–1 teaspoon ground cumin
salt and pepper	salt and pepper
1 large cucumber	1 large cucumber
3 tomatoes, sliced	3 tomatoes, sliced
watercress to garnish	watercress to garnish

Rub the cottage cheese through a sieve or blend it in a liquidiser or blender to achieve a thick, smooth consistency. Add a drop of milk if necessary. Stir in the cumin and salt and pepper to taste. Dice the cucumber and mix it into the cheese dressing; let it stand a short while before serving topped with tomato slices and garnished with watercress. **Serves 4**

Sweet Celery Salad

METRIC/IMPERIAL	AMERICAN
1 small head celery	1 small head celery
50 g/2 oz canned sweet corn	⅓ cup canned corn
1 small red pepper, deseeded	1 small red pepper, deseeded
1 (227-g/8-oz) can pineapple pieces in natural juice	1 (8-oz) can pineapple pieces in natural juice
4–6 tablespoons Coconut Dressing (page 110), made without honey	⅓–½ cup Coconut Dressing (page 110), made without honey
50 g/2 oz desiccated coconut	⅔ cup shredded coconut
½ Webb's Wonder lettuce, shredded (optional)	½ Bibb lettuce, shredded (optional)

Wash the celery, divide it into sticks and trim away the leaves. Chop the celery. Drain the sweet corn and dice the red pepper. Mix these ingredients together in a bowl. Drain the pineapple, reserving the juice, chop it coarsely, and add it to the mixture. Stir some of the pineapple juice into the Coconut Dressing, if liked, to sweeten it and pour the dressing over the salad ingredients. Sprinkle with desiccated coconut and serve on a bed of lettuce, if used. **Serves 4**

Celeriac Salad

METRIC/IMPERIAL	AMERICAN
1 large root celeriac	1 large root celeriac
1 large orange	1 large orange
½ small onion	½ small onion
6 tablespoons Yogurt Watercress Dressing (page 111)	½ cup Yogurt Watercress Dressing (page 111)
salt and pepper	salt and pepper

Peel and grate the celeriac. Peel the orange, divide it into segments and chop the segments. Grate the onion as finely as possible. Combine all the ingredients and toss them in the dressing. Season to taste with salt and pepper. **Serves 4**

Potato and Broad Bean Salad

Illustrated on page 108

METRIC/IMPERIAL	AMERICAN
450 g/1 lb shelled broad beans	2¼ cups shelled Lima beans
225 g/8 oz very small new potatoes	½ lb very small new potatoes
2 teaspoons capers	2 teaspoons capers
2 spring onions	2 scallions
about 4 tablespoons soured cream or	about 5 tablespoons dairy sour cream or
Mayonnaise (page 109)	Mayonnaise (page 109)
salt and pepper	salt and pepper

Cook the broad beans in boiling salted water for 15 minutes or until just tender. Rinse through with cold water, drain and leave on one side. Wash the potatoes, cut the larger ones in half and cook them in the same way for 15–20 minutes.

Drain and chop the capers. Trim and finely chop the spring onions (scallions). In a bowl combine the beans and potatoes while they are still warm and stir in the capers and soured cream or mayonnaise. Season with salt and pepper to taste and sprinkle with chopped spring onion. **Serves 4**

Curried Apple Cole Slaw

METRIC/IMPERIAL	AMERICAN
¼ small white cabbage	¼ small white cabbage
2 carrots	2 carrots
½ small onion	½ small onion
2 dessert apples	2 dessert apples
50 g/2 oz sultanas	⅓ cup seedless white raisins
2 teaspoons curry powder or to taste	2 teaspoons curry powder or to taste
about 6 tablespoons natural yogurt,	about ½ cup plain yogurt, dairy sour
soured cream or Mayonnaise (page 109)	cream or Mayonnaise (page 109)
squeeze of lemon	squeeze of lemon

Finely grate the cabbage, carrots and onion and mix well. Quarter, core and coarsely chop the apples and add them to the salad with the sultanas (seedless white raisins). Stir enough curry powder into the yogurt, soured cream or mayonnaise to give it a mild flavour, add the lemon juice and mix the dressing into the cole slaw.

This salad is best served soon after it is prepared. **Serves 4**

Beetroot Raita

METRIC/IMPERIAL	AMERICAN
225 g/8 oz cooked beetroot	1⅓ cups cooked beets
1 teaspoon ground cumin	1 teaspoon ground cumin
4–6 tablespoons natural yogurt or soured	⅓–½ cup plain yogurt or dairy sour cream
cream	salt and pepper
salt and pepper	

Dice the beetroot (beets) and drain very thoroughly. Mix the cumin into the yogurt or soured cream with salt and pepper to taste and add the mixture to the beetroot. Chill briefly but do not stir more than necessary. **Serves 4**

Broccoli and Egg Salad

Illustrated on page 45

METRIC/IMPERIAL	AMERICAN
450 g/1 lb broccoli	1 lb broccoli
2 large tomatoes	2 large tomatoes
6 spring onions	6 scallions
about 4 tablespoons Mayonnaise	about 5 tablespoons Mayonnaise
(page 109)	(page 109)
2 hard-boiled eggs, sliced	2 hard-cooked eggs, sliced
sprinkling of paprika	sprinkling of paprika

Break the broccoli into sprigs and cook them in a little boiling salted water for 10 minutes or until just tender. Rinse them in cold water, drain and put them into a bowl. Quarter the tomatoes, trim and chop the spring onions and add them to the bowl. Mix in enough mayonnaise to moisten the salad ingredients and top with the sliced eggs. Sprinkle with paprika. **Serves 4**

Winter Salad

METRIC/IMPERIAL	AMERICAN
$\frac{1}{2}$ small head Chinese leaves	$\frac{1}{2}$ small head Chinese leaves
2 sticks celery	2 stalks celery
100 g/4 oz Brussels sprouts	$\frac{1}{4}$ lb Brussels sprouts
1 large dessert pear	1 large dessert pear
100 g/4 oz parsnips, grated	1 cup grated parsnip
4–6 tablespoons Tahini Garlic Dressing	$\frac{1}{3}$–$\frac{1}{2}$ cup Tahini Garlic Dressing
(page 111)	(page 111)
salt and pepper	salt and pepper
2 tomatoes	2 tomatoes
$\frac{1}{4}$ curly endive	$\frac{1}{4}$ head chicory

Trim and chop the Chinese leaves and celery; grate the Brussels sprouts; dice the pear. Mix all the prepared ingredients including the grated parsnip together in a bowl and add tahini dressing and salt and pepper to taste.

Quarter the tomatoes. Wash the endive (chicory), separate the leaves, drain well and arrange them on a salad platter. Heap the salad on top and garnish with the tomatoes. **Serves 4**

Globe Artichoke and Cheese Salad

METRIC/IMPERIAL	AMERICAN
4 globe artichokes	4 globe artichokes
4 tomatoes, quartered	4 tomatoes, quartered
100 g/4 oz hard cheese (Edam, Cheddar, Gruyère), diced	$\frac{2}{3}$ cup diced hard cheese (Edam, Cheddar, Gruyère)
about 150 ml/$\frac{1}{4}$ pint Mayonnaise (page 109)	about $\frac{2}{3}$ cup Mayonnaise (page 109)

Slice the stalk ends off the artichokes and soak the artichokes for a while in water to clean. Cook them in boiling salted water for 30–40 minutes, until it is easy to pull out a leaf, drain well and leave to cool. Remove all the leaves and the choke from each one, reserving the heart. Cut the hearts into halves or quarters as liked and arrange them in a shallow dish with the tomatoes. Sprinkle the diced cheese over the top and serve the salad with the mayonnaise. **Serves 4**

Rice Salad

METRIC/IMPERIAL	AMERICAN
½ crisp lettuce	½ crisp lettuce
2 courgettes	2 zucchini
2 tomatoes	2 tomatoes
1 green pepper	1 green pepper
3 tablespoons vegetable oil	4 tablespoons vegetable oil
675 g/1½ lb cooked brown rice	4 cups cooked brown rice
2 spring onions	2 scallions
½ small cucumber	½ small cucumber
6–8 tablespoons Italian Dressing (page 109)	½–⅔ cup Italian Dressing (page 109)
salt and pepper	salt and pepper
50 g/2 oz grated Parmesan cheese or chopped almonds	½ cup grated Parmesan cheese or chopped almonds

Wash the lettuce, separate it into leaves and allow to drain. Slice the courgettes (zucchini) and tomatoes. Trim and slice the green pepper, removing the seeds. Heat the oil in a pan and sauté the sliced vegetables very gently for 5–10 minutes or until tender but still crisp. Drain the vegetables, allow them to cool and put them in a bowl with the rice. Chop the spring onions (scallions) and cucumber and add them to the bowl. Toss all the ingredients in the dressing, season with salt and pepper to taste and serve the salad on a bed of lettuce, sprinkled with the cheese or nuts. **Serves 4**

Crunchy Cauliflower Salad

METRIC/IMPERIAL	AMERICAN
100 g/4 oz soya beans, soaked in water overnight	½ cup soy beans, soaked in water overnight
vegetable oil for frying	vegetable oil for frying
1 small cauliflower	1 small cauliflower
1–2 sticks celery	1–2 stalks celery
1 small cucumber	1 small cucumber
1–2 carrots	1–2 carrots
50 g/2 oz dried apricots, soaked in water overnight	⅓ cup dried apricots, soaked in water overnight
4–6 tablespoons Green Goddess Dressing (page 111)	⅓–½ cup Green Goddess Dressing (page 111)

Begin by making the soya bean crunch nuts. Drain the beans and dry them well. Heat the oil in a pan to 185 C (360 F) and drop in the beans, a few at a time. They will crisp up in 1 minute, becoming deep golden in colour. Drain the crunch nuts and let them cool while you prepare the salad.

Trim the cauliflower and break it into florets. Blanch the florets first in a little boiling salted water for 5 minutes, if liked, or put them straight into your salad bowl. Finely chop the celery and cucumber. Peel or scrape the carrots and cut them into fine strips. Drain and coarsely chop the apricots. Mix all the ingredients together in a bowl, pour in the dressing and serve topped with the soya nuts. **Serves 4**

Dressings

Home-made salad dressings are infinitely nicer than shop-bought ones and amazingly easy to make. They also give you a great opportunity to be creative. The only disadvantage is that most of them will not stay fresh for long and should be made up as and when they are needed. Still, make them in a liquidiser or blender and it will take literally seconds; whisk them by hand and it won't take you longer than a minute or two.

Here are some ideas to get you going. All of them are made from natural, wholesome ingredients; all of them make more of a salad. But don't forget, the idea is that they cling to the salad ingredients and therefore enhance their flavour – not drown it!

French Dressing (Oil and Vinegar)

The classic dressing and probably the simplest of all.

METRIC/IMPERIAL	AMERICAN
6 tablespoons vegetable oil	½ cup vegetable oil
3 tablespoons wine vinegar	4 tablespoons wine vinegar
salt and pepper to taste	salt and pepper to taste

Whisk the ingredients together or shake them thoroughly in a screw-top jar until blended. Store in the refrigerator until needed (this is one dressing that will keep quite well).

Vinaigrette Dressing

METRIC/IMPERIAL	AMERICAN
3 tablespoons wine vinegar or lemon juice	4 tablespoons wine vinegar or lemon juice
6 tablespoons vegetable oil	½ cup vegetable oil
½ teaspoon made mustard or to taste	½ teaspoon made mustard or to taste
2 teaspoons chopped fresh herbs (parsley, tarragon, mint) or to taste	2 teaspoons chopped fresh herbs (parsley, tarragon, mint) or to taste
salt and pepper to taste	salt and pepper to taste

Whisk all the ingredients thoroughly together. Store in the refrigerator until needed.

Lemon and Honey Dressing

METRIC/IMPERIAL	AMERICAN
2 tablespoons vegetable oil	3 tablespoons vegetable oil
2 tablespoons clear honey	3 tablespoons clear honey
2 tablespoons lemon juice	3 tablespoons lemon juice
salt and pepper to taste	salt and pepper to taste

Whisk all the ingredients together well and keep in a cool place until needed.

From the top *Chinese Leaves and Avocado Salad (page 98); Three Bean Salad (page 96).*
Overleaf from the left: *Pakora (page 90); Sweet Corn Ratatouille (page 84); Foil-baked Potatoes (page 92) with Nut-stuffed Aubergines (page 91).*

Italian Dressing

METRIC/IMPERIAL	AMERICAN
½ clove garlic or to taste	½ clove garlic or to taste
4 tablespoons olive oil	5 tablespoons olive oil
2 tablespoons wine vinegar or lemon juice	3 tablespoons wine vinegar or lemon juice
1 teaspoon chopped fresh or ½ teaspoon dried basil	1 teaspoon chopped fresh or ½ teaspoon dried basil
salt and pepper to taste	salt and pepper to taste

Finely chop or crush the garlic and combine it with all the other ingredients. Leave the dressing to stand for a while before serving to allow all the flavours to mingle.

Mayonnaise

METRIC/IMPERIAL	AMERICAN
1 large egg yolk	1 large egg yolk
pinch of mustard powder	pinch of mustard powder
salt and pepper to taste	salt and pepper to taste
150 ml/¼ pint vegetable oil	⅔ cup of vegetable oil
2 teaspoons wine vinegar	2 teaspoons wine vinegar
2 teaspoons warm water	2 teaspoons warm water

In a bowl stir together the egg yolk, mustard and seasoning. Add the oil, drop by drop, beating continuously as you do so. When the mixture begins to thicken you can go a little faster, but be sure to beat the mixture energetically so that it does not curdle. If the worst happens and the egg does curdle, beat another egg yolk in a second bowl and gradually beat the mayonnaise into it, then continue as before. If it seems too thick beat in a drop of vinegar and water as you go along; otherwise add it at the end.

Mayonnaise is best used when freshly made, but it will keep for a few days in the refrigerator.

VARIATIONS

Add any of the following to the finished mayonnaise: 1–2 teaspoons finely grated horseradish; a few finely chopped capers, black olives and gherkins to taste; a lightly beaten egg white, stirred in just before serving.

Thousand Island Dressing

METRIC/IMPERIAL	AMERICAN
300 ml/½ pint Mayonnaise (above)	1 cup Mayonnaise (above)
2 tablespoons finely chopped stuffed olives	3 tablespoons finely chopped stuffed olives
1 tablespoon finely chopped onion	1 tablespoon finely chopped onion
1 finely chopped hard-boiled egg	1 finely chopped hard-cooked egg
1–2 tablespoons chilli sauce or tomato ketchup	1–2 tablespoons chili sauce or tomato ketchup
salt and pepper	salt and pepper

Combine all the ingredients very thoroughly together, taste and adjust seasoning. Serve at once.

From the top California Salad (page 97); Potato and Broad Bean Salad (page 101).

Blue Cheese Dressing

METRIC/IMPERIAL	AMERICAN
75 g/3 oz blue cheese (Stilton, Dolcelatte, Roquefort)	½ cup blue cheese (Stilton, Dolcelatte, Roquefort)
150 ml/¼ pint Mayonnaise (page 109) or French Dressing (page 104)	⅔ cup Mayonnaise (page 109) or French Dressing (page 104)

Crumble the cheese and mash it to a cream before mixing it thoroughly with the mayonnaise or French Dressing.

Mousseline Dressing

METRIC/IMPERIAL	AMERICAN
150 ml/¼ pint double cream	⅔ cup heavy cream
150 ml/¼ pint Mayonnaise (page 109)	⅔ cup Mayonnaise (page 109)
1 tablespoon tomato purée	1 tablespoon tomato purée
1 tablespoon lemon juice	1 tablespoon lemon juice
1 teaspoon chopped fresh chives	1 teaspoon chopped fresh chives
soy sauce to taste	soy sauce to taste

Lightly whip the cream, add the mayonnaise and stir in the remaining ingredients. Serve as soon as possible.

Vegan Salad Cream

METRIC/IMPERIAL	AMERICAN
2 tablespoons lemon juice	3 tablespoons lemon juice
2 tablespoons vegetable oil	3 tablespoons vegetable oil
about 2 tablespoons concentrated soya milk	about 3 tablespoons concentrated soy milk

Whisk together the lemon juice and oil and stir in enough concentrated soy milk to reach the desired consistency.

Tofu Dressing

METRIC/IMPERIAL	AMERICAN
175 g/6 oz tofu	¾ cup tofu
2 tablespoons vegetable oil	3 tablespoons vegetable oil
2 tablespoons cider vinegar	3 tablespoons cider vinegar
soy sauce or salt and pepper to taste	soy sauce or salt and pepper to taste

Drain and dice the tofu and beat it with the other ingredients until you have a smooth, creamy dressing. A liquidiser or blender is the best thing to use for this. Tofu dressing will keep for a few days if stored in the refrigerator.

VARIATIONS
Add any of the following to basic Tofu Dressing: 1 teaspoon curry powder, cumin or turmeric; 1–2 cloves garlic, finely crushed; 1 small onion, finely chopped; 2 tablespoons (3 tablespoons US) tomato purée and some chopped fresh parsley; 1–2 teaspoons chopped fresh basil; ½ teaspoon dried oregano; 1 teaspoon crushed caraway or celery seeds.

Coconut Dressing

METRIC/IMPERIAL	AMERICAN
100 g/4 oz cottage cheese	$\frac{1}{2}$ cup cottage cheese
1 tablespoon desiccated coconut	1 tablespoon shredded coconut
honey to taste	honey to taste

Pass the cottage cheese through a sieve and mash it until very smooth. Combine it with the coconut and honey to taste.

Yogurt Watercress Dressing

METRIC/IMPERIAL	AMERICAN
150 ml/$\frac{1}{4}$ pint natural yogurt	$\frac{2}{3}$ cup plain yogurt
squeeze of lemon	squeeze of lemon
$\frac{1}{2}$ teaspoon finely grated lemon rind	$\frac{1}{2}$ teaspoon finely grated lemon rind
$\frac{1}{2}$ teaspoon clear honey or to taste	$\frac{1}{2}$ teaspoon clear honey or to taste
finely chopped watercress to taste	finely chopped watercress to taste

Mix all the ingredients well together and serve as soon as possible.

Green Goddess Dressing

METRIC/IMPERIAL	AMERICAN
1 ripe avocado	1 ripe avocado
generous squeeze of lemon	generous squeeze of lemon
50 g/2 oz cream cheese or 3 tablespoons soured cream	$\frac{1}{4}$ cup cream cheese or dairy sour cream
2 tablespoons Mayonnaise (page 109)	3 tablespoons Mayonnaise (page 109)
$\frac{1}{2}$ clove garlic, crushed	$\frac{1}{2}$ clove garlic, crushed
1–2 teaspoons finely chopped parsley	1–2 teaspoons finely chopped parsley
1 teaspoon chopped fresh tarragon	1 teaspoon chopped fresh tarragon
pinch of cayenne	pinch of cayenne
salt to taste	salt to taste

Peel and dice the avocado and mash it with the lemon juice. Combine thoroughly with all the other ingredients, taste and add salt if necessary.

Tahini Garlic Dressing

METRIC/IMPERIAL	AMERICAN
4 tablespoons tahini	$\frac{1}{3}$ cup tahini
4 tablespoons vegetable oil	$\frac{1}{3}$ cup vegetable oil
2 tablespoons lemon juice	3 tablespoons lemon juice
$\frac{1}{2}$–1 clove garlic, crushed	$\frac{1}{2}$–1 clove garlic, crushed
salt and pepper	salt and pepper

Stir all the ingredients together and whisk until they are thoroughly mixed or blend them in a liquidiser or blender. If the dressing seems too thick, add more oil.

VARIATION
Sprinkle in a little soy sauce or 1 teaspoon chopped fresh mixed herbs to give the dressing a special bite without detracting from its unique flavour.

Happy Endings

Buckwheat Crêpes
with Maple Sauce

Illustrated on pages 126–7

METRIC/IMPERIAL
Crêpes
75 g/3 oz buckwheat flour
75 g/3 oz plain wholemeal flour
2 small eggs
about 600 ml/1 pint water
2 tablespoons oil
Sauce
100 g/4 oz pure maple syrup
50 g/2 oz chopped almonds (optional)
2 oranges

AMERICAN
Crêpes
¾ cup buckwheat flour
¾ cup wholemeal flour
2 small eggs
about 2½ cups water
3 tablespoons oil
Sauce
⅓ cup pure maple syrup
⅓ cup chopped almonds (optional)
2 oranges

Combine the two flours in a bowl. Beat the eggs lightly and stir them into the flour, adding enough water to give a thin, creamy texture. Beat the batter until completely smooth and leave it to stand in a cool place for at least 30 minutes.

Meanwhile, make the sauce. Heat the maple syrup gently in a pan with the nuts, if used, and simmer the mixture for 5 minutes. Allow to cool. Peel the oranges and divide them into segments, removing all the skin from each segment.

Heat some of the oil in a frying pan or skillet and when very hot, pour in a little of the batter – the thinner the covering, the crisper your crêpe will be. Cook for a few minutes, then toss or turn the crêpe with a spatula and cook the other side. Keep the crêpes warm while you use the rest of the batter in the same way. Arrange them folded on a plate and top them with the orange segments. Pour over the maple sauce and serve. **Serves 4**

Strawberry Soufflé

Make this at the end of the season when strawberries are no longer at their best – nor their most expensive – or early in the season if you want to impress.
At other times use the same simple recipe with whatever fruit is available: peaches, gooseberries, bananas, or combinations like apples and blackberries. Even dried fruits like apricots and prunes will work well as long as you soak them in water first.

METRIC/IMPERIAL
450 g/1 lb strawberries
4 egg whites
100 g/4 oz light Muscovado raw brown
sugar

AMERICAN
1 lb strawberries
4 egg whites
⅔ cup light raw brown sugar

Set the oven at moderate (180 C, 350 F, gas 4). Clean and hull the strawberries and press them through a sieve or blend them in a liquidiser or blender to make a thick purée. Whisk the egg whites until stiff enough to hold firm peaks, carefully add the sugar and fold the mixture into the strawberry purée. Pour into a lightly greased 1.75-litre/3-pint (4-pint US) soufflé dish and bake the soufflé for about 30 minutes, until well risen. Serve at once. **Serves 4**

Almond Cheesecake

Illustrated on page 128

METRIC/IMPERIAL	AMERICAN
90 g/3½ oz butter or margarine	scant ¼ cup butter or margarine
100 g/4 oz cake crumbs	2 cups cake crumbs
50 g/2 oz light Muscovado raw brown sugar	⅓ cup light raw brown sugar
grated rind of 1 lemon	grated rind of 1 lemon
grated rind of 1 orange	grated rind of 1 orange
3 eggs, beaten	3 eggs, beaten
450 g/1 lb cottage cheese	1 lb cottage cheese
50 g/2 oz ground almonds	½ cup ground almonds
pinch of salt	pinch of salt
50 g/2 oz flaked almonds	¼ cup flaked almonds

Set the oven at moderate (180 C, 350 F, gas 4). Melt 40 g/1½ oz (3 tablespoons) of the fat in a pan and mix it with the cake crumbs. Grease an 18-cm/7-in springclip cake tin and sprinkle in the crumbs so that they are evenly distributed.

Cream together the rest of the butter or margarine, the sugar and the lemon and orange rind. Work in the beaten egg, a little at a time. Pass the cottage cheese through a sieve and add it to the mixture, followed by the ground almonds and salt. Spoon the cheese and almond mixture into the tin, smooth the top and sprinkle with the flaked almonds. Bake the cheesecake for 45–50 minutes or until it has set.

Leave the cheesecake to cool in the oven with the door open to help prevent it from cracking. If, however, your cake still cracks, you can disguise the fault by adding a light dusting of more cake crumbs or sugar, by spooning drained stewed fruit on top or by layering the top with fresh fruit laid in a pattern. **Serves 4**

Hot Stuffed Peaches

Illustrated on pages 126–7

METRIC/IMPERIAL	AMERICAN
4 large firm peaches	4 large firm peaches
75 g/3 oz dried wholemeal breadcrumbs	¾ cup dried wholewheat breadcrumbs
50 g/2 oz demerara raw brown sugar	⅓ cup light raw brown sugar
50 g/2 oz butter or margarine	¼ cup butter or margarine
25 g/1 oz walnuts, flaked almonds or desiccated coconut	¼ cup walnuts, flaked almonds or shredded coconut

Wash the peaches, cut them in half and remove the stones. Scoop out some of the flesh from each with a teaspoon, leaving a strong shell. Chop the flesh and mix it in a bowl with the breadcrumbs, sugar and 40 g/1½ oz (3 tablespoons) of the butter or margarine.

Fill the peach shells with the mixture, piling it high, and arrange them in an ovenproof dish. Sprinkle with the nuts, dot with the remaining butter or margarine and heat through under a gentle grill until lightly browned on top. **Serves 4**

VARIATION

I like the crisp texture of almost raw peaches, but if you prefer them soft, bake them in a moderate oven (180 C, 350 F, gas 4) for about 20 minutes.

Lemon Steamed Sponge Pudding

Illustrated on pages 126–7

METRIC/IMPERIAL	AMERICAN
75 g/3 oz demerara raw brown sugar	½ cup light raw brown sugar
75 g/3 oz butter or margarine	⅓ cup butter or margarine
2 eggs	2 eggs
grated rind of 1 lemon	grated rind of 1 lemon
100 g/4 oz self-raising wholemeal flour	1 cup wholewheat flour sifted with 1
1 tablespoon lemon juice	teaspoon baking powder
3 tablespoons lemon curd	1 tablespoon lemon juice
	4 tablespoons lemon curd

Grind the sugar to a powder in a liquidiser or blender, if liked, to give the pudding a finer texture, and cream it with the butter or margarine. Lightly beat the eggs. Add the lemon rind to the pudding mixture, then beat in the egg a little at a time, until well blended. Sift the flour, reserving the bran for use in another recipe, and stir it into the mixture, followed by the lemon juice.

Grease a 900-ml/1½-pint (2-pint US) pudding basin, spoon in the lemon curd and turn the basin to distribute it across the bottom. Carefully pour in the pudding mixture. Cover the top with greaseproof (waxed) paper or cooking foil, securing it firmly round the edge with string. Stand the basin in a steamer. Bring a large saucepan of water to a fast boil and put the steamer inside. The water should reach two-thirds up the side of the basin. Steam the pudding for at least 1½ hours. Check from time to time that the water has not dried up. When ready, tip the pudding out on to a warmed plate and serve with Lemon Sauce (see below). **Serves 4**

Lemon Sauce

METRIC/IMPERIAL	AMERICAN
2 lemons	2 lemons
about 150 ml/¼ pint water	about ⅔ cup water
50 g/2 oz demerara raw brown sugar	⅓ cup light raw brown sugar
15 g/½ oz arrowroot	2 teaspoons arrowroot
pinch of grated nutmeg	pinch of grated nutmeg

Thinly peel the lemons and leave the peel on one side. Cut the lemons in half and squeeze out as much of the juice as you can into a bowl. Add enough water to make the liquid up to 300 ml/½ pint (1¼ cups) and put all but 2 tablespoons of this into a saucepan with the sugar. Heat gently, stirring continually, until the sugar dissolves.

Mix the arrowroot in a bowl with the remaining lemon juice to a smooth paste and slowly pour on the hot syrup, stirring well. Return this to the pan. Add the nutmeg and gently heat the sauce until it thickens and becomes clear. Snip some of the lemon peel into very fine shreds, transfer the sauce to a jug and sprinkle the lemon peel on top. Serve with Lemon Sponge Pudding (see above). **Serves 4**

Deep Dish Plum Pie

Illustrated on pages 126–7

METRIC/IMPERIAL	AMERICAN
Pastry	*Dough*
75 g/3 oz butter or margarine	⅓ cup butter or margarine
175 g/6 oz plain wholemeal flour	1½ cups wholewheat flour
2–3 tablespoons cold water	3–4 tablespoons cold water
Filling	*Filling*
675 g/1½ lb plums	1½ lb plums
175 g/6 oz demerara raw brown sugar	1 cup light raw brown sugar
1–2 teaspoons cinnamon	1–2 teaspoons cinnamon
squeeze of lemon	squeeze of lemon
1 tablespoon water	1 tablespoon water

Set the oven at moderately hot (200 C, 400 F, gas 6). Rub the butter or margarine into the flour until the mixture resembles fine breadcrumbs. Add enough cold water to bind the dough together, knead briefly and chill in the refrigerator for 30 minutes. On a lightly floured surface roll the dough out as thinly as possible to a shape 2.5 cm/1 in larger all round than the top of your deep pie dish. Cut a 2.5–cm/1-in strip off this to give you a border of pastry for the rim of the dish, moisten the rim with water and press the strip on to it. (This border is not absolutely necessary, but does tend to give you a better result.)

Wash, halve and stone the plums before layering them in the dish. Sprinkle each layer with a little sugar, cinnamon and lemon juice, reserving some of the sugar and cinnamon on one side. (In deep dish pies the filling should reach the top to support the pastry. Even so, a pie funnel can help ensure attractive results). Trickle the water over the fruit and cover the dish with the pastry shape, pressing it firmly to the pastry rim. Roll out any remaining pastry and cut leaves from it to decorate the pie. Arrange these on top, brush the whole pie top with water and sprinkle generously with the remaining sugar and cinnamon. Bake in the preheated oven for 20 minutes, then turn the oven down to moderate (180 C, 350 F, gas 4) for 20 more minutes. **Serves 4**

Chocolate and Lime Crunch Pie

METRIC/IMPERIAL	AMERICAN
175 g/6 oz chocolate digestive biscuits	1½ cups chocolate Graham crackers
75 g/3 oz butter or margarine, melted	⅓ cup butter or margarine, melted
¾ packet lime-flavoured agar-agar	¾ packet lime-flavoured agar-agar
200 ml/7 fl oz whipping cream	¾ cup heavy cream
few drops of green food colouring	few drops of green food colouring
(optional)	(optional)

Crush the biscuits, coat them well with the melted butter or margarine and use the mixture to line an 18-cm/7-in flan dish or pie pan. Set on one side.

Dissolve the agar-agar in 200 ml/7 fl oz (¾ cup) boiling water and leave it to cool. Whip the cream until thick and fold it into the cooled, but not set, agar-agar. Add the colouring, if you are using it, to give a delicate lime colour. Spoon the mixture into the prepared flan base, smooth the top and put it in the refrigerator to set completely. **Serves 4**

NOTE If you cannot obtain lime-flavoured agar-agar, make your own by bringing 200 ml/7 fl oz (¾ cup) diluted lime juice cordial – or the juice of 1 lime made up to this quantity with water – to boiling point and sprinkling in 1 teaspoon powdered unflavoured agar-agar. Stir until dissolved, then proceed as above.

Tofu Apricot Slices

I first learned to love tofu by using it in recipes like this one. Now I cannot praise it enough. How smooth and creamy it can be, how cleverly it absorbs the most subtle flavours. Once you've learned to love tofu, you'll want to use it in all sorts of desserts.

METRIC/IMPERIAL	AMERICAN
Base	*Base*
225 g/8 oz digestive biscuits	½ lb Graham crackers
75 g/3 oz butter or margarine, melted	⅓ cup butter or margarine, melted
¼ teaspoon cinnamon	¼ teaspoon cinnamon
¼ teaspoon grated nutmeg	¼ teaspoon grated nutmeg
Topping	*Topping*
100 g/4 oz creamy tofu	½ cup creamy tofu
2 large ripe bananas	2 large ripe bananas
2–3 tablespoons maple syrup	3–4 tablespoons maple syrup
100 g/4 oz dried apricots	¾ cup dried apricots
¼–½ teaspoon cinnamon	¼–½ teaspoon cinnamon
¼–½ teaspoon grated nutmeg	¼–½ teaspoon grated nutmeg
grated rind of 1 orange	grated rind of 1 orange
2 tablespoons apricot jam	3 tablespoons apricot jam

To make the base, crush the biscuits as finely as possible and combine them with the melted fat and the spices. Line a 33 × 23-cm/13 × 9-in Swiss roll tin (jelly roll pan) with cooking foil and press the mixture into it. Set aside to firm up.

Drain the tofu and mash it with the bananas to make a smooth, creamy mixture; sweeten to taste with the maple syrup. Spread this cream across the crumb base. Wash the apricots, put them in a pan with the spices, orange rind and 1–2 tablespoons water and simmer for 10–15 minutes, until just tender. Drain off and reserve any excess liquid and allow to cool before spooning the fruit over the tofu mixture. Warm the apricot jam very gently in a saucepan to make a sauce, adding a little of the apricot liquid or water if it is too dry. Cool and pour it over the fruit. Chill before cutting into generous slices. **Makes 8**

Summer Fruit Salad

Illustrated on page 125

Ideal in summer not just because some of the fruits are at their best then, but because it is one the crispest, freshest-tasting combinations you can throw together. The secret, of course, is the cucumber . . . .

METRIC/IMPERIAL	AMERICAN
1 grapefruit	1 grapefruit
1 orange	1 orange
1 crisp green apple	1 crisp green apple
100 g/4 oz strawberries	1 cup strawberries
1 small pineapple	1 small pineapple
1 cucumber	1 cucumber
1 teaspoon clear honey	1 teaspoon clear honey
150 ml/¼ pint orange juice	⅔ cup orange juice

Peel the grapefruit and orange and divide them into segments. Core and slice the apple. Clean, hull and halve the strawberries. Cut the pineapple into quarters, slice the flesh from the shell and dice it. Peel and dice the cucumber. Mix all the fruit carefully together. Dissolve the honey in the orange juice and pour it over the salad. Chill in the refrigerator and serve in tall glasses, if liked. **Serves 4**

Lemon Yogurt Jelly

METRIC/IMPERIAL	AMERICAN
2 lemons	2 lemons
1 packet lemon-flavoured agar-agar or	1 packet lemon-flavoured agar-agar or
2 teaspoons powdered agar-agar	2 teaspoons powdered agar-agar
50 g/2 oz demerara raw brown sugar	$\frac{1}{3}$ cup demerara raw brown sugar
1 (150-g/5.3-oz) carton natural yogurt	$\frac{2}{3}$ cup plain yogurt
25 g/1 oz grated chocolate or chopped walnuts	3 tablespoons grated chocolate or chopped walnuts

Squeeze the lemons and put the juice on one side. Peel the lemons, chop the peel very coarsely and put it in a pan with 600 ml/1 pint (2½ cups) water. Bring to the boil and simmer over a low heat for 10 minutes. Strain to remove the peel, then dissolve the agar-agar in the hot liquid. Add the sugar and stir until it, too, has completely dissolved. Add the lemon juice. Leave the jelly until cold but not set, then whisk in the yogurt and spoon the mixture into four individual glasses. Chill to set firm and decorate with grated chocolate or chopped nuts before serving. **Serves 4**

Dried Fruit Compote

METRIC/IMPERIAL	AMERICAN
100 g/4 oz dried apricots	$\frac{2}{3}$ cup dried apricots
100 g/4 oz dried prunes	$\frac{2}{3}$ cup dried prunes
100 g/4 oz raisins	$\frac{2}{3}$ cup raisins
100 g/4 oz dried pears	$\frac{2}{3}$ cup dried pears
2 tablespoons honey	3 tablespoons honey
grated rind of 1 small lemon	grated rind of 1 small lemon
50 g/2 oz flaked almonds	$\frac{1}{4}$ cup flaked almonds

Wash the fruit carefully, put it into a bowl and cover it with hot water. Stir in the honey and lemon rind, cover the bowl and leave overnight for the fruit to plump up. There is no need to cook dried fruit – in fact, to do so takes away much of the goodness, flavour and texture.

Serve sprinkled with the flaked almonds. **Serves 4**

Scots Cream-crowdie

METRIC/IMPERIAL	AMERICAN
50 g/2 oz oatmeal	$\frac{1}{2}$ cup oatmeal
300 ml/½ pint double cream	1¼ cups heavy cream
4 tablespoons whisky or to taste	5 tablespoons whiskey or to taste
1 teaspoon lemon juice	1 teaspoon lemon juice
100 g/4 oz light Muscovado raw brown sugar	$\frac{2}{3}$ cup light raw brown sugar

Dry-roast the oatmeal in a saucepan or under the grill for a few minutes, stirring frequently, until crisp and golden. Whip the cream until thick and able to hold its shape. Combine the whisky and lemon juice and fold the liquid gently into the cream with the sugar. Add all but 1 tablespoon of the oatmeal. Divide the mixture between four individual glasses and chill in the refrigerator before serving them topped with the remaining oatmeal. **Serves 4**

Vanilla Mousse

METRIC/IMPERIAL	AMERICAN
25 g/1 oz demerara raw brown sugar	2 tablespoons light raw brown sugar
300 ml/½ pint whipping cream	1¼ cups heavy cream
½ teaspoon vanilla essence	½ teaspoon vanilla extract
1 egg white	1 egg white
4 teaspoons crème de menthe or 25 g/1 oz grated mint chocolate	2 tablespoons crème de menthe or grated mint chocolate

Grind the sugar to a powder in a liquidiser or blender. Whip the cream until firm enough to hold its shape and stir in the vanilla essence and sugar, making sure they are thoroughly mixed. Beat the egg white and fold it into the cream mixture. Divide the mousse between four individual glasses and chill. Just before serving, spoon a little crème de menthe over each glass or top it with a sprinkling of grated mint chocolate. **Serves 4**

Carob Jamaican Mousse

METRIC/IMPERIAL	AMERICAN
1 (175-g/6-oz) carob 'chocolate' bar	1 (6-oz) carob 'chocolate' bar
1 tablespoon strong coffee or	1 tablespoon strong coffee or
1 tablespoon instant coffee dissolved in	1 tablespoon instant coffee dissolved in
1 tablespoon hot water	1 tablespoon hot water
4 eggs, separated	4 eggs, separated
2 tablespoons rum	3 tablespoons rum
300 ml/½ pint whipping cream	1¼ cups heavy cream

In a double saucepan or a bowl held over a pan of hot water, gently melt the carob bar with the coffee and allow to cool slightly. Beat the egg yolks and add them to the sauce with the rum. Whip the cream until thick and fold it into the sauce with a metal spoon; whisk the egg whites until stiff and fold these in too.

Divide the mousse between four or six individual glasses and chill it thoroughly, preferably overnight. **Serves 4–6**

Honey Ice Cream with Ginger

Illustrated on page 125

METRIC/IMPERIAL	AMERICAN
2 eggs, separated	2 eggs, separated
300 ml/½ pint milk	1¼ cups milk
100 g/4 oz clear honey	⅓ cup clear honey
1 teaspoon vanilla essence or ginger wine	1 teaspoon vanilla extract or ginger wine
about 100 g/4 oz preserved stem ginger, chopped	about ½ cup chopped preserved stem ginger
300 ml/½ pint whipping cream	1¼ cups heavy cream
4 tablespoons ginger wine to decorate (optional)	⅓ cup ginger wine to decorate (optional)

In a saucepan mix together the egg yolks and milk and heat gently, stirring continually, until you have a sauce just thick enough to coat the back of a spoon. Do not allow it to boil. Stir in the honey and vanilla essence or ginger wine, followed by half the chopped ginger. Cool the mixture slightly, pour it into a freezing tray and freeze for ½–2 hours, depending on the temperature of your freezer, until the ice cream is beginning to set round the edges.

Whisk the egg whites until stiff and fold them into the ice cream. Whip the cream until thick and fold this in too. Return the ice cream to the freezing tray and freeze it for several hours until set. Serve in chilled glasses or dishes topped with the remaining chopped ginger with a little of its syrup or the ginger wine, if used. **Serves 4**

Blackberry Yogurt Ice Cream

Illustrated on page 125

METRIC/IMPERIAL	AMERICAN
175 g/6 oz demerara raw brown sugar	1 cup light raw brown sugar
275 g/10 oz fresh or frozen blackberries	2 cups fresh or frozen blackberries
300 ml/½ pint double cream	1¼ cups heavy cream
2 (150-g/5.3-oz) cartons natural yogurt	1⅓ cups plain yogurt
1 teaspoon rosewater	1 teaspoon rosewater

Grind the sugar to a powder in a liquidiser or blender. Thaw the blackberries if necessary, keep about 50 g/2 oz (½ cup) on one side for decoration and blend the rest in the liquidiser until smooth. Strain the juice into a bowl.

In an enamel saucepan heat the cream very gently, without letting it boil. Take the pan off the heat, add the sugar and stir until it has dissolved completely. Allow the mixture to cool and stir in the yogurt. When well mixed, add the blackberry juice and rosewater. Chill the mixture for a few hours in the refrigerator, then pour it into a freezing tray and freeze it for several hours until set. Serve in chilled glasses or dishes topped with the reserved blackberries and more yogurt or whipped cream, if liked. **Serves 4**

Cassata Dessert

Illustrated on page 128

Not an ice cream, as you would expect, but a smooth, creamy, crunchy, bitter-sweet mixture that is quite unique. Based on low-fat ricotta cheese, it is nowhere near as fattening as it tastes.

METRIC/IMPERIAL	AMERICAN
50 g/2 oz demerara raw brown sugar	⅓ cup light raw brown sugar
225 g/8 oz ricotta cheese	1 cup ricotta cheese
150 ml/¼ pint whipping cream	⅔ cup heavy cream
50 g/2 oz candied peel	⅓ cup candied peel
50 g/2 oz chopped almonds, toasted, or pistachio nuts	⅓ cup chopped almonds, toasted, or pistachio nuts
50 g/2 oz plain dessert chocolate, coarsely grated or chopped	⅓ cup coarsely grated or chopped plain dessert chocolate
15 g/½ oz glacé cherries (optional)	1 tablespoon glacé cherries (optional)
2 tablespoons Cointreau liqueur (optional)	3 tablespoons Cointreau liqueur (optional)

Grind the sugar to a powder in a liquidiser or blender and beat it gently with the ricotta cheese to make a smooth sauce. Lightly whip the cream. Chop the peel into small pieces. Mix the cream, peel, chopped nuts and grated or chopped chocolate into the ricotta sauce and chill before spooning the cassata into four individual glasses. Chop the glacé cherries, if used, and sprinkle them on top to decorate, together with the Cointreau, if liked. You can also decorate with a little more chopped chocolate, nuts or candied peel. **Serves 4**

Fresh-from-the-Oven

Quick Wholemeal Bread

Illustrated on page 145

METRIC/IMPERIAL	AMERICAN
1.4 kg/3 lb plain wholemeal flour	12 cups wholewheat flour
generous pinch of salt	generous pinch of salt
25 g/1 oz fresh yeast or 15 g/½ oz dried yeast	1 cake compressed yeast or 1 package active dry yeast
1 litre/1¾ pints lukewarm water	4¼ cups lukewarm water
1 teaspoon raw brown sugar, honey or molasses	1 teaspoon raw brown sugar, honey or molasses

Mix the flour and salt together in a warmed bowl and set on one side. Cream the fresh (compressed) yeast with about one third of the water and the sugar, honey or molasses; or sprinkle the dried (active dry) yeast on to the same amount of water, add the sweetening and stir until dissolved. Set the yeast mixture aside in a warm place for 5 minutes, until frothy.

Make a well in the centre of the flour and pour in the yeast liquid, followed by the rest of the water. Mix the flour gradually into the liquid with a wooden spoon, adding a little more warm water if it seems too dry. Stir thoroughly for several minutes; use your hands if you find it easier. Set the oven at hot (230 C, 450 F, gas 8). Thoroughly grease two 1-kg/2-lb (8½ × 4½ × 2-in) loaf tins and turn the dough into them. Leave the tins in a warm, draught-free spot until the dough has risen to the top of each tin (this can take anything up to 1 hour). Carefully put the bread in the preheated oven and bake it for 5 minutes, then lower the heat to moderately hot (200 C, 400 F, gas 6) and continue to bake for 30 minutes more. Turn the bread out of the tins and test to see if it is done by tapping each loaf with your knuckles – if it sounds hollow, put it on a wire rack to cool; if not, do not replace it in its tin, but return it to the oven, stand it upside down, and bake it for a further 5 minutes. Do this anyway if you like a crisper crust. **Makes two 1-kg/2-lb loaves**

NOTE A tea towel (dish cloth) placed over the bread during cooling makes the inside of the loaf softer.

Wholemeal Baps

Follow the recipe for Quick Wholemeal Bread given above but using two 450-g/1-lb (7 × 3½ × 2½-in) loaf tins instead of two 1-kg/2-lb (8½ × 4½ × 2-in) ones. Turn half the dough into these tins and leave to rise.

Knead the remaining dough briefly, put it in a covered bowl and leave it also to rise until doubled in size. Now knead the dough again, divide it into small portions and shape these into 6–8 baps. Dust them with flour and place them on a greased baking sheet until doubled in size. Bake them in a hot oven (220 C, 425 F, gas 7) for 15 minutes. **Makes 6–8**

Soda Bread

Illustrated on page 145

This bread used to be particularly popular in Ireland when yeast was hard to obtain. Now it's popular everywhere because it's so quick to make and good to eat.

METRIC/IMPERIAL	AMERICAN
450 g/1 lb plain wholemeal flour	4 cups wholewheat flour
1 teaspoon bicarbonate of soda	1 teaspoon baking soda
1 teaspoon cream of tartar	1 teaspoon cream of tartar
pinch of salt	pinch of salt
about 300 ml/½ pint milk and warm water mixed	about 1¼ cups milk and warm water mixed

Set the oven at moderately hot (190 C, 375 F, gas 5). In a bowl mix together thoroughly the flour, soda, cream of tartar and salt. Stir in enough liquid to give a moist dough – you may need to adjust the quantity to get the right consistency.

Turn the dough on to a floured board, dust it with flour and, using your hands, pat it into one large or two small rounds – the traditional shape for soda bread. Put the bread on a lightly greased baking sheet, flatten it slightly and cut a large cross in the top of each loaf. Bake for 40 minutes or until the bread is firm to the touch and sounds hollow when tapped. Cool on a wire rack. Eat while fresh as this bread does not keep very well. **Makes 1 large or 2 small loaves**

NOTE This recipe is an excellent way of using up milk that has gone sour – in fact if you use sour milk instead of fresh the bread will taste even more delicious.

Malt Bread

Illustrated on page 145

METRIC/IMPERIAL	AMERICAN
25 g/1 oz fresh yeast or 15 g/½ oz dried yeast	1 cake compressed yeast or 1 package active dry yeast
about 400 ml/14 fl oz lukewarm water	about 1¾ cups lukewarm water
3 tablespoons malt extract	4 tablespoons malt extract
2 tablespoons molasses	3 tablespoons molasses
25 g/1 oz butter or margarine	2 tablespoons butter or margarine
450 g/1 lb plain wholemeal flour	4 cups wholewheat flour
1 teaspoon salt	1 teaspoon salt
250 g/9 oz mixed dried fruit	1⅔ cups mixed dried fruit

Cream the fresh (compressed) yeast, if used, with the water. Sprinkle dried (active dry) yeast into the water and stir until dissolved. Leave the yeast liquid in a warm place for 5 minutes to become frothy. Put the malt extract, molasses and butter or margarine in a pan together and melt them over a low heat, stirring occasionally so that they blend completely.

Mix the flour and salt together in a warmed bowl. Make a well in the centre and pour in the yeast liquid. Add the melted ingredients and the dried fruit and mix everything together, stirring energetically for at least a few minutes. Set the oven at moderately hot (200 C, 400 F, gas 6). Grease two 450-g/1-lb (7 × 3½ × 2-in) loaf tins and divide the dough between them. Cover and leave to rise in a warm place for 30 minutes or until the dough has nearly reached the tops of the tins. Bake for 45 minutes. **Makes two 450-g/1-lb loaves**

Courgette Bread

Illustrated on page 145

*An unusual American-style bread which tastes much better than it sounds. It
also makes a great conversation piece!*

METRIC/IMPERIAL	AMERICAN
about 225 g/8 oz courgettes	about $\frac{1}{2}$ lb zucchini
about 6 tablespoons vegetable oil	$\frac{1}{2}$ cup vegetable oil
225 g/8 oz light raw brown sugar	$1\frac{1}{3}$ cups light raw brown sugar
1 large egg	1 large egg
175 g/6 oz plain wholemeal flour	$1\frac{1}{2}$ cups wholewheat flour
$\frac{1}{2}$ teaspoon bicarbonate of soda	$\frac{1}{2}$ teaspoon baking soda
pinch of baking powder	pinch of baking powder
$\frac{1}{2}$ teaspoon ground cinnamon	$\frac{1}{2}$ teaspoon ground cinnamon
pinch of salt	pinch of salt
50 g/2 oz mixed chopped nuts	$\frac{1}{3}$ cup mixed chopped nuts

Set the oven at moderate (180 C, 350 F, gas 4). Wash, trim and grate the courgettes
(zucchini) as finely as possible.

In a bowl beat together the oil, sugar and egg until well mixed and add the
courgettes. Combine the dry ingredients in another bowl and stir them into the
first mixture. Add the nuts and distribute them evenly.

Lightly grease a 1-kg/2-lb ($8\frac{1}{2} \times 4\frac{1}{2} \times$ 2-in) loaf tin and pour in the mixture,
smoothing the top. Bake it for about 1 hour, turn out and leave to cool. Serve
lightly buttered. **Makes one 1-kg/2-lb loaf**

Yogurt Muffins

Illustrated on page 145

METRIC/IMPERIAL	AMERICAN
225 g/8 oz plain wholemeal flour	2 cups wholewheat flour
2 teaspoons baking powder	2 teaspoons baking powder
pinch of salt	pinch of salt
100 g/4 oz light Muscovado raw brown sugar	$\frac{2}{3}$ cup light raw brown sugar
50 g/2 oz butter or margarine	$\frac{1}{4}$ cup butter or margarine
1 egg, beaten	1 egg, beaten
1 (150-g/5.3-oz) carton natural yogurt	$\frac{2}{3}$ cup plain yogurt
1 tablespoon finely grated orange peel	1 tablespoon finely grated orange peel

Set the oven at moderately hot (200 C, 400 F, gas 6). In a bowl mix together the
flour, baking powder and salt. Stir in the sugar. Melt the butter or margarine and
combine it in another bowl with the beaten egg and yogurt. Add the orange peel,
pour the liquid mixture into the dry ingredients and stir briefly (the mixture does
not need to be smooth).

Grease 12 patty tins (muffin pans), divide the muffin mixture between them and
bake for 20–25 minutes or until light golden in colour. **Makes 12**

Hot Cross Buns

Illustrated on page 145

METRIC/IMPERIAL	AMERICAN
25 g/1 oz fresh or 15 g/½ oz dried yeast	1 cake compressed yeast or 1 package active dry yeast
300 ml/½ pint lukewarm milk and water, mixed	1¼ cups lukewarm milk and water, mixed
50 g/2 oz light Muscovado raw brown sugar	⅓ cup light raw brown sugar
450 g/1 lb plain wholemeal flour	4 cups wholewheat flour
1 teaspoon cinnamon	1 teaspoon cinnamon
1 teaspoon mixed spice	1 teaspoon mixed spice
pinch of salt	pinch of salt
100 g/4 oz currants	⅔ cup currants
50 g/2 oz candied peel	⅓ cup candied peel
1 egg	1 egg
50 g/2 oz butter or margarine, melted	¼ cup butter or margarine, melted
Glaze	*Glaze*
25 g/1 oz light Muscovado raw brown sugar	2 tablespoons light raw brown sugar
1 tablespoon milk	1 tablespoon milk

Crumble the fresh yeast, if used, into a small bowl and mix it to a paste with a little of the warm liquid and a teaspoon of sugar. Pour in the rest of the liquid and set the mixture aside in a warm place for 5 minutes or until frothy. Sprinkle dried yeast on to the liquid with 1 teaspoon sugar, stir until dissolved and set aside until frothy.

In a large, warmed bowl thoroughly mix together the flour, spices and salt. Add the rest of the sugar, the currants and candied peel and make a well in the centre. Beat the egg and stir it into the yeast mixture, followed by the melted butter or margarine, and pour the liquid into the well in the centre of the dry ingredients. Use a wooden spoon to mix thoroughly, then turn the dough out on to a well-floured board and knead it for at least 5 minutes until firm but elastic. Return the dough to the bowl, cover with a tea towel (dish cloth), and leave it in a warm spot for about 1 hour or until well risen.

Set the oven at moderately hot (200 C, 400 F, gas 6). Grease and flour 1–2 baking sheets. Lightly knead the dough again and divide it into 12–16 pieces. Shape these into buns, arrange them on the sheets and use a knife to mark each one with a cross. Again, set them aside in a warm, draught-free place to rise for 30–45 minutes, until doubled in size. If necessary lightly re-mark the crosses. Bake the buns for 15–20 minutes, until golden.

Make the glaze by dissolving the sugar in the milk over a low heat to form a syrup and brush this over the tops of the buns immediately they are taken from the oven. Cool slightly on a wire rack – they are best eaten warm. If not for immediate consumption, hot cross buns can always be popped into the oven again for a few minutes to re-heat. **Makes 12–16**

VARIATIONS

Personally, I think these buns are far too tasty to be served only once a year. These variations will allow you to enjoy them whenever you like.

Hot Cross Squares Omit the spices, add 50 g/2 oz sultanas (⅓ cup seedless white raisins) and turn the dough into a greased 20-cm/8-in or 23-cm/9-in square baking tin or pan instead of shaping it into buns. Leave to rise for 30–45 minutes, then bake as above and cut into squares when done.

Chelsea Buns Make the dough as above but leaving out the dried fruit. Leave it to rise, knead lightly and roll it out to two 30 × 23-cm/12 × 9-in rectangles. Brush these with 25 g/1 oz (2 tablespoons) melted butter or margarine, sprinkle with dried fruit and 50 g/2 oz (⅓ cup) light raw brown sugar and roll them up from the longest edge. Cut each roll into 9 slices and place these on greased baking sheets. Allow to rise, then bake and glaze them as above.

Oatmeal Scones

METRIC/IMPERIAL	AMERICAN
100 g/4 oz plain wholemeal flour	1 cup wholewheat flour
100 g/4 oz medium oatmeal	$\frac{2}{3}$ cup medium oatmeal
1 teaspoon baking powder	1 teaspoon baking powder
pinch of salt	pinch of salt
$\frac{1}{2}$ teaspoon chopped fresh mixed herbs or	$\frac{1}{2}$ teaspoon chopped fresh mixed herbs or
$\frac{1}{4}$ teaspoon dried mixed herbs	$\frac{1}{4}$ teaspoon dried mixed herbs
50 g/2 oz butter or margarine	$\frac{1}{4}$ cup butter or margarine
150 ml/$\frac{1}{4}$ pint milk	$\frac{2}{3}$ cup milk

Set the oven at hot (220 C, 425 F, gas 7). Mix well together the flour, oatmeal, baking powder and salt. Stir in the herbs. Rub in the fat with your fingertips and bind the mixture to a dough with the milk. Knead the dough lightly on a floured board, then roll it out to 1 cm/$\frac{1}{2}$ in thick. Cut out 12 (5-cm/2-in) rounds using a pastry (cookie) cutter or glass. Brush the tops with a little extra milk, arrange the scones on a greased baking sheet and bake them for 15 minutes. Leave to cool on a wire rack and eat the scones warm or cold with butter or margarine, creamy cheeses or nut butter. **Makes 12**

VARIATION
You can eat these scones with sweet toppings – jam, honey, molasses and so on – if you omit the herbs.

Banana Fruit Loaf

Illustrated on page 145

This is a rather heavy, moist loaf, very filling – but also very more-ish.

METRIC/IMPERIAL	AMERICAN
2 large ripe bananas	2 large ripe bananas
225 g/8 oz self-raising wholemeal flour	2 cups wholewheat flour mixed with
$\frac{1}{2}$ teaspoon nutmeg	2 teaspoons baking powder
1 teaspoon cinnamon	$\frac{1}{2}$ teaspoon nutmeg
100 g/4 oz light Muscovado raw brown	1 teaspoon cinnamon
sugar	$\frac{2}{3}$ cup light raw brown sugar
225 g/8 oz mixed dried fruit	1$\frac{1}{3}$ cups mixed dried fruit
300 ml/$\frac{1}{2}$ pint milk	1$\frac{1}{4}$ cups milk

Set the oven at moderate (180 C, 350 F, gas 4). Mash the bananas. Mix together the flour and spices, stir in the sugar and dried fruit and pour in the milk. Mix with the bananas and spoon the dough into a greased 1-kg/2-lb (8$\frac{1}{2}$ × 4$\frac{1}{2}$ × 2-in) loaf tin. Bake for about 1 hour or until a skewer inserted in the centre of the loaf comes out clean. Cool on a wire rack and serve sliced, spread with butter.

For a more decorative loaf, take it from the oven after 45 minutes and sprinkle the top with 25 g/1 oz (3 tablespoons) chopped walnuts and 25 g/1 oz (2 tablespoons) demerara raw brown sugar. Return it to the oven and cook until firm. **Makes one 1-kg/2-lb loaf**

Summer Fruit Salad (page 116); Honey Ice Cream with Ginger (page 118);
Blackberry Yogurt Ice Cream (page 119).

Overleaf *Deep Dish Plum Pie (page 115); Buckwheat Crêpes with Maple Sauce (page 112);*
Lemon Steamed Sponge Pudding (page 114); Hot Stuffed Peaches (page 113).

Blondies

METRIC/IMPERIAL	AMERICAN
100 g/4 oz butter or margarine	$\frac{1}{2}$ cup butter or margarine
275 g/10 oz light Muscovado raw brown sugar	$1\frac{2}{3}$ cups light raw brown sugar
1 teaspoon vanilla essence	1 teaspoon vanilla extract
pinch of salt	pinch of salt
2 eggs	2 eggs
225 g/8 oz self-raising wholemeal flour	2 cups wholewheat flour mixed with 2 teaspoons baking powder
2 egg whites	2 egg whites

Set the oven at moderate (180 C, 350 F, gas 4). Cream together the butter or margarine with 175 g/6 oz (1 cup) of the sugar, the vanilla and salt. Add the eggs and beat well. Stir in the flour and mix all the ingredients with your fingertips. Lightly grease a shallow 25-cm/10-in square tin or pan and press the mixture into it evenly.

Make the meringue topping by whisking the egg whites until stiff but not too dry and gradually and gently folding in the remaining sugar. Spread the meringue quickly and evenly over the blondie base and bake for 30 minutes. Mark it into 25 (5-cm/2-in) squares and cut them out when cool. **Makes 25**

Fruit and Nut Slices

METRIC/IMPERIAL	AMERICAN
Pastry	*Dough*
100 g/4 oz butter or margarine	$\frac{1}{2}$ cup butter or margarine
225 g/8 oz plain wholemeal flour	2 cups wholewheat flour
about 2 tablespoons water	about 2 tablespoons water
a little milk to glaze	a little milk to glaze
Filling	*Filling*
175 g/6 oz stoned dates	1 cup pitted dates
2 large dessert apples	2 large dessert apples
squeeze of lemon	squeeze of lemon
50 g/2 oz walnut pieces or chopped hazelnuts	$\frac{1}{3}$ cup walnut pieces or chopped hazelnuts
25 g/1 oz sunflower seeds	$\frac{1}{4}$ cup sunflower seeds

Set the oven at moderately hot (200 C, 400 F, gas 6). Rub the butter or margarine into the flour with your fingertips until the mixture resembles fine breadcrumbs. Add just enough water to bind it to a dough and knead it gently for a minute or two. Divide the dough into two pieces and roll them out as thinly as possible on a floured board to make two rectangles measuring roughly 20 × 15 cm/8 × 6 in.

Chop the dates. Peel, core and slice the apples and simmer them with the dates and lemon juice in a pan for 15–20 minutes until you have a thick purée. Add a little water during cooking if necessary and stir the mixture frequently so that it doesn't stick or burn. Leave to cool.

Lay one sheet of pastry in a greased shallow baking tin or pan or on a baking sheet and use a knife to spread the filling over it. Sprinkle the nuts and sunflower seeds evenly over the top, cover with the remaining pastry and brush with a drop of milk. Bake for 20–30 minutes or until golden brown. Cut into slices and eat warm or cold. **Makes 9–12**

Cassata Dessert (page 119); Almond Cheesecake (page 113).

Lemon Date Sponge Squares

Illustrated on pages 146–7

METRIC/IMPERIAL	AMERICAN
100 g/4 oz butter or margarine	½ cup butter or margarine
100 g/4 oz raw brown sugar	⅔ cup raw brown sugar
2 eggs	2 eggs
2 tablespoons lemon curd	3 tablespoons lemon curd
50 g/2 oz stoned dates	⅓ cup pitted dates
100 g/4 oz self-raising wholemeal flour	1 cup wholewheat flour mixed with
50 g/2 oz walnuts, coarsely chopped	1 teaspoon baking powder
	⅓ cup coarsely chopped walnuts

Set the oven at moderately hot (190 C, 375 F, gas 5). Cream the butter or margarine and sugar together in a bowl. Beat the eggs lightly and stir them into the mixture with the lemon curd. Finely chop the dates and add them to the bowl. Fold in the flour gently and mix so that all the ingredients are evenly distributed, adding a little water if the mixture seems dry.

Grease a 25 × 15-cm/10 × 6-in shallow tin or pan and pour in the mixture. Smooth the top with a knife and scatter with the chopped nuts, pressing them down lightly.

Bake the sponge for 20–30 minutes or until you can press your finger on top and not leave a mark. Cool slightly in the tin and cut into squares. **Makes 15**

Walnut Layer Cake

Illustrated on pages 146–7

METRIC/IMPERIAL	AMERICAN
Cake	*Cake*
175 g/6 oz butter or margarine	¾ cup butter or margarine
100 g/4 oz demerara raw brown sugar	⅔ cup light raw brown sugar
3 eggs, beaten	3 eggs, beaten
75 g/3 oz chopped walnuts	½ cup chopped walnuts
175 g/6 oz self-raising wholemeal flour	1½ cups wholewheat flour mixed with
Filling	1¼ teaspoons baking powder
75 g/3 oz butter	*Filling*
175 g/6 oz demerara raw brown sugar,	⅓ cup butter
ground to a powder	1 cup light raw brown sugar, ground to a
2 tablespoons coffee essence or to taste	powder
American Frosting	3 tablespoons coffee extract or to taste
175 g/6 oz light raw brown sugar, ground	*Boiled Frosting*
to a powder	1 cup light raw brown sugar, ground to a
1 egg white	powder
2 tablespoons water	1 egg white
pinch of cream of tartar	3 tablespoons water
8–10 walnut halves to decorate	pinch of cream of tartar
	8–10 walnut halves to decorate

Set the oven at moderately hot (190 C, 375 F, gas 5). To make the cake, cream together the fat and sugar and add the beaten egg, a little at a time, blending thoroughly. Stir in the chopped nuts, then fold in the flour. Grease and line the bases of three 18-cm/7-in sandwich tins (layer cake pans) and spoon the mixture into them, spreading the tops so that they are level. Bake the cakes for about 20 minutes or until beginning to come away from the sides of the tins. Turn out and leave to cool.

Make the filling by first creaming the butter, then gradually adding the sugar and coffee essence until the mixture is thick and creamy. Use this to sandwich the three layers of sponge together and stand the cake on a plate.

Put all the ingredients for the frosting into a bowl over a saucepan of hot water. Whisk them together over a gentle heat for as long as it takes for the mixture to thicken – this usually takes at least 5 minutes. Remove from the heat, continue whisking for 1–2 minutes, then spread the frosting at once over the top and side of the cake, using a warm knife to smooth the surface. Decorate with the walnut halves.

Strawberry Shortcakes

Illustrated on pages 146–7

A really traditional summer-tea-on-the-lawn treat. You could always cheat and have them mid-winter with frozen strawberries . . . .

METRIC/IMPERIAL	AMERICAN
250 g/9 oz plain wholemeal flour	2¼ cups wholewheat flour
1 teaspoon baking powder	1 teaspoon baking powder
100 g/4 oz light Muscovado raw brown sugar	⅔ cup light raw brown sugar
175 g/6 oz butter or margarine	¾ cup butter or margarine
300 ml/½ pint double or single cream (optional)	1¼ cups heavy or light cream (optional)
350 g/12 oz strawberries	2½ cups strawberries

Set the oven at moderately hot (190 C, 370 F, gas 5). Mix together the flour and baking powder. Cream 75 g/3 oz (½ cup) of the sugar with the butter or margarine in a bowl until light and fluffy. Stir in the dry ingredients, mix well and knead the dough for a few minutes.

Transfer the dough to a floured board and roll it out to a depth of about 5 mm/¼ in. Using two biscuit (cookie) cutters or glasses, one measuring 7.5 cm/3 in. in diameter and the other slightly smaller, cut out an equal number of rounds of each size. The exact number will depend on the depth of your dough and the diameters of your circles. Arrange these on a greased and floured baking sheet and bake them for about 15 minutes, until golden brown. Carefully remove them from the sheet and leave to cool.

Whip the double (heavy) cream, if used, until thick. Set aside the smallest strawberries and coarsely chop the rest. Put a portion on each of the larger shortbreads with a little whipped cream, if liked, sprinkle with a little of the remaining sugar and sandwich them with the smaller shortbreads. Garnish with the remaining whole strawberries, pour over the single (light) cream, if used, and serve with a fork (they're impossible to eat with fingers). **Makes 4–5**

Apple Crumble Cake

METRIC/IMPERIAL	AMERICAN
Cake	*Cake*
225 g/8 oz self-raising wholemeal flour	2 cups wholewheat flour mixed with
1 teaspoon cinnamon	2 teaspoons baking powder
100 g/4 oz butter or margarine	1 teaspoon cinnamon
2 dessert apples, peeled and cored	½ cup butter or margarine
100 g/4 oz demerara raw brown sugar	2 dessert apples, peeled and cored
2 eggs, beaten	⅔ cup light raw brown sugar
Crumble Topping	2 eggs, beaten
25 g/1 oz butter or margarine	*Crumble Topping*
50 g/2 oz plain wholemeal flour	2 tablespoons butter or margarine
pinch of cinnamon	½ cup wholewheat flour
25 g/1 oz demerara raw brown sugar	pinch of cinnamon
50 g/2 oz chopped walnuts	3 tablespoons light raw brown sugar
4 tablespoons apricot jam	⅓ cup chopped walnuts
	5 tablespoons apricot jam

Set the oven at moderate (180 C, 350 F, gas 4). To make the cake, mix the flour and cinnamon together in a bowl and rub in the fat to produce a crumb-like mixture. Grate or finely chop the apples and stir them into the mixture with the sugar. Add the beaten egg to make a stiff dough. Turn the mixture into a greased 450-g/1-lb (7 × 3½ × 2-in) loaf tin and set it aside.

Make the crumble topping by rubbing the butter or margarine into the flour and spice, then sprinkling in the sugar and chopped walnuts. Flatten the surface of the cake, spread it with jam and spoon the topping on top, pressing down lightly. Bake the cake for about 45 minutes or until firm to the touch. Allow to cool slightly before removing it from the tin, taking care not to lose all the crumble topping as you do so!

Pineapple Swiss Roll

Illustrated on pages 146–7

Besides being a tea-time favourite, this Swiss roll can be sliced and topped with cream, ice cream or custard for dessert. It also does amazing things for trifle . . . .

METRIC/IMPERIAL	AMERICAN
50 g/2 oz demerara raw brown sugar	⅓ cup light raw brown sugar
2 eggs	2 eggs
50 g/2 oz self-raising wholemeal flour	½ cup wholewheat flour mixed with
¼ small pineapple or 1 (227-g/8-oz) can	½ teaspoon baking powder
pineapple pieces in natural juice	¼ small pineapple or 1 (8-oz) can
150 ml/¼ pint double cream	pineapple pieces in natural juice
	⅔ cup heavy cream

Set the oven at moderately hot (200 C, 400 F, gas 6). Grind the sugar to a powder in a liquidiser or blender. Beat the eggs vigorously with the sugar in a bowl until the mixture is thick and smooth. This is easiest with an electric hand-beater. Sift the flour, reserving the bran for use in another recipe, and fold it gently into the egg mixture with a metal spoon.

Grease and line the base of a 28 × 18-cm/11 × 7-in Swiss roll tin (jelly roll pan), pour in the mixture and level the surface. Bake for 8–10 minutes or until you can press the sponge lightly without leaving an impression. Remove it from the oven immediately and tip it out on to a sheet of lightly sugared greaseproof (waxed) paper. Peel off and discard the lining paper, trim the edges of the sponge with a

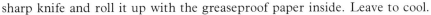

sharp knife and roll it up with the greaseproof paper inside. Leave to cool.

Cut the fresh pineapple from its shell or drain the canned pineapple. Chop the fruit. Whip the cream until thick. Unroll the Swiss roll, discarding the greaseproof paper, and spread it with cream, reserving a little on one side for decoration. Top with all but six pieces of pineapple, reroll the sponge and arrange it on a plate. Put all the remaining cream in a piping bag fitted with a star-shaped nozzle (fluted tip) and pipe a decorative line down the centre of the Swiss roll. Place the remaining pineapple pieces at intervals in the cream.

VARIATION

Other fruit can be substituted for the pineapple: fresh strawberries, cooked gooseberries, apricots, blackcurrant and apple, whatever you fancy.

Cherry Chocolate Gâteau

A light, creamy gâteau that isn't too heavy on the calories – as gâteaux go, that is. This one has a tendency to go very fast.

METRIC/IMPERIAL	AMERICAN
Cake	*Cake*
100 g/4 oz butter or margarine	$\frac{1}{2}$ cup butter or margarine
100 g/4 oz light Muscovado raw brown sugar	$\frac{2}{3}$ cup light raw brown sugar
3 eggs, beaten	3 eggs, beaten
150 g/5 oz self-raising wholemeal flour	$1\frac{1}{4}$ cups wholewheat flour mixed with $1\frac{1}{4}$ teaspoons baking powder
25 g/1 oz cocoa powder	$\frac{1}{4}$ cup cocoa powder
Filling	*Filling*
200 ml/7 fl oz whipping cream	1 cup heavy cream
50 g/2 oz glacé cherries, chopped	$\frac{1}{4}$ cup candied cherries, chopped
50 g/2 oz chopped hazelnuts	$\frac{1}{3}$ cup chopped hazelnuts
Coating	*Coating*
75 g/3 oz dessert chocolate	$\frac{1}{2}$ cup dessert chocolate
3 tablespoons milk	4 tablespoons milk
50 g/2 oz flaked almonds or chocolate vemicelli	$\frac{1}{4}$ cup flaked almonds or chocolate vermicelli
50 g/2 oz glacé cherries, halved	$\frac{1}{4}$ cup candied cherries, halved

Set the oven at moderate (180 C, 350 F, gas 4). Grease and flour two 18-cm/7-in sandwich tins (layer cake pans). In a bowl cream together the butter or margarine and sugar and beat until light and fluffy. Add the beaten egg, a little at a time. Mix the flour and cocoa together and fold carefully but thoroughly into the mixture. Divide between the prepared tins. Bake the cakes for 20 minutes or until you can press each one gently and leave no impression. Turn them out of the tins and cool on a wire rack.

Whip the cream until thick enough to hold its shape, stir in the chopped cherries and hazelnuts and use the mixture to sandwich the two cakes together.

Chop or grate the chocolate and melt it in a heavy pan with the milk, stirring frequently to make a thick sauce. Allow to cool slightly, then pour or spread it with a knife over the top and side of the cake. Sprinkle the flaked almonds or chocolate vermicelli on top of the cake, arranging the halved cherries at intervals round the edge. Chill the gâteau before serving and eat within 24 hours.

Chocolate Digestive Biscuits

Illustrated on page 148

Crisp, crunchy biscuits that taste much better than the ones you get from a packet. If you really believe in healthy eating, coat them with carob instead of chocolate.

METRIC/IMPERIAL	AMERICAN
100 g/4 oz plain wholemeal flour	1 cup wholewheat flour
½ teaspoon baking powder	½ teaspoon baking powder
pinch of salt	pinch of salt
25 g/1 oz light Muscovado raw brown sugar	3 tablespoons light raw brown sugar
25 g/1 oz medium oatmeal	3 tablespoons medium oatmeal
50 g/2 oz butter or margarine	¼ cup butter or margarine
a little milk	a little milk
75 g/3 oz dessert chocolate or carob bar	½ cup dessert chocolate or carob bar

Set oven at moderate (180 C, 350 F, gas 4). Mix together the flour, baking powder and salt; stir in the sugar and oatmeal. Rub the fat in with your fingertips to give a fine crumbly mixture, then bind the ingredients with 1–2 tablespoons of milk and knead to a dough. On a lightly floured board, roll the dough out to a thickness of about 5 mm/¼ in and cut it into rounds with a 6-cm/2½-in biscuit (cookie) cutter or glass.

Arrange the biscuits on a greased baking sheet and prick each one with a fork. Bake them for 15 minutes or until crisp. Leave to cool on a baking sheet.

Break up or grate the chocolate or carob bar and put it in a bowl over a saucepan of hot water to melt. Dip the biscuits into the chocolate to coat them on one side or spread the chocolate with a knife. Leave to set. **Makes 12–15**

Cinnamon Peanut Butter Cookies

American-style cookies that are protein-rich. Kids aren't the only ones who love them!

METRIC/IMPERIAL	AMERICAN
50 g/2 oz peanut butter	3 tablespoons peanut butter
50 g/2 oz butter or margarine	¼ cup butter or margarine
75 g/3 oz light Muscovado raw brown sugar	½ cup light raw brown sugar
1 egg	1 egg
100 g/4 oz self-raising wholemeal flour	1 cup wholewheat flour mixed with
50 g/2 oz raisins, chopped	1 teaspoon baking powder
1 teaspoon cinnamon or to taste	⅓ cup raisins, chopped
	1 teaspoon cinnamon or to taste

Set the oven at moderate (180 C, 350 F, gas 4). In a bowl cream together the peanut butter, fat and sugar. When soft and completely blended, add the egg and the flour to make a dough. Mix in the chopped raisins and spice.

Divide the mixture into 12–15 pieces and roll these into small balls. Flatten them slightly and arrange them on an ungreased baking sheet, leaving room between each to spread. Bake the cookies for 15–20 minutes and leave them to cool on a wire rack. **Makes 12–15**

Coconut Macaroons

Illustrated on page 148

METRIC/IMPERIAL	AMERICAN
2 egg whites	2 egg whites
150 g/5 oz desiccated coconut	1⅔ cups shredded coconut
150 g/5 oz demerara raw brown sugar	¾–1 cup light raw brown sugar
rice paper	rice paper
glacé cherries and angelica leaves to decorate (optional)	candied cherries and angelica leaves to decorate (optional)
beaten egg white to glaze	beaten egg white to glaze

Set the oven at moderate (180 C, 350 F, gas 4). Whisk the egg whites together lightly until firm enough to hold soft peaks. Carefully fold in the coconut and sugar. The mixture should be soft but not too soft – if it is too wet, add a little more coconut; if too dry, add a drop of water.

Line a baking sheet with the rice paper and arrange spoonfuls of the coconut mixture on top, leaving room in between for the macaroons to spread. Decorate each one with a cherry and a little angelica, if liked, and brush the surface with egg white to give a glazed finish. Bake for about 20 minutes. Leave to cool on the baking sheet for a few minutes before tearing or cutting the rice paper around the macaroons and placing them on a wire rack to cool completely. **Makes 18–20**

VARIATION

Substitute an equal quantity of ground almonds for the coconut to make traditional macaroons, topping each one with a few split almonds instead of glacé cherries.

Christmas Flapjacks

Illustrated on page 148

A welcome change from mince pies.

METRIC/IMPERIAL	AMERICAN
75 g/3 oz butter or margarine	⅓ cup butter or margarine
25 g/1 oz clear honey	1½ tablespoons clear honey
25 g/1 oz Muscovado raw brown sugar	3 tablespoons raw brown sugar
175 g/6 oz medium oat flakes	2 cups medium oat flakes
100 g/4 oz vegetarian mincemeat	½ cup vegetarian mincemeat
25 g/1 oz glacé cherries, chopped	2 tablespoons candied cherries, chopped

Set the oven at moderate (180 C, 350 F, gas 4). Grease a 20 × 15-cm/8 × 6-in Swiss roll tin (jelly roll pan). In a saucepan melt the fat gently, then stir in the honey and sugar. Cool slightly before mixing in the oat flakes. Add the mincemeat and cherries and combine all the ingredients thoroughly together.

Spread the mixture evenly in the prepared tin and bake for 25–30 minutes or until golden brown. Cut it into fingers or squares while still warm and leave the flapjacks to cool in the tin. **Makes 16**

Orange Creams

Illustrated on page 148

METRIC/IMPERIAL	AMERICAN
Biscuits	*Cookies*
1 tablespoon frozen concentrated orange juice	1 tablespoon frozen concentrated orange juice
225 g/8 oz Muscovado raw brown sugar	1⅓ cups light raw brown sugar
100 g/4 oz butter or margarine	½ cup butter or margarine
1 egg	1 egg
1 teaspoon vanilla essence	1 teaspoon vanilla extract
350 g/12 oz plain wholemeal flour	3 cups wholewheat flour
2 teaspoons baking powder	2 teaspoons baking powder
Filling	*Filling*
175 g/6 oz demerara raw brown sugar	1 cup light raw brown sugar
50 g/2 oz butter or margarine, softened	¼ cup butter or margarine, softened
about 2 tablespoons frozen concentrated orange juice	about 3 tablespoons frozen concentrated orange juice

Allow the frozen orange juice to thaw at room temperature. In a bowl cream together the sugar and fat until soft and thoroughly combined. Add the egg, vanilla essence and orange juice. Mix the flour and baking powder together and stir the dry ingredients into the mixture. Knead to a dough, shape it into two long rolls and wrap these in cooking foil or cling-film (saran wrap). Chill in the refrigerator for as long as possible – preferably overnight.

Set the oven at moderately hot (190 C, 375 F, gas 5). Unwrap the dough rolls and reshape them gently, if necessary. Carefully slice them as thinly as possible, arrange the slices on a lightly greased baking sheet and bake them for 6–8 minutes. Leave to cool on a wire rack.

For the filling, grind the sugar to a powder in a liquidiser or blender. Beat it with the softened butter or margarine, adding enough orange juice to give a thick, spreadable cream. If it is too soft, add more sugar; if too firm, add a little more juice. Beat the cream until very smooth. Spread a small amount of the cream over half the cold biscuits and top with the remaining biscuits, pressing down gently. Leave to set. **Makes 20–24**

Health-nut Cookies

Protein-packed cookies you can nibble all day long without feeling guilty. Children love them, too.

METRIC/IMPERIAL	AMERICAN
100 g/4 oz sunflower seeds	⅔ cup sunflower seeds
100 g/4 oz medium oat flakes or oatmeal	1 cup rolled oats or ⅔ cup oatmeal
1 tablespoon vegetable oil	1 tablespoon vegetable oil
2 tablespoons honey	3 tablespoons honey
1 large ripe banana	1 large ripe banana
1 egg, beaten	1 egg, beaten

Set the oven at moderate (180 C, 350 F, gas 4). Grind both the seeds and oat flakes (rolled oats), if used, and combine them to make a flour-like mixture. Gently heat the oil and honey together in a pan and mix into the dry ingredients. Mash the banana and stir it into the mixture with the beaten egg. Combine all the ingredients thoroughly.

Lightly grease a baking sheet and drop heaped teaspoons of the mixture on to it. Bake the cookies for 15 minutes or until golden. Cool on a wire rack. **Makes 20**

Ginger Crisps

Illustrated on page 148

METRIC/IMPERIAL	AMERICAN
175 g/6 oz plain wholemeal flour	1½ cups wholewheat flour
1 heaped teaspoon ground ginger	1 heaped teaspoon ground ginger
1 heaped teaspoon mixed spice	1 heaped teaspoon mixed spice
pinch of salt	pinch of salt
75 g/3 oz butter or margarine	⅓ cup butter or margarine
75 g/3 oz Muscovado raw brown sugar	½ cup raw brown sugar
1 egg, lightly beaten	1 egg, lightly beaten

Set the oven at moderately hot (190 C, 375 F, gas 5). Mix the flour with the spices and salt in a bowl. Rub the fat in with your finger tips until the mixture resembles fine breadcrumbs. Stir in the sugar and add enough beaten egg to bind all the ingredients to a firm dough.

On a floured board roll the dough out as thinly as possible and cut out various shapes using biscuit (cookie) cutters or a sharp knife and a steady hand. Arrange these on a baking sheet and bake for about 10 minutes. Leave the biscuits to cool thoroughly before removing them from the baking sheet – this makes them crisper.
Makes 20–24 different shapes

Sesame Wheatgerm Crackers

Illustrated on page 148

As I'm crackers about sesame seeds, I find these irresistible with cheese, yeast extract, nut butters, pâtés and spreads, honey and jam . . . not to mention on their own and unadorned.

METRIC/IMPERIAL	AMERICAN
50 g/2 oz butter or margarine	¼ cup butter or margarine
75 g/3 oz plain wholemeal flour	¾ cup wholewheat flour
25 g/1 oz wheatgerm	¼ cup wheatgerm
about 3 tablespoons milk	about 4 tablespoons milk
50 g/2 oz sesame seeds	⅓ cup sesame seeds
beaten egg to glaze	beaten egg to glaze

Set the oven at moderately hot (190 C, 375 F, gas 5). Grease a baking sheet with a little of the butter or margarine. Mix the flour and wheatgerm together in a bowl and rub in the remaining fat with your finger tips to make a mixture resembling coarse breadcrumbs. Pour in the milk, add the sesame seeds and continue stirring until you have a stiff dough (if it is too firm, add a little more milk).

On a lightly floured board, roll the dough out as thinly as possible and cut it into 5-cm/2-in squares. Arrange them on the baking sheet, glaze them with a little beaten egg and prick each one lightly with a fork. Bake the crackers for 12–15 minutes or until just firm to the touch. Leave them to cool on the baking sheet for a few minutes before transferring them to a wire rack. **Makes 25–30**

Menus for Special Occasions

No matter how many delicious recipes you know, when it comes to putting together a selection of dishes for a particular occasion you can often find yourself stuck for ideas. Here to help you is a variety of menus to suit all kinds of entertaining. Follow them if you like, or simply use them as inspiration to create your own mouth-watering feasts!

Patio Brunch for 4

My favourite meal is brunch. It's a Sunday meal, prepared and eaten at a leisurely pace and usually shared with someone special. A patio brunch is, of course, best of all because it means it's a summer Sunday.

Strawberry Fruit Salad

or

Shredded Wheat Dish

Wholemeal Croissants

Savoury Pancake Pie with Fried Mushrooms

Coffee or Tea

Strawberry Fruit Salad

METRIC/IMPERIAL	AMERICAN
225 g/8 oz small strawberries	1⅔ cups small strawberries
1 small melon	1 small melon
2 bananas	2 bananas
generous squeeze of lemon	generous squeeze of lemon
about 2 tablespoons fresh orange juice	about 3 tablespoons fresh orange juice

Clean and hull the strawberries. Slice the top off the melon with a zig-zag motion, remove the seeds and scoop out the flesh with a melon baller or a teaspoon. Keep the shell on one side. Slice the bananas and toss in the lemon juice. Mix all the fruit together in a bowl and stir in any remaining lemon juice with the orange juice. Transfer the fruit salad to the melon shell and serve at once with natural (plain) yogurt and a little sugar, if liked.

Shredded Wheat Dish

METRIC/IMPERIAL	AMERICAN
50 g/2 oz dried apricots	⅓ cup diced apricots
4 large shredded wheat biscuits	4 large shredded wheat biscuits
50 g/2 oz toasted wheatgerm	½ cup toasted wheatgerm
50 g/2 oz raisins	⅓ cup raisins
50 g/2 oz coarsely chopped almonds	⅓ cup coarsely chopped almonds
about 600 ml/1 pint milk or fruit juice	2¼ cups milk or fruit juice

Soak the apricots in water to cover for 1 hour, then drain and chop them. Crumble the shredded wheat into large pieces and mix it with the toasted wheatgerm. Sprinkle in the raisins, apricots and chopped almonds. Divide the mixture between four individual dishes and serve with the milk or fruit juice.

Wholemeal Croissants

METRIC/IMPERIAL	AMERICAN
25 g/1 oz fresh yeast or ½ oz dried yeast	1 cake compressed yeast or 1 package active dry yeast
just under 300 ml/½ pint warm water	scant 1¼ cups warm water
1 teaspoon raw brown sugar	1 teaspoon raw brown sugar
450 g/1 lb plain wholemeal flour	4 cups wholewheat flour
pinch of salt	pinch of salt
150 g/5 oz butter or margarine	⅔ cup butter or margarine
1 large egg	1 large egg

Cream the fresh yeast with a little of the water, pour in the remaining water with the sugar and leave to rise in a warm place for 10 minutes or until frothy. Dissolve dried yeast in the water with the sugar and leave to rise for 10 minutes.

Sift the flour and salt into a mixing bowl, reserving the bran left in the sieve for use in another recipe. Rub in 25 g/1 oz (2 tablespoons) of the fat to make a crumb-like mixture. Lightly beat the egg, keep a little on one side for glazing and stir the rest into the yeast liquid. Pour the mixture into the dry ingredients. Mix well together, turn the dough on to a floured board and knead until smooth and elastic – if it seems too dry or too wet, adjust the consistency with a little more water or flour. Leave to rise in a warm place for about 30 minutes, until doubled in size. Knead it again lightly, wrap it in kitchen foil and chill it for 20 minutes.

Roll the dough out to a large rectangle about 5 mm/¼ in thick and mark it lightly into three sections. Divide the remaining fat into three pieces and cut each piece into small cubes. Sprinkle one portion of cubes evenly over the top two-thirds of the dough, leaving a narrow border round the edges. Fold the bottom third over the middle section and the top third over that, so that the fat is divided equally between the layers. Turn the dough so that the side edges are now facing you, press these edges together to seal and roll out again to a similar rectangle. Repeat this process twice more to use up the two remaining portions of fat, then wrap the dough in silver foil or cling film and chill it in the refrigerator for 15 minutes. Repeat this rolling and folding process three more times and return the dough to the cool again for 1 hour or overnight, if preferred.

Set the oven at hot (220 C, 425 F, gas 7). Roll the dough out to a large rectangle measuring about 46 × 30 cm/18 × 12 in and cut it into six 15-cm/6-in squares. Cut each square in half to form two triangles. Roll the triangles up from the right angles and curve them to make the traditional croissant shape. Place the croissants on a baking sheet and leave them to rise in a warm spot for 30–45 minutes.

Brush the croissants with the remaining beaten egg and bake them for about 15 minutes. Serve while still warm with butter, honey or jam.

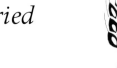

Savoury Pancake Pie with Fried Mushrooms

METRIC/IMPERIAL	AMERICAN
Pancakes	*Crêpes*
100 g/4 oz plain wholemeal flour	1 cup wholewheat flour
pinch of salt	pinch of salt
1 large egg, beaten	1 large egg, beaten
300 ml/½ pint mixed milk and water	1¼ cups mixed milk and water
vegetable oil for frying	vegetable oil for frying
butter and chopped fresh parsley to garnish	butter and chopped fresh parsley to garnish
Filling 1	*Filling 1*
4 large tomatoes	4 large tomatoes
1 onion	1 onion
1 tablespoon vegetable oil	1 tablespoon vegetable oil
generous pinch of dried thyme	generous pinch of dried thyme
salt and pepper	salt and pepper
Filling 2	*Filling 2*
25 g/1 oz butter or margarine	2 tablespoons butter or margarine
3 eggs, beaten	3 eggs, beaten
salt and pepper	salt and pepper
1 tablespoon chopped fresh parsley	1 tablespoon chopped fresh parsley
Filling 3	*Filling 3*
2 large sticks celery	2 large stalks celery
50 g/2 oz dried skimmed milk	⅔ cup dried milk solids
25 g/1 oz butter or margarine	2 tablespoons butter or margarine
25 g/1 oz plain wholemeal flour	¼ cup wholewheat flour
salt and pepper	salt and pepper
Fried Mushrooms	*Fried Mushrooms*
225 g/8 oz button mushrooms	2 cups button mushrooms
50 g/2 oz butter	¼ cup butter
salt and pepper	salt and pepper

Mix together the flour and salt, make a well in the centre and pour in the egg. Stir the ingredients together, gradually add the milk and water and beat thoroughly to make a soft, creamy batter. Allow to stand for 30 minutes and add a drop more milk if it seems too thick.

Now make the fillings. Peel the tomatoes (see Tomato Soup with Tofu, page 23) and chop the flesh. Slice the onion. Heat the oil in a pan and sauté the onion for 5 minutes, then add the chopped tomatoes, the thyme and salt and pepper to taste and cook to make a dry-ish sauce.

Melt the fat in a pan and scramble the beaten egg until beginning to set. Season with salt and pepper to taste and mix in the chopped parsley.

Clean, trim and chop the celery and cook it in a little boiling water for 15–20 minutes. Drain, reserving the water, and leave the celery on one side. Make the celery water up to 200 ml/7 fl oz (¾ cup) with a little more water and whisk in the dried milk. Make a white sauce (see page 72) with the butter or margarine, the flour and the celery liquid, stir in the celery pieces and season well with salt and pepper.

Clean and trim the mushrooms. Melt the butter in a pan, toss in the mushrooms and cook for 5–10 minutes, stirring frequently. Season to taste with salt and pepper and keep warm while you make the pancakes.

Heat a very little oil in a frying pan and ladle in a quarter of the batter. Cook the pancake quickly until light brown underneath, flip it over and cook the other side. Use the rest of the batter to make three more pancakes in the same way, adding a little more oil if necessary. Stack them on top of each other with a filling between each layer, finishing with the fourth pancake. Garnish with parsley and a few knobs of butter, cut into four wedges and serve hot with the fried mushrooms.

Children's Tea Party for 12

As a child, the thing I loved most about parties was the food. No, I didn't have an enormous appetite. My joy came from seeing a table laden with so many good things – most of them everyday foods, but dressed up for the occasion in bright colours and pretty packaging. This, then, is the kind of spread that would have made a party a success for me. Despite their sophistication, I think many of today's children will agree . . . .

Cabbage Hedgehog

Nutty Cheese Aigrettes

Savoury Tarts

Gingerbread Sandwiches

Madeleines

Decorated Biscuits

Chocolate Peppermint Cake

Party Drinks

Cabbage Hedgehog

METRIC/IMPERIAL	AMERICAN
1 large, firm white cabbage or 2 small ones	1 large, firm white cabbage or 2 small ones
12 cherry tomatoes	12 cherry tomatoes
350 g/12 oz firm grapes, preferably some black and some white	¾ lb firm grapes, preferably some purple and some white
4 large carrots	4 large carrots
1 large cucumber	1 large cucumber
4 sticks celery	4 stalks celery
½ fresh pineapple or 1 (225-g/8-oz) can pineapple pieces in natural juice	½ fresh pineapple or 1 (8-oz) can pineapple pieces in natural juice
2 (155-g/5½-oz) cans wheat or nut 'luncheon meat'	1 (11-oz) can textured vegetable protein 'luncheon meat'
3 dessert apples	3 dessert apples
generous squeeze of lemon	generous squeeze of lemon
50 g/2 oz cream cheese	¼ cup cream cheese
50 g/2 oz roasted peanuts, chopped	½ cup roasted peanuts, chopped
450 g/1 lb Cheddar or Edam cheese	1 lb Cheddar or Edam cheese

Pull off any discoloured leaves from the outside of the cabbage and cut a slice off the stalk end so that it will stand firm. Place it on a pretty plate.

Wash and dry the cherry tomatoes and grapes. Peel the carrots and cut them into bite-sized pieces, together with the cucumber and celery. Slice the fresh pineapple, if used, into rings, cut away the shell and slice the fruit into cubes. Drain the canned pineapple. Cut the 'meat' into cubes – it tastes a bit like luncheon meat, and most children love it! Quarter, core and thickly slice the apples and dip the slices in lemon juice. Divide the cream cheese into small balls and roll them in the chopped peanuts. Cut the Cheddar or Edam into cubes. Thread all the prepared ingredients on to cocktail sticks (toothpicks), combining them or leaving them separate as liked. Stick the cocktail sticks on to the cabbage to cover it evenly and serve your Cabbage Hedgehog soon after preparing it.

Nutty Cheese Aigrettes

METRIC/IMPERIAL	AMERICAN
100 g/4 oz plain wholemeal flour	1 cup wholewheat flour
150 ml/¼ pint water	⅔ cup water
50 g/2 oz butter or margarine	¼ cup butter or margarine
2 eggs	2 eggs
75–100 g/3–4 oz finely grated Cheddar or Parmesan cheese	¾–1 cup finely grated Cheddar or Parmesan cheese
25–50 g/1–2 oz roasted peanuts, chopped	¼–½ cup roasted peanuts, chopped
salt and pepper	salt and pepper
oil for deep-frying	oil for deep-frying
parsley sprigs to garnish	parsley sprigs to garnish

Sift the flour, reserving the bran for use in another recipe. Combine the water and butter or margarine in a saucepan and heat gently until the fat melts. Bring to the boil and immediately add the flour. Take the pan off the heat and beat well until the mixture comes clean away from the side of the pan. Cool slightly, then gradually beat in the eggs and continue beating until the dough is completely smooth. Stir in the grated cheese, chopped nuts and salt and pepper to taste.

Heat the oil in a deep pan to 180 C/350 F and drop small spoonfuls of the mixture into it, a few at a time. Deep-fry them for about 8 minutes, until puffed up and brown. Drain the aigrettes on absorbent kitchen paper, pile them on to a serving dish and garnish them with parsley. Serve while still quite warm, though not too hot or impatient fingers (and mouths) may get burned!

Savoury Tarts

METRIC/IMPERIAL	AMERICAN
Pastry	*Dough*
175 g/6 oz plain wholemeal flour	1½ cups wholewheat flour
pinch of salt	pinch of salt
75 g/3 oz butter or margarine	⅓ cup butter or margarine
2–3 tablespoons cold water	3–4 tablespoons cold water
Fillings	*Fillings*
75 g/3 oz butter or margarine	⅓ cup butter or margarine
40 g/1½ oz plain wholemeal flour	⅓ cup wholewheat flour
300 ml/½ pint creamy milk	1¼ cups creamy milk
salt and pepper	salt and pepper
100 g/4 oz Cheddar cheese, grated	1 cup grated Cheddar cheese
50 g/2 oz cooked peas	⅓ cup cooked peas
50 g/2 oz walnut pieces	½ cup walnut pieces
100 g/4 oz mushrooms	1 cup mushrooms
50 g/2 oz canned sweet corn	⅓ cup canned corn
paprika for sprinkling	paprika for sprinkling
lettuce leaves, chopped fresh chives, quartered tomatoes and watercress to garnish	lettuce leaves, chopped fresh chives, quartered tomatoes and watercress to garnish

Set the oven at moderately hot (190 C, 375 F, gas 5). Make the pastry shells first. Mix together the flour and salt and rub in the fat to give a crumb-like texture. Add enough water to bind the mixture together, knead to a dough and wrap it in cooking foil or cling film (saran wrap). Chill the dough in the refrigerator for at least 30 minutes.

Now roll the dough out and use it to line 12 plain or fluted patty tins or muffin pans. Prick the bases and bake the pastry shells for 10–12 minutes, until golden and crisp. Leave them on one side to cool.

For the fillings, make a white sauce (see page 72) using half the butter or margarine, the flour and the milk. Season to taste with salt and pepper. Use this sauce as a basic filling for the tarts, adding other ingredients to it so that you have a variety of flavours.

Divide the cheese into three portions. Mix one portion with the peas and a little white sauce and fill three tart shells with the mixture. Mix another portion with the walnuts and some sauce and use this to fill three more tart shells.

Clean, trim and slice the mushrooms and sauté them for a few minutes in the remaining butter or margarine. Stir in some more white sauce, fill a further three tarts with the mixture and sprinkle with the remaining portion of grated cheese. Brown these under the grill for 1–2 minutes.

For the last three tarts, drain the sweet corn and mix it with the rest of the sauce. Spoon the mixture into the tarts and top each with a sprinkling of paprika.

Arrange the savoury tarts on one or two large plates and garnish generously with lettuce, chives, tomatoes and watercress so that the plates make a splash of colour on the table.

Gingerbread Sandwiches

Try and make the gingerbread a few days before your party as the flavour improves with time.

METRIC/IMPERIAL	AMERICAN
Gingerbread	*Gingerbread*
100 g/4 oz butter or margarine	$\frac{1}{2}$ cup butter or margarine
225 g/8 oz molasses	$\frac{2}{3}$ cup molasses
150 ml/$\frac{1}{4}$ pint milk	$\frac{2}{3}$ cup milk
2 eggs, beaten	2 eggs, beaten
225 g/8 oz plain wholemeal flour	2 cups wholewheat flour
1 teaspoon mixed spice	1 teaspoon mixed spice
2 teaspoons ground ginger	2 teaspoons ground ginger
$\frac{1}{2}$ teaspoon bicarbonate of soda	$\frac{1}{2}$ teaspoon baking soda
50 g/2 oz raw brown sugar	$\frac{1}{3}$ cup raw brown sugar
100 g/4 oz sultanas	$\frac{2}{3}$ cup seedless white raisins
Fillings	*Fillings*
grated Cheddar cheese	grated Cheddar cheese
ricotta or cream cheese	ricotta or cream cheese
1–2 dessert apples	1–2 dessert apples
Apple Spread (page 75)	Apple Spread (page 75)

Set the oven at moderate (160 C, 325 F, gas 3). Grease and line an 18-cm/7-in square cake tin. In a saucepan gently heat the butter or margarine, the molasses and milk and stir well. Allow to cool slightly, then add the beaten eggs. Mix the flour, spices, soda, sugar and sultanas (seedless white raisins) together in a bowl and gradually pour in the liquid mixture, beating continuously so that everything is well blended. Turn the mixture into the prepared tin and bake for 1–1$\frac{1}{4}$ hours, until firm to the touch. Leave the gingerbread to cool for a while in the tin before transferring it to a wire rack.

To make the sandwiches, cut the gingerbread into 12 fingers and slice these horizontally in half. Spread the bottom halves with grated Cheddar, ricotta or cream cheese, apple slices or apple butter as liked, or a combination of any of these. Sandwich the fillings with the remaining gingerbread halves and arrange on a plate.

Madeleines

METRIC/IMPERIAL	AMERICAN
100 g/4 oz self-raising wholemeal flour	1 cup wholewheat flour mixed with
100 g/4 oz butter or margarine	1 teaspoon baking powder
100 g/4 oz demerara raw brown sugar	$\frac{1}{2}$ cup butter or margarine
2 eggs	$\frac{2}{3}$ cup light raw brown sugar
100 g/4 oz strawberry or raspberry jam	2 eggs
50–75 g/2–3 oz desiccated coconut	$\frac{1}{3}$ cup strawberry or raspberry jam
12 glacé cherries	$\frac{2}{3}$–1 cup shredded coconut
24 angelica leaves	12 candied cherries
	24 angelica leaves

Set the oven at moderately hot (200 C, 400 F, gas 6). Sift the flour, reserving the bran for use in another recipe. Cream together the fat and sugar until fluffy and soft, beat in the eggs and mix thoroughly. Fold in the flour.

Grease 12 dariole moulds and divide the mixture between them, filling each one just over half way. Bake the madeleines for 10–15 minutes, until golden brown, turn out carefully and leave to cool. If they have risen too high and are misshaped, cut them so that all the tops are even.

Gently heat the jam and use a pastry brush to apply a thin coating of it to the side and top of each cake. Roll the cakes in the coconut and decorate the tops with the cherries and angelica leaves.

VARIATION

Traditionally, madeleines are covered in a red jam but if you have other varieties in the cupboard as well (apricot, greengage or gooseberry, blackcurrant), you can make a plateful of different coloured cakes.

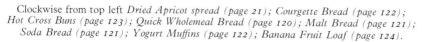

Clockwise from top left *Dried Apricot spread (page 21); Courgette Bread (page 122); Hot Cross Buns (page 123); Quick Wholemeal Bread (page 120); Malt Bread (page 121); Soda Bread (page 121); Yogurt Muffins (page 122); Banana Fruit Loaf (page 124).*

Overleaf *Walnut Layer Cake (page 131); Strawberry Shortcakes (page 130); Lemon Date Sponge Squares (page 130); Pineapple Swiss Roll (page 132).*

Decorated Biscuits

METRIC/IMPERIAL	AMERICAN
Biscuits	*Cookies*
225 g/8 oz plain wholemeal flour	2 cups wholewheat flour
100 g/4 oz butter or margarine	½ cup butter or margarine
100 g/4 oz raw brown sugar	⅔ cup raw brown sugar
1 egg	1 egg
Glacé Icing	*Glacé Frosting*
225 g/8 oz demerara raw brown sugar	1¼ cups light raw brown sugar
2–3 tablespoons hot water or orange,	3–4 tablespoons hot water or orange,
blackcurrant or lemon juice	blackcurrant or lemon juice
Butter Icing	*Butter Cream Frosting*
75 g/3 oz demerara raw brown sugar	½ cup light raw brown sugar
50 g/2 oz unsalted butter	¼ cup unsalted butter
Decorations	*Decorations*
Chocolate vermicelli or grated dessert chocolate; nuts, whole, flaked and chopped; raisins; finely grated orange and lemon peel; glacé cherries; angelica leaves; desiccated coconut; edible silver balls; marzipan; jam	Chocolate vermicelli or grated dessert chocolate; nuts, whole, flaked and chopped; raisins; finely grated orange and lemon peel; candied cherries; angelica leaves; shredded coconut; edible silver balls; almond paste; jam

Sift the flour, putting aside the bran for use in another recipe. Rub in the fat with your finger tips until the mixture resembles breadcrumbs. Stir in the sugar followed by the egg and knead briefly. Wrap the dough in silver foil or cling-film (saran wrap) and chill for 30 minutes.

Set the oven at moderately hot (190 C, 375 F, gas 5). Roll the dough out to about 3 mm/⅜ in thick and use pastry cutters to cut out a variety of shapes – rounds, hearts, crescents, diamonds, stars, rectangles, even animal shapes. If you are intending to sandwich some of them, make sure you have an even number of the same size and shape. Arrange the biscuits on ungreased baking sheets and bake them for 15 minutes. Leave to cool on the sheets so that they stay crisp.

For the glacé icing, grind the sugar to a fine powder in a liquidiser or blender and mix it with the hot water or any of the fruit juices listed. They all give different coloured results – if you have time, divide the sugar and make up some icing in each colour. Blend thoroughly. Grind the sugar for the butter icing, too, and combine it with the butter until smooth.

Use the glacé icing, butter icing and assorted decorations to top the biscuits in whatever way you like. Here are some suggestions to get you started:

Cover some biscuits with glacé or butter icing and sprinkle them with chocolate vermicelli, grated chocolate, orange or lemon peel or desiccated coconut.

Make faces on round biscuits by first spreading them with glacé icing, then using a sliver of glacé cherry for a smiling mouth and two raisins or nuts for eyes.

Top some heart-shaped biscuits with pink glacé icing and make a border with silver balls and a flower with cherry halves and angelica leaves.

Sandwich other biscuits together with butter icing, jam or marzipan and decorate the tops as liked.

NOTE If you are making these biscuits in advance, store them in an airtight tin to prevent them from going soft. Decorate them on the day of your party.

Clockwise from the top *Christmas Flapjacks (page 135)*; *Ginger Crisps (page 137)*;
Orange Creams (page 136); *Chocolate Digestive Biscuits (page 134)*;
Coconut Macaroons (page 135) Bottom right *Sesame Wheatgerm Crackers (page 137)*.

Chocolate Peppermint Cake

METRIC/IMPERIAL	AMERICAN
Cake	*Cake*
100 g/4 oz butter or margarine	½ cup butter or margarine
100 g/4 oz demerara raw brown sugar	⅔ cup light raw brown sugar
2 large eggs, beaten	2 large eggs, beaten
½ teaspoon vanilla essence	½ teaspoon vanilla extract
150 g/5 oz self-raising wholemeal flour	1¼ cups wholewheat flour mixed with
50 g/2 oz cocoa powder	1¼ teaspoons baking powder
1 tablespoon warm water or milk	½ cup cocoa powder
(optional)	1 tablespoon warm water or milk
Icing	(optional)
175 g/6 oz demerara raw brown sugar	*Icing*
75 g/3 oz unsalted butter, softened	1 cup light raw brown sugar
about ½ teaspoon peppermint essence	⅓ cup unsalted butter, softened
	about ½ teaspoon peppermint extract

Set the oven at moderate (180 C, 350 F, gas 4). Grease and flour two (20-cm/8-in) sandwich tins (layer cake pans).

In a mixing bowl cream the butter or margarine and sugar together until light and soft. Add the beaten eggs gradually, mixing them in well, then add the vanilla essence. Mix together the flour and cocoa and fold them gently into the rest of the ingredients. If the mixture seems a little dry – it should have a soft dropping consistency – add a little warm water or milk.

Divide the mixture between the two prepared tins and bake for 25–30 minutes, until firm to the touch. Turn the cakes out on to a wire rack and leave to cool.

For the filling, grind the sugar to a powder in a liquidiser or blender and beat all but 25 g/1 oz (3 tablespoons) of it with the butter and peppermint essence to taste. Sandwich the two cakes together with the peppermint cream, sprinkle the top with the remaining powdered sugar and arrange the cake on a plate or a stand. This chocolate cake will keep for a few days in an airtight tin, but do not add the filling until just before you serve it.

VARIATIONS

Most children love the taste of peppermint but if you feel your crowd might not, use whipped cream as a filling instead, possibly mixed with some chopped fresh strawberries.

Party Drinks

Banana Yogurt Drink

METRIC/IMPERIAL	AMERICAN
1 large banana	1 large banana
2 (150-g/5.3-oz) cartons natural yogurt	1⅓ cups plain yogurt
300 ml/½ pint pineapple juice	1¼ cups pineapple juice
25–50 g/1–2 oz toasted coconut flakes (optional)	2–4 tablespoons toasted coconut flakes (optional)

Mash the banana and whisk it into the yogurt with the pineapple juice. (A liquidiser or blender will do the job more quickly with smoother results.) Serve in three individual glasses, scattered with toasted coconut flakes, if liked. **Serves 3**

Strawberry Milk Shake

METRIC/IMPERIAL	AMERICAN
50 g/2 oz honey or demerara raw brown sugar	3 tablespoons honey or ⅓ cup light raw brown sugar
225 g/8 oz fresh strawberries	1⅔ cups fresh strawberries
1.15 litres/2 pints milk	5 cups milk
100 g/4 oz strawberry jam (optional)	⅓ cup strawberry jam (optional)

Grind the sugar, if used, to a powder in a liquidiser or blender. Mash the strawberries with the honey or sugar and whisk in the milk to make a frothy drink. If you have a liquidiser, simply combine all the ingredients and blend until smooth. Serve chilled in six individual glasses, with a spoonful or two of strawberry jam in each, if liked. **Serves 6**

VARIATION

Raspberries, crushed pineapple, apricots and blackcurrants can all be substituted for the strawberries.

Carob Milk Shake (Vegan)

METRIC/IMPERIAL	AMERICAN
2 heaped tablespoons carob powder	3 heaped tablespoons carob powder
600 ml/1 pint soya milk	2½ cups soy milk
15 g/½ oz raw brown sugar or to taste	1 tablespoon light raw brown sugar or to taste
25 g/1 oz plain dessert chocolate, finely grated	2 tablespoons finely grated plain dessert chocolate

Combine the carob powder with a little of the soya milk, then pour in the rest of the milk and whisk until light and frothy. Sweeten with sugar to taste. Transfer to three individual glasses and serve each carob shake topped with some finely grated chocolate. **Serves 3**

Formal Dinner Party for 4

Illustrated on page 165

There is no denying that this meal is rather fiddly to prepare. But when you want to impress your guests, it's well worth the effort. Middle Eastern in character, each dish is an experience – and even those who insist no meal is complete without meat are unlikely to leave the table feeling hungry.

Felafels

Hummus

Aubergine with Yogurt

Stuffed Vine Leaves

Pan-fried Pitta Bread

Mixed Salad

Strawberry Dessert with Caramel Topping

Felafels

METRIC/IMPERIAL	AMERICAN
225 g/8 oz chickpeas, soaked in water overnight	1 cup garbanzos beans, soaked in water overnight
½ small green pepper, deseeded	½ small green pepper, deseeded
1 clove garlic, crushed	1 clove garlic, crushed
1 teaspoon coriander	1 teaspoon coriander
½ teaspoon cumin	½ teaspoon cumin
generous pinch of dried thyme	generous pinch of dried thyme
generous pinch of dried sage	generous pinch of dried sage
salt and pepper	salt and pepper
a little plain wholemeal flour	a little wholewheat flour
oil for deep-frying	oil for deep-frying

Drain the chickpeas (garbanzos), put them in a pan with plenty of fresh water, bring them to the boil and simmer for 1–2 hours, until soft. Drain, reserving the water. Finely chop the green pepper or – better still – mince it; make sure the garlic, too, is crushed as finely as possible.

Coarsely grind or blend the chickpeas to a paste in a liquidiser or blender and transfer this to a bowl. Stir in the green pepper, garlic, spices, herbs and salt and pepper to taste, with just enough flour to make the mixture smooth. Bind the ingredients together with a little of the chickpea water and, using floured hands, divide it into small balls. Heat the oil in a deep pan to 190 C/375 F and deep-fry the felafels for just a few minutes, until crisp and golden. Drain on absorbent kitchen paper and serve with Hummus (see opposite) – the creamy, delicate sauce goes well with the spicy, crunchy felafels.

Hummus

METRIC/IMPERIAL	AMERICAN
225 g/8 oz chickpeas, soaked in water overnight	1 cup garbanzos beans, soaked in water overnight
2–3 tablespoons tahini	3–4 tablespoons tahini
1 clove garlic, crushed, or to taste	1 clove garlic, crushed, or to taste
juice of one lemon	juice of one lemon
about 4 tablespoons vegetable or olive oil	about ⅓ cup vegetable or olive oil
salt and pepper	salt and pepper
mint sprigs or black olives to garnish	mint sprigs or ripe olives to garnish

Drain the chickpeas (garbanzos) and cook them in plenty of fresh, boiling water for 1–2 hours, until quite soft. Drain, retaining the liquid.

Use a liquidiser or blender to grind the chickpeas into a thick powder – you can also do this by mashing them with a fork but it is a long job, especially as they must be ground really fine. In a bowl, combine the chickpea powder with the tahini, garlic, lemon juice and enough oil to turn the ingredients into a smooth purée. If you feel there is enough oil in the hummus but that it is still too thick, adjust the consistency with a little of the chickpea water. Beat well so that the texture is light and airy.

Season with salt and pepper to taste, pile the hummus into a shallow serving dish and garnish with fresh mint or black olives.

Aubergine with Yogurt

METRIC/IMPERIAL	AMERICAN
2 large aubergines	2 large eggplants
salt and pepper	salt and pepper
about 4 tablespoons vegetable oil	about ⅓ cup vegetable oil
2 onions, sliced	2 onions, sliced
1 clove garlic, crushed, or to taste	1 clove garlic, crushed, or to taste
450 g/1 lb tomatoes or 1 (425-g/15-oz) can tomatoes	1 lb tomatoes or 1 (15-oz) can tomatoes
½ teaspoon cayenne	½ teaspoon cayenne
1 teaspoon ground cumin	1 teaspoon ground cumin
1 (150-g/5.3-oz) carton natural yogurt	⅔ cup plain yogurt

Slice the aubergines (eggplants), lay them on a plate and sprinkle with salt. Set aside for 30 minutes, then rinse in cold water and pat dry with absorbent kitchen paper.

Set the oven at moderate (180 C, 350 F, gas 4). Heat the oil in a saucepan and add the aubergine slices. Cook gently for 10 minutes, turning the aubergine over after 5 minutes, drain and set aside. Now put the sliced onions and garlic in the pan, adding more oil if necessary. Sauté until the onion becomes transparent. Peel the fresh tomatoes, if used (see Tomato Soup with Tofu, page 23). Chop the fresh or canned tomatoes and add them to the pan with the spices and salt and pepper to taste. Continue cooking gently for 5 more minutes.

Put half the aubergine slices in a shallow ovenproof dish and cover with half the tomato mixture. Repeat these layers and top with the yogurt. Bake for 40–50 minutes, until the aubergine is tender.

Stuffed Vine Leaves

METRIC/IMPERIAL	AMERICAN
100 g/4 oz brown rice	½ cup brown rice
2 tablespoons vegetable oil	3 tablespoons vegetable oil
1 small onion, finely chopped	1 small onion, finely chopped
50 g/2 oz pine nuts or hazelnuts	½ cup pine nuts or hazelnuts
1 teaspoon chopped fresh mint	1 teaspoon chopped fresh mint
salt and pepper	salt and pepper
12 large vine leaves	12 large vine leaves
25 g/1 oz butter	2 tablespoons butter

Set the oven at moderate (180 C, 350 F, gas 4). Wash the rice thoroughly, drain and cook it in boiling water for 30–40 minutes, until soft. Meanwhile, heat the oil and sauté the onion for a few minutes. Drain the rice and mix it into the onion, followed by the nuts, mint and a little salt and pepper. Remove the pan from the heat.

Wash the vine leaves and blanch them in boiling water for 1 minute. Drain well. Spread the leaves out and spoon some of the rice and nut mixture on to each one. Roll up each leaf, tucking in the ends to keep the filling securely in place, and arrange the rolls close together in a greased shallow ovenproof dish. Cover with silver foil and bake for 30 minutes. Serve topped with a few knobs of butter.

NOTE If you cannot obtain vine leaves, use cabbage or cos (romaine) lettuce leaves instead.

Pan-fried Pitta Bread

METRIC/IMPERIAL	AMERICAN
225 g/8 oz plain wholemeal flour	2 cups wholewheat flour
pinch of salt	pinch of salt
150 ml/¼ pint warm water	⅔ cup warm water
7 g/¼ oz fresh yeast	¼ cake compressed yeast
½ teaspoon honey or raw brown sugar	½ teaspoon honey or raw brown sugar

Mix together the flour and salt. In another bowl, combine the warm water with the yeast and honey or sugar, stir well and leave the mixture in a warm spot for 10–15 minutes, or until frothy.

Pour the yeast liquid into the flour, mix thoroughly and knead until the dough is smooth and elastic. Put it into a covered bowl and place it in a warm spot for 30 minutes or until doubled in size. Knead the dough again lightly, divide it into four pieces and roll each piece out to a large, thin oval. Lightly grease a heavy-based pan and pre-heat it until hot right through. Slip a pitta bread into the pan and cook it for a few minutes over a medium heat, pressing on it with a knife or spatula and turning the bread when the underside is golden. Cook the remaining breads in the same way, greasing the pan a little more if necessary.

Pitta bread can also be cooked in a moderately hot oven (200 C, 400 F, gas 6) for 10 minutes. As this is a much higher temperature than that needed to cook the other dishes being served at this meal, you would have to cook your pitta breads in advance and heat them through just before serving.

Mixed Salad

METRIC/IMPERIAL	AMERICAN
Salad	*Salad*
1 small Webbs lettuce	1 small Bibb lettuce
1 small soft lettuce	1 small soft lettuce
4 sticks celery	4 stalks celery
4 tomatoes	4 tomatoes
8 radishes	8 radishes
¼ small cauliflower	¼ small cauliflower
50 g/2 oz button mushrooms	½ cup button mushrooms
1 bunch of watercress or some chopped fresh parsley	1 bunch of watercress or some chopped fresh parsley
Dressing	*Dressing*
1 tablespoon white wine or cider vinegar	1 tablespoon white wine or cider vinegar
3 tablespoons vegetable oil	3 tablespoons vegetable oil
generous pinch of mustard powder	generous pinch of mustard powder
generous pinch of demerara raw brown sugar	generous pinch of light raw brown sugar
salt and pepper	salt and pepper

Wash all the salad ingredients and allow to drain. The two lettuces should be very different in colour and texture; tear them into bite-size pieces and combine them to line a serving dish. Slice the celery, tomatoes and radishes and place them on top. Break the cauliflower into florets and scatter them over the salad with the mushrooms. Garnish with the watercress or parsley.

Make the dressing by combining all the ingredients in a screw-top jar and shaking well. Add to the salad just before serving, and toss the ingredients so that everything is evenly coated with the dressing.

Strawberry Dessert with Caramel Topping

This sweet crunchy topping makes what is basically strawberries and cream into something even more special.

METRIC/IMPERIAL	AMERICAN
450 g/1 lb fresh or frozen strawberries	1 lb fresh or frozen strawberries
2 tablespoons sherry	3 tablespoons sherry
1 tablespoon orange juice	1 tablespoon orange juice
1 (142-ml/5-fl oz) carton whipping cream	⅔ cup heavy cream
75–100 g/3–4 oz demerara raw brown sugar	½–¾ cup light raw brown sugar

Allow the frozen strawberries, if used, to thaw at room temperature. Clean and hull the fruit and divide it between four small ovenproof dishes. Pour a little sherry and orange juice over each one. Alternatively, if the strawberries are over-ripe, mash them to a purée with the juice and sherry and spoon the purée into the dishes.

Whip the cream until thick and spread it over the strawberries. Sprinkle the sugar over the cream in a thick and even layer. Chill the dishes for 1–2 hours.

To make the caramel topping, place the strawberries under a hot grill and leave them just long enough for the sugar to melt. Chill them again before serving; the tops will be crisp and golden.

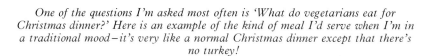

Christmas Dinner for 8

Illustrated on pages 166–7

One of the questions I'm asked most often is 'What do vegetarians eat for Christmas dinner?' Here is an example of the kind of meal I'd serve when I'm in a traditional mood – it's very like a normal Christmas dinner except that there's no turkey!

Avocado and Tomato Cocktail

Cashew and Red Pepper Loaf

Crunchy Cauliflower

Jacket Potatoes

Carrots Julienne

Chicory and Tomato Salad

Lemon Sorbet

Christmas Pudding

Brandy Butter

Nuts, fresh fruit

Avocado and Tomato Cocktail

METRIC/IMPERIAL	AMERICAN
4 large avocados	4 large avocados
5 tablespoons lemon juice	6 tablespoons lemon juice
8 firm tomatoes	8 firm tomatoes
24 green olives	24 green olives
1 small onion, finely chopped	1 small onion, finely chopped
225 g/8 oz mozzarella cheese, diced	$1\frac{1}{3}$ cups mozzarella cheese, diced
8 tablespoons vegetable oil	$\frac{2}{3}$ cup vegetable oil
salt and freshly ground black pepper	salt and freshly ground black pepper
50 g/2 oz walnuts, coarsely chopped	$\frac{1}{3}$ cup coarsely chopped walnuts

Cut the avocados in half and remove the stones. Scoop out some of the flesh from each half and toss it in 1 tablespoon of the lemon juice. Sprinkle lemon juice also over the avocado halves.

Slice the tomatoes into wedges. Halve and stone the olives. Mix these with the chopped onion, diced cheese and avocado flesh in a bowl. Whisk the remaining lemon juice with the oil and salt and pepper to taste and pour the dressing over the salad. Chill for 1 hour, then divide the cocktail between the eight avocado halves and sprinkle with the chopped walnuts.

Cashew and Red Pepper Loaf

METRIC/IMPERIAL	AMERICAN
2 sticks celery, finely chopped	2 stalks celery, finely chopped
2 red peppers, deseeded and chopped	2 red peppers, deseeded and chopped
1 small onion, finely sliced	1 small onion, finely sliced
50 g/2 oz fresh wholemeal breadcrumbs	1 cup fresh wholewheat breadcrumbs
225 g/8 oz coarsely ground cashew nuts	1⅓ cups coarsely ground cashew nuts
½–1 teaspoon dried marjoram	½–1 teaspoon dried marjoram
pinch each of salt and pepper	pinch each of salt and pepper
3 eggs	3 eggs
300 ml/½ pint milk	1¼ cups milk
50 g/2 oz butter or margarine, melted	¼ cup butter or margarine, melted

Set the oven at moderately hot (190 C, 375 F, gas 5). Mix the chopped vegetables with the breadcrumbs, nuts, herbs and seasoning. Beat together the eggs, milk and three quarters of the melted fat and pour the liquid into the rest of the ingredients. Leave to stand for a short time. The mixture should be moist and heavy; adjust the texture if necessary with more milk or breadcrumbs.

Use the rest of the fat to grease a 1-kg/2-lb (8½ × 4½ × 2-in) loaf tin, pour in the nut and pepper mixture and smooth the top. Bake the loaf for 40–50 minutes, until cooked; do not overcook it or it may be rather dry. Turn it out of the tin and serve.

Crunchy Cauliflower

METRIC/IMPERIAL	AMERICAN
2 medium cauliflowers	2 medium cauliflowers
75 g/3 oz butter or margarine	⅓ cup butter or margarine
2 large onions, sliced	2 large onions, sliced
100 g/4 oz medium or coarse oat flakes	1 cup rolled oats
salt and pepper	salt and pepper
chopped fresh parsley to garnish	chopped fresh parsley to garnish

Wash the cauliflowers and break or cut them into large florets. Steam these or cook them in a little boiling water for 10 minutes or until tender but still firm. Drain and arrange them in a shallow dish.

Melt the fat and sauté the sliced onions for 5 minutes. Stir in the oats and cook briefly until they turn golden and crisp. Season the mixture with salt and pepper to taste and sprinkle over the cauliflower. Serve garnished with parsley.

Jacket Potatoes

METRIC/IMPERIAL	AMERICAN
8 medium potatoes	8 medium potatoes
a little vegetable oil	a little vegetable oil
50 g/2 oz blue cheese (optional)	⅓ cup diced blue cheese
1 (150-g/5.3-oz) carton natural yogurt	⅔ cup plain yogurt
salt and pepper	salt and pepper

Set the oven at moderately hot (200 C, 400 F, gas 6). Scrub the potatoes, dry well and prick with a fork. Brush the skins with some vegetable oil before placing them near the top of the oven. Bake the potatoes for 1 hour or until soft to the touch.

Meanwhile, mash the blue cheese, if used, and mix it into the yogurt with a little salt and pepper. When ready, remove the potatoes from the oven and cut a cross on top of each. Spoon some of the yogurt mixture inside and serve at once.

Carrots Julienne

METRIC/IMPERIAL	AMERICAN
8 large carrots	8 large carrots
75 g/3 oz butter or margarine	⅓ cup butter or margarine
1 tablespoon raw brown sugar	1 tablespoon raw brown sugar
celery salt and freshly ground pepper	celery salt and freshly ground pepper
watercress to garnish (optional)	watercress to garnish (optional)

Using a sharp knife, peel and slice the carrots into julienne strips about 2.5 cm/1 in long and 5 mm/¼ in thick. Soak them in iced water for 1–2 hours, or until needed – this will make them crisper.

When almost ready to eat the carrots, drain and pat them dry with absorbent kitchen paper. Melt the fat and, when hot, toss in the carrot strips and cook, stirring frequently, over a medium heat until they are tender, but still firm. This will only take a few minutes. Sprinkle in the sugar and seasoning to taste, stir well again and pile the carrots into a serving dish. Serve garnished with watercress, if liked.

Chicory and Tomato Salad

METRIC/IMPERIAL	AMERICAN
4 large heads chicory	4 large heads Belgian endive
8 tomatoes, sliced	8 tomatoes, sliced
Dressing	*Dressing*
1 tablespoon lemon juice	1 tablespoon lemon juice
4 tablespoons vegetable oil	4 tablespoons vegetable oil
¼ teaspoon French mustard	¼ teaspoon French mustard
generous pinch of raw brown sugar or	generous pinch of raw brown sugar or
1 teaspoon clear honey	1 teaspoon clear honey
salt and pepper	salt and pepper

In a screw-top jar, shake together the lemon juice, oil, mustard, sugar and salt and pepper to taste.

Wash the chicory (endive) and separate the leaves. Arrange them in a circle around the edge of a dish, fill the centre with sliced tomatoes and pour a little of the dressing over the salad ingredients.

Lemon Sorbet

METRIC/IMPERIAL	AMERICAN
300 ml/½ pint water	1¼ cups water
175 g/6 oz demerara raw brown sugar	1 cup light raw brown sugar
300 ml/½ pint lemon juice	1¼ cups lemon juice
finely grated rind of 1 lemon	finely grated rind of 1 lemon
2 egg whites	2 egg whites

Put the water and sugar together in a saucepan and cook over a low heat, stirring occasionally, until the sugar melts completely. Leave to cool.

Stir in the lemon juice and rind, pour the liquid into a freezing tray and put it into the freezer for 1 hour or until it begins to harden round the edges. Remove it from the freezer and beat well. Whisk the egg whites until stiff and fold them into the mixture. Refreeze the sorbet for a few hours until firm but not too hard.

Christmas Pudding

METRIC/IMPERIAL	AMERICAN
225 g/8 oz seedless raisins	1⅓ cups seedless raisins
225 g/8 oz currants	1⅓ cups currants
225 g/8 oz sultanas	1⅓ cups seedless white raisins
225 g/8 oz dried apricot pieces or prunes	1¼ cups dried apricot pieces or prunes
100 g/4 oz candied peel	⅔ cup candied peel
50 g/2 oz blanched almonds, chopped	⅓ cup chopped blanched almonds
100 g/4 oz plain wholemeal flour	1 cup wholewheat flour
½ teaspoon ground nutmeg	½ teaspoon ground nutmeg
½ teaspoon ground cinnamon	½ teaspoon ground cinnamon
1 teaspoon ground mixed spice	1 teaspoon ground mixed spice
225 g/8 oz raw brown sugar	1⅓ cups raw brown sugar
100 g/4 oz fresh wholemeal breadcrumbs	2 cups fresh wholewheat breadcrumbs
225 g/8 oz vegetarian suet, grated, or margarine	1 cup vegetable shortening, grated, or margarine
2 eggs, beaten	2 eggs, beaten
about 150 ml/¼ pint orange and lemon juice or juice and dry sherry, mixed	about ⅔ cup orange and lemon juice or juice and dry sherry, mixed

Wash the dried fruit, if necessary, and dry it thoroughly before using it. Chop the apricots or prunes into small pieces and mix them in a large bowl with all the rest of the fruit, the peel and chopped nuts. Mix together the flour and spices and stir them into the fruit with the sugar, breadcrumbs and grated suet (shortening). Add the beaten egg, followed by enough of the fruit juice liquid to make a soft, heavy mixture. Allow to stand for a few hours, preferably overnight. Adjust the liquid again, as the flour and bread will absorb a good deal of it, and you don't want the pudding to be too dry.

Pack the mixture tightly into 2–3 well-greased 1-litre/1½-pint (2-pint US) pudding basins. Cover these with pieces of greased greaseproof (waxed) paper, then with greased cooking foil or pudding cloths. Put each pudding into a large pan containing enough boiling water to reach two-thirds up the side of the basin and boil for 4 hours. Top up the pans with boiling water from time to time if necessary. Uncover the puddings and leave them to cool. Cover again with fresh greaseproof paper and foil or pudding cloths and store in a cool, dry place until needed.

On Christmas Day, steam the puddings in the same way for 3 more hours, turn them out and decorate them with holly. Serve with Brandy Butter and Lemon Sorbet.

NOTE Vegans can easily adapt this pudding to their diet by omitting the eggs and simply using more fruit juice instead.

Brandy Butter

METRIC/IMPERIAL	AMERICAN
175 g/6 oz demerara raw brown sugar	1 cup light raw brown sugar
100 g/4 oz butter, softened	½ cup butter, softened
a little grated orange rind (optional)	a little grated orange rind (optional)
2 tablespoons brandy	3 tablespoons brandy

Grind the sugar to a powder in a liquidiser or blender. Cream the butter until light and soft and gradually add the sugar and orange rind, if used. Finally add the brandy and continue beating to give the butter a smooth, creamy texture. Chill in the refrigerator until needed.

Buffet Supper for 12

Inviting friends round for a buffet supper is a nice compromise between offering them drinks and 'something to nibble' and sitting them down to a formal dinner. The food can be quite simple. Just make sure you include a choice of savoury dishes, a fresh salad – and a scrumptious dessert. This menu will give you the idea, then go on and think up some of your own.

Vegetable and Bean Hotpot

Chestnut Croquettes

Endive and Egg Salad

Red Cabbage Slaw

Cheese Mousse with Melba Toast

Tarragon Rice

Cheese Twists

Bananas with Rum

Vegetable and Bean Hotpot

METRIC/IMPERIAL	AMERICAN
2 tablespoons vegetable oil	3 tablespoons vegetable oil
50 g/2 oz butter or margarine	$\frac{1}{4}$ cup butter or margarine
3 large onions, sliced	3 large onions, sliced
1 large cabbage	1 large cabbage
8 large tomatoes	8 large tomatoes
1 large marrow	1 large summer squash
2–3 teaspoons crushed dried rosemary or to taste	2–3 teaspoons crushed dried rosemary or to taste
salt and pepper	salt and pepper
350 g/12 oz cooked butter beans	2 cups cooked lima beans
350 g/12 oz Cheddar cheese, grated	3 cups grated Cheddar cheese

Set the oven at moderate (180 C, 350 F, gas 4). In a large saucepan, heat the oil and butter or margarine together, add the sliced onions and sauté them until they begin to soften. Coarsely shred the cabbage. Chop the tomatoes. Peel and dice the marrow (summer squash), removing the seeds, and add all the prepared vegetables to the pan with the rosemary and salt and pepper to taste. Cook for 5 minutes, stirring frequently. Stir in the butter (lima) beans, transfer the mixture to an earthenware casserole (or any attractive ovenproof dish) and bake it for about 30 minutes, until the vegetables are tender but not overcooked.

Top the hotpot with the grated cheese and return it to the oven until the cheese melts. Alternatively, if you think some of your guests may not eat cheese, just serve the grated cheese in a large dish on the table so that those who want it can help themselves.

Chestnut Croquettes

METRIC/IMPERIAL	AMERICAN
675 g/1½ lb chestnuts	1½ lb chestnuts
50 g/2 oz butter or margarine	¼ cup butter or margarine
2 onions, finely chopped	2 onions, finely chopped
about 150 ml/¼ pint milk or Vegetable Stock (page 22)	about ⅔ cup milk or Vegetable Stock (page 22)
3 large eggs	3 large eggs
225 g/8 oz chopped walnuts	1⅓ cups chopped walnuts
salt and pepper	salt and pepper
dried wholemeal breadcrumbs	dried wholewheat breadcrumbs
vegetable oil for deep-frying	vegetable oil for deep-frying

Cut a cross in the chestnut shells and place the chestnuts in a pan of cold water. Bring to the boil, lower the heat and simmer for 10 minutes. Drain and allow to cool slightly, then carefully remove the outer shells and inner skins.

Melt the fat, add the chopped onion and cook for just a few minutes, then add the chestnuts and enough milk or vegetable stock to cover. Simmer for 20–40 minutes until the chestnuts are tender and the liquid has been absorbed. Mash the mixture or blend it in a liquidiser or blender to a thick purée. Cool slightly.

Beat the eggs and add three-quarters of the frothy mixture to the purée, followed by the chopped walnuts and salt and pepper to taste. Leave to cool completely. The mixture should be soft but firm enough to hold its shape – if it seems too wet, add more nuts or some fresh breadcrumbs or wheatgerm. Shape the mixture into small croquettes and roll them first in dried breadcrumbs, then in the remaining beaten egg and finally in more breadcrumbs.

Heat the oil in a deep pan to 180 c (350 f) and deep-fry the croquettes for no more than 5 minutes, until brown and crisp. Drain them on absorbent kitchen paper and keep them hot until needed.

Endive and Egg Salad

METRIC/IMPERIAL	AMERICAN
1 lettuce	1 lettuce
1 curly endive	1 head chicory
1 large head chicory	1 large Belgian endive
1 bunch radishes	1 bunch radishes
4 hard-boiled eggs, quartered	4 hard-cooked eggs, quartered
watercress to garnish	watercress to garnish
Dressing	*Dressing*
6 tablespoons vegetable oil	½ cup vegetable oil
3 tablespoons white wine vinegar	⅓ cup white wine vinegar
generous pinch of mustard powder	generous pinch of mustard powder
generous pinch of raw brown sugar	generous pinch of raw brown sugar
salt and pepper to taste	salt and pepper to taste

Wash the lettuce and endive (chicory) and tear the leaves into small pieces. Trim and slice the chicory (Belgian endive) and radishes. Combine all the prepared ingredients in a salad bowl.

Make the salad dressing by putting all the ingredients in a screw-top jar and shaking well. Just before serving the salad, pour some of the dressing over it and toss so that everything is evenly coated. Arrange the quartered eggs on top of the salad and garnish with the watercress. Serve the remaining dressing in a jug alongside.

Red Cabbage Slaw

METRIC/IMPERIAL	AMERICAN
1 large red cabbage	1 large red cabbage
1 small white cabbage	1 small white cabbage
2 dessert apples	2 dessert apples
1 (142-ml/5-fl oz) carton soured cream	⅔ cup dairy sour cream
4 tablespoons Mayonnaise (page 109)	⅓ cup Mayonnaise (page 109)
salt and pepper	salt and pepper
75 g/3 oz walnut halves	¾ cup walnut halves

Cut the cabbages into quarters, remove the centre stalks and finely shred the rest. Quarter, core and slice the apples and mix them in a bowl with the shredded cabbage.

Combine the cream and mayonnaise with salt and pepper to taste and pour the dressing over the salad ingredients. Toss lightly, and chill for at least 1 hour. Serve the slaw with the nuts scattered over the top.

Cheese Mousse

METRIC/IMPERIAL	AMERICAN
25 g/1 oz butter or margarine	2 tablespoons butter or margarine
25 g/1 oz plain wholemeal flour	¼ cup wholewheat flour
300 ml/½ pint milk	1¼ cups milk
50 g/2 oz Gruyère or Cheddar cheese, grated	½ cup grated Gruyère or Cheddar cheese
50 g/2 oz Parmesan cheese, grated	½ cup grated Parmesan cheese
pinch of cayenne	pinch of cayenne
pinch of mustard powder	pinch of mustard powder
salt and pepper	salt and pepper
1 tablespoon powdered agar-agar	1 tablespoon powdered agar-agar
3 tablespoons water	4 tablespoons water
2 large eggs	2 large eggs
finely sliced cucumber to garnish	finely sliced cucumber to garnish

Make the cheese sauce first. Melt the fat and sauté the flour for a few minutes, add the milk and bring to the boil, stirring continuously. Boil for 1 minute, until the sauce thickens, take the pan off the heat and add the Gruyère or Cheddar and the Parmesan. Continue stirring until all the cheese has melted. Sprinkle in the cayenne, mustard and salt and pepper to taste.

Stir the agar-agar into half the water, then bring the rest of the water to the boil and stir it into the agar-agar mixture. Separate the eggs and add the yolks to the cheese sauce with the dissolved agar-agar. Heat very gently for 5 minutes, stirring all the time, then set aside to cool.

Beat the egg whites until stiff and fold them into the cheese mixture just as it is beginning to set. Turn the mixture into a 600-ml/1-pint (1½-pint US) mould and put it in a cool place to set completely. When you are ready to serve the mousse, dip the base of the mould briefly in hot water to loosen the side and tip the mousse out on to a plate. Garnish with wafer-thin slices of cucumber and surround with wholemeal Melba Toast (see page 29).

Tarragon Rice

METRIC/IMPERIAL	AMERICAN
450 g/1 lb brown rice	2⅓ cups brown rice
1.4 litres/2½ pints water	6¼ cups water
25 g/1 oz butter	2 tablespoons butter
1 tablespoon chopped fresh tarragon	1 tablespoon chopped fresh tarragon
salt and pepper	salt and pepper
few sprigs of fresh tarragon to garnish	few sprigs of fresh tarragon to garnish

Wash and drain the rice and put it into a saucepan with the cold water. Bring to the boil, add the butter and simmer covered over a low heat for 30–40 minutes, until the rice is tender and all the water has been absorbed. Stir in the tarragon and salt and pepper to taste and set the rice aside in a warm spot for a short time for the flavours to mingle. Serve in a heated dish, preferably with a cover, and with a few more sprigs of tarragon scattered on top.

Cheese Twists

METRIC/IMPERIAL	AMERICAN
100 g/4 oz butter or margarine	½ cup butter or margarine
225 g/8 oz plain wholemeal flour	2 cups wholewheat flour
225 g/8 oz Cheddar cheese, finely grated	2 cups finely grated Cheddar cheese
about 2 tablespoons cold water	about 3 tablespoons cold water
a little paprika	a little paprika
50 g/2 oz poppy, sesame or caraway seeds	⅓ cup poppy or sesame seeds or ½ cup caraway seeds

In a bowl rub the fat into the flour until the mixture resembles fine breadcrumbs. Stir in 175 g/6 oz (1½ cups) of the cheese, together with just enough water to bind the ingredients to a dough. Knead briefly, wrap in kitchen foil or cling-film (saran wrap) and chill the dough for at least 30 minutes.

Set the oven at moderately hot (190 C, 375 F, gas 5). Roll the dough out as thinly as possible on a floured board and cut it into strips measuring about 6 cm/2½ in long and 1 cm/½ in wide. Twist two strips together at a time, flatten slightly and dust with paprika. Sprinkle the twists with seeds and a little more grated cheese and place them on a greased baking sheet. Bake for 10–15 minutes, until crisp.

Bananas with Rum

METRIC/IMPERIAL	AMERICAN
12 firm, ripe bananas	12 firm, ripe bananas
50 g/2 oz light muscovado raw brown sugar	⅓ cup light raw brown sugar
½ teaspoon grated nutmeg or to taste	½ teaspoon grated nutmeg or to taste
6–8 tablespoons rum	⅓–½ cup rum
25 g/1 oz butter	2 tablespoons butter
300 ml/½ pint whipping cream	1¼ cups heavy cream

Set the oven at moderately hot (180 C, 350 F, gas 4). Peel and halve the bananas and slice them lengthways. Arrange them in a large, shallow, well-greased ovenproof dish and sprinkle them with the sugar, nutmeg and rum. Dot with butter. Bake for 20 minutes or until the bananas are cooked. Lightly whip the cream. Serve the bananas hot or cold, with the cream and crisp biscuits, if liked.

Basic Techniques

Sprouting Seeds and Grains

Why sprout?

Sprouted seeds have long been an important part of Oriental cookery, but it is only in recent years that they have gradually come to be accepted in the western world.

When you sprout a seed, enzymes are activated and the starches are converted to simple sugars. The calorie count is lowered greatly. Protein and fats in the seed become easier to digest; valuable amino acids are increased; so are vitamins, especially B and C.

If all that means little to you, think instead of the way sprouted seeds taste – crisp and sweet and moist, like freshly picked summer salad. But you can enjoy this all the year through.

What to sprout

Most seeds can be sprouted, but the fresher they are, the better will be the results. Also, don't buy your seeds from a horticulturist, unless they are specifically sold for sprouting. Others may well have been treated with chemicals. Your local wholefood shop will probably have the widest choice.

Some seeds are much easier to sprout than others, and I must admit I tend to stick to two or three favourites. Mung beans are easy, so are whole lentils and alfalfa. Aduki beans and dried sugar peas usually sprout well. In theory you can sprout any beans – including kidneys, chickpeas (garbanzos) and soyas. Grains can also be turned into 'vegetables' in this way; triticale wheat (a cross between wheat and rye, often just called 'sprouting wheat') is one of the easiest. It has a delicate, sweet flavour. Or try ordinary wheat, barley or rye grains. Experiment, too, with vegetable seeds like celery and lettuce; with tiny sesame and fenugreek seeds; and even with mixtures of your favourites (you can, in fact, buy seeds chosen to sprout well together ready-mixed in packets).

Equipment you will need

What you are aiming for is a container with a porous covering so that you can turn it upside down to drain the sprouts, thereby avoiding the necessity of handling them – they're fragile and can easily be damaged. An ideal container is a wide-necked jar with a piece of nylon or muslin (cheesecloth) secured over the top with a rubber band. You can also use a vegetable basket, colander or large strainer.

You can now buy specially made sprouting trays. I have one that consists of three trays that stack on top of each other which means I can fill each one with a different kind of seed and drain them all together at one time. Sometimes I fill them with just one variety of seed but at different stages of growth, so there are always some ready when I need them.

How to sprout seeds

First choose your seeds, then spread the amount you need on a plate or a flat surface. Three or four tablespoons will be enough to fill a quart jar – they may not look much to start with, but they can increase their bulk as much as six times or even more. Pick out any broken seeds or foreign objects such as tiny stones.

Rinse the seeds well and leave them to soak in plenty of water for about 8 hours (overnight if possible) after which they will probably have doubled in size. Discard the water, rinse the seeds through again, put them into your chosen container and tip the container upside down to drain. Leave it in a warm spot.

Now simply rinse the seeds in clean water and drain them well 2–3 times a day. Some beans (soya for example) may need more frequent rinsing.

Most sprouts should be ready to eat within 4–5 days, by which time they will be anything from $1 \text{ cm}/\frac{1}{2}$ in to $6 \text{ cm}/2\frac{1}{2}$ in long, depending on the kind of seeds used. Do not let them grow too long. If they are ready but you don't want to eat them for a couple of days, just put them in the refrigerator to stop their growth.

Using your sprouts

You get the most nutrients from raw sprouts. They make a super, fresh-tasting addition to salads and sandwiches and a quick and easy garnish for all sorts of savoury dishes. Light cooking does, however, make them easier to digest, but be careful not to overcook them. Add a handful or two at the last moment to soups, stews, grain or bean dishes, omelettes or scrambled eggs. Alternatively, stir-fry them in a little oil for 2–3 minutes, add soy sauce, crushed garlic or sliced fresh root ginger, and within minutes you have a vegetable accompaniment to go with most dishes. Or steam them lightly and serve them with a knob of butter.

Once you start experimenting with sprouts, you may find yourself using them as a basic ingredient in your daily cooking as I do.

Formal Dinner Party. From the top *Stuffed Vine Leaves (page 154); Mixed Salad (page 155);*
Hummus (page 153); Felafels (page 152);
Strawberry Dessert with Caramel Topping (page 155); Aubergine with Yogurt (page 153).

Overleaf Christmas Dinner. Cashew and Red Pepper Loaf (page 157) with
Carrots Julienne (page 158), Jacket Potatoes (page 157) and Crunchy Cauliflower (page 157);
Christmas Pudding (page 159) with Brandy Butter (page 159); Lemon Sorbet (page 158);
Chicory and Tomato Salad (page 158); Avocado and Tomato Cocktail (page 156).

Home-made Yogurt

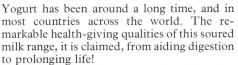

Yogurt has been around a long time, and in most countries across the world. The remarkable health-giving qualities of this soured milk range, it is claimed, from aiding digestion to prolonging life!

Unfortunately, the mass-produced variety most people now consume in this country is a long way from natural yogurt. Quite apart from the way the yogurt is produced, flavoured ones in particular contain so many additives that they can hardly be called health (or diet!) foods. Certainly simple, unadulterated yogurt is low in calories and high in nutrients, but most of the fruit-flavoured supermarket varieties may well be quite the opposite.

The answer is to make your own protein and calcium-rich yogurt at home. It means you can always have some in the refrigerator, and you can add your own jam, honey or fresh fruit to make it as delicious as any you can buy (if not more so).

Equipment you will need
You can use small, wide-necked jam jars or pots to make individual portions, putting them into a well-insulated tin or box (or the airing cupboard) while the souring process takes place. Or you can use a wide-necked thermos flask. There are also now many electric yogurt makers on the market. Usually simple in design, they keep the milk at an even temperature until it sours, so guaranteeing good results.

Yogurt

METRIC/IMPERIAL	AMERICAN
600 ml/1 pint milk (whole, skimmed, longlife or a combination of any of these)	2½ cups milk (whole, skimmed, longlife or a combination of any of these)
1–2 tablespoons dried skimmed milk or single cream (optional)	1–2 tablespoons dried milk solids or light cream (optional)
1 tablespoon natural yogurt (home-made or shop-bought)	1 tablespoon plain yogurt (home-made or shop-bought)

Clean all your equipment and sterilize it in boiling water. Leave the water in the container or flask until just before you pour in the yogurt so that it will still be warm.

Put the milk in a pan with the milk powder or cream (if you want your yogurt to be thicker and smoother). Bring to the boil, stirring as you do so to prevent a skin forming. Allow the milk to cool until it reaches blood heat (about 42 C/110 F). Stir in the yogurt. When well blended, pour the mixture into your warmed container, cover and store it in a warm spot such as an airing cupboard. If you are using an electric yogurt maker, switch it on. The yogurt should be ready in 6–8 hours. Put it into the refrigerator at once and leave, if possible, for at least four hours to become quite firm. Serve as it is or mix in honey, raw brown sugar, molasses or chopped fresh fruit.

Stored in a covered container the yogurt should keep for about 1 week. Don't forget to reserve a few spoonfuls on one side so that you can make a new batch when this one nears its end. **Makes 600 ml/1 pint (2½ cups)**

NON-DAIRY YOGURT
Anyone who wishes to avoid dairy products, for whatever reason, can make a yogurt-like product by using plant or nut milks in the same way. Special starters can be purchased at some wholefood or health food shops which enable you to dispense with the tablespoonful of milk yogurt. The results will not taste exactly like yogurt, but will have a similar consistency, will be high in nutrients and can be served in the same wide variety of ways.

Making your own yogurt and bean sprouts is both fun and rewarding. Shown here are mung beans and sprouts, natural yogurt, strawberry and cherry flavoured yogurts and alfalfa seeds and sprouts. Molasses and honey go well with natural yogurt.

Glossary

Agar-agar A gelling agent made from seaweed; vegetarians use it instead of gelatine. Unflavoured agar-agar comes in a powdered form of which 1 teaspoon will set 300 ml/½ pint (1¼ cups) liquid. Flavoured agar-agar comes as granules in packets usually designed to make up to 600 ml/1 pint (2½ cups) jelly.

Barley Flakes These are barley grains which have been steamed and flattened, a process which makes them quick to cook.

Bean Sprouts Generally this term refers to mung bean sprouts, but sprouts can be obtained from other beans and grains such as alfalfa and wheat.

Bran This is the hard, protective skin of the wheat grain, very good as fibre to combat constipation and other connected ailments. It can be added to savoury or sweet dishes or sprinkled over breakfast cereal.

Bulgur see Cracked Wheat

Butter A natural and nutritious food but, being an animal product, high in saturated fats which, it is thought, can build up in the body and cause health problems. Used in reasonable quantities however it is unlikely to harm you, especially as a vegetarian diet includes very few other foods which contain these fats.

Carob Rich in nutrients, this chocolate-like powder can be used in sweet dishes and drinks.

Cheese A protein-rich food that is popular with vegetarians, but should be used in restricted amounts as it is high in fats. Many cheeses are made with animal rennet (the lining of a calf's stomach), so make sure you know which these are. You can obtain most of the popular varieties in forms made specially for vegetarians.

Chocolate Not quite as bad as people think – it does supply some iron. Raw sugar chocolate can be bought in many wholefood shops.

Cornmeal This is made from ground maize grains. Stoneground is the best to buy as this will always contain the whole grain.

Cracked Wheat Whole wheatgrains are cracked between rollers to enable them to cook faster. Bulgur is parboiled cracked wheat and cooks even more quickly.

Dried Fruits A good source of minerals and an excellent way to satisfy a sweet tooth without resorting to sugar. Apricots are especially rich in iron, while prunes are the lowest in calories.

Eggs Try to use free-range eggs whenever possible as battery-farm chickens don't have a happy existence. Do not rely heavily on eggs for protein as they are high in cholesterol.

Flour Use wholemeal whenever possible, both plain and self-raising. It contains many natural nutrients and valuable fibre that white flour lacks. If you find 100% wholemeal flour difficult to bake with, use 81% flour instead; this is wholemeal flour from which the bran has been sifted. Smarter still, sift the bran from your own supply of flour. Wholemeal flour must be used when fresh so buy it in small quantities and store it in a cool, dry place.

Fruit Vegetarians and non-vegetarians alike should eat plenty of fruit, preferably picked fresh, eaten raw and chewed well. Frozen fruits make a good alternative for cooking if fresh are hard to obtain.

Ghee This is clarified butter, often used in Indian cooking. You can make your own (see page 74) or you can buy it in cans.

Grains An underrated source of protein in this country, grains are cheap, filling and delicious.

Herbs Best when fresh, but unless you have some growing in a window box, fresh herbs may be hard to obtain during much of the year. If you substitute dried herbs always use half quantity, as they are more concentrated than fresh.

Honey A healthy alternative to sugar, naturally produced honey is rich in vitamins and minerals.

Jams It is now possible to buy raw sugar jams or – even better – jams made without any sugar at all.

Kasha Another name for roasted buckwheat. You can buy it as it is or roast uncooked buckwheat.

Lemon Curd Raw sugar lemon curd can be obtained from many wholefood shops.

Maple Syrup Collected from maple trees, mainly in New England and Canada, this is another good – if expensive – alternative to sugar. Use it sparingly but do use it. Its taste is quite unique.

Margarine It used to be considered the 'poor man's butter', then recently became very popular as a good source of polyunsaturated oils. These are thought to break down easily in your body as opposed to saturated fats which build up. Many margarines, however, contain animal ingredients which are not listed, making them hidden traps for vegetarians. The softer ones are more likely to be entirely vegetarian in content.

Marzipan Raw sugar marzipan is obtainable in most wholefood shops.

Milk An excellent food for growing children, milk should not, however, feature too strongly in the diets of adults. Being very concentrated and nutritious, a small amount will go a long way. Think of it as a food rather than a drink. The low-fat variety works well in cooking (unless you want creamy results).

Mincemeat You can buy raw sugar, vegetarian mincemeat from most wholefood shops. Or you can make your own, substituting vegetable suet or margarine for beef suet.

Miso This is a thick soya bean purée that has been fermented for years to produce a very nutritious food to flavour soups and stews.

Molasses A dark, heavy syrup, high in minerals and low in calories. The darkest variety, blackstrap, has half the calories of sugar.

Nuts A wonderful food, packed with energy and taste, nuts should be used often as a principle source of protein, vitamin B and minerals. Nut butters are especially easy to digest and are popular with children.

Oat Flakes Also known as rolled oats, these are oats which have been steamed and rolled to flatten them and make them quick to cook. You can buy fine, medium and jumbo oat flakes.

Oatmeal Made from ground whole oat grains, oatmeal comes as fine, medium and coarse.

Oils The best – and most expensive – oils to buy are unrefined oils, that is, those that have simply been cold-pressed before being bottled. Refined oils have been produced under pressure at a high temperature and have lost many nutrients in the process. Either way, pure vegetable oils are still rich in polyunsaturates and vitamin E.

Pasta This is, of course, traditionally made with refined white flour but wholewheat pasta is better for you as it contains all the nutrients white pasta has lost.

Pearl Barley These are barley grains which have been polished and lost some of the bran and germ in the process. They have the advantage however of taking only $1-1\frac{1}{2}$ hours to cook.

Pot Barley Consisting of the whole grain except for the outer husk, pot barley is very nutritious. It requires 2–3 hours of cooking before it is tender.

Pulses Beans, peas and lentils are all pulses and between them they offer at least 20 different varieties to choose from. They are a delicious and underrated source of protein.

Rice Brown rice is far more nutritious than white as it consists of the whole grain with just the husk removed. Polished white rice has lost the bran and germ and thereby many valuable nutrients, particularly vitamin B.

Rye Flakes Whole rye grains are steamed and flattened to make them cook more quickly.

Soya Grits The soya bean is broken into several small pieces, a process which greatly shortens the cooking time.

Soya 'Meat' Made from the high-protein bean, soya meat substitutes are, nutritionally,

exceptional value for money. They are also low in fats and calories and quick to prepare.

Soya Milk A nutritious milk, useful for vegetarian, non-vegetarian and vegan alike since it is high in protein but contains no animal fats and is therefore low in saturates (see **Butter**). It comes either ready to be used, as a powder, or in concentrated form, needing to be diluted with water.

Sugar If you are really keen on healthy eating, you should eat as little sugar as possible. It contains a good deal of calories without any protein, vitamins or minerals. Raw brown sugar is slightly better for you than white sugar as it does contain a very small amount of nutrients, but more important, it has more flavour, which means you need to use less of it. Demerara, light and dark muscovado are all types of raw brown sugar. Beware of any packets labelled simply 'soft brown sugar', as these are invariably white sugars which have been dyed with syrup or molasses.

Suet You can buy vegetarian suet from most good wholefood shops. Otherwise try using margarine.

Tahini This is a very nutritious paste made from sesame seeds, available usually in a lighter (milder) and darker (stronger) version. Stir it into soups or sauces, mix it with vegetables, beans or grains or – most delicious of all – blend it with honey and use it in sweet dishes.

Tofu Perhaps the most versatile soya bean product of all, tofu is comparatively new to the West, though it's been part of the cuisine of the East for thousands of years. A bland-tasting soya curd, it can be used in countless ways to add protein to all sorts of dishes, savoury and sweet, without adding calories.

Vegetables *Not* the only things vegetarians eat, as some people seem to think, but certainly they form a large part of the meatless diet. Best cooked for the minimum time, either steamed or boiled in a very little water. Frozen vegetables are better than canned, fresh better than frozen and those picked straight from your own garden best of all.

Wheatgerm The germ or heart of the wheat, rich in nutrients, particularly vitamins B and E, wheatgerm is eliminated in the process of making refined white flour. You can buy it as a powder to sprinkle on dishes but buy it in small amounts as it does not keep well.

Yogurt Another excellent food, yogurt is not only full of nutrients but also easy to digest. Use the natural variety often, whether you buy it or make it yourself (see page 169); it goes well with both sweet and savoury foods.

Cooking Charts

Pulses

Pulse	Cooking Method	Cooking Time	Comments
Slow-cooking varieties:			
Butter (lima) **beans**	All dried beans will cook more quickly if you soak them first overnight.	About 1–2 hours, except soya beans which can take 3 or more hours	Do not add salt until the beans are nearly cooked as this toughens the skin. Cook till completely soft or they may be hard to digest.
Kidney beans *	Then drain them and put them into a large pan with at least twice the volume of fresh water, bring to the boil and simmer covered until cooked.		Soya bean flakes can be used instead of the whole bean in many dishes – they cook in minutes and contain all the goodness of the whole bean.
Soya beans			
Chickpeas (Garbanzos beans)	These may need more water during cooking.		
Black beans			
Dried broad beans			

* Kidney beans should be brought to the boil and boiled for at least 10 minutes before turning down the heat and simmering until tender.

Pulse	Cooking Method	Cooking Time	Comments
Quicker-cooking varieties:			
Black-eye beans	Soak overnight, or bring to the boil, set aside for 1 hour and drain. In fresh water to cover bring the beans to the boil and simmer covered until cooked.	About 45 minutes	Some people believe it is good to cook the beans in the water in which they have been soaked as it is full of nutrients. However, if you cook them in fresh water, you reduce the problem of flatulence.
Aduki beans			
Dried whole green peas			
Haricot (navy) **beans**			
Flageolets			

Pulse	Cooking Method	Cooking Time	Comments
Ready-in-next-to-no-time pulses:			
Whole lentils	The split varieties need no soaking; whole pulses can be cooked without, but soaking quickens the cooking process.	About 20–30 minutes (staler lentils or mung beans might take a little longer)	Lentils and split peas provide the quickest and easiest way to add pulses to your dishes.
Split peas			
Split lentils			
Mung beans			

Grains

Grain	Soaking	Amount of water for cooking	Cooking method	Cooking Time	Comments
Whole-wheat (Whole berry wheat)	Overnight in water to cover.	Keep the grains covered with water.	Bring to the boil and simmer in a covered pan.	1¼ hours or until the grains burst	Both are heavy, chewy grains with a distinctive flavour.
Rye	Follow instructions given above				
Brown rice	No soaking needed, but wash the grains thoroughly.	Twice the volume of rice.	Bring to the boil and simmer covered. Stir once.	30–40 minutes or until all the water is absorbed	The cooking time may vary slightly depending on whether you use short or long grain.
Millet	No soaking needed.	Three times the volume of millet.	Dry roast the grains for a few minutes, if liked, before adding the water. Bring to the boil, cover and simmer, stirring as necessary.	15–20 minutes	A very light, delicately flavoured grain.
Pot Barley	Overnight in plenty of water.	Three times the volume of barley. More water may be needed during cooking.	Bring to the boil and simmer in a lidded pan, stirring occasionally.	at least 2–3 hours	Pot barley is especially easy to digest, and a good grain with winter dishes.
Pearl Barley	No soaking needed.	Keep the grains covered with water.	Bring to the boil, cover the pan and simmer.	1–1½ hours	This is the polished grain, not quite so nutritious as pot barley.
Buck-wheat / **Kasha** (Roasted buck-wheat)	No soaking needed.	Twice the volume of buckwheat. More water may be needed during cooking.	Dry roast the grains (unless you are using kasha) for a few minutes before adding water. Bring to the boil and simmer in a covered pan.	10–20 minutes	Not strictly a grain, but buckwheat is used as one.
Cracked wheat	No soaking needed.	Twice the volume of wheat.	As buckwheat.	20–30 minutes	
Bulgur (Parboiled cracked wheat)	No soaking needed.	Twice the volume of bulgur.	As buckwheat.	15–20 minutes	

Index